BESTIA

BESTIA

ITALIAN RECIPES CREATED IN THE HEART OF L.A.

Ori Menashe &
Genevieve Gergis
with Lesley Suter

Photographs by Nicole Franzen

CONTENTS

COCKTAILS

CHARCUTERIE

SALADS

STARTERS & SIDES

BREAD & PIZZA

PASTA

MAIN DISHES

DESSERTS

BEST

OUR STORY

Genevieve: Bestia is a restaurant that never should have worked.

To start, we were two self-taught unknowns. Ori had cooked in many great restaurants around Los Angeles, but he's not the type to take credit or be showy—that's just not his style—and as a result, few people outside of the restaurant industry knew who he was. I had never worked in a professional kitchen in my life, so I brought nothing to the table at all.

Then there's the location. We chose to open an ambitiously sized restaurant on a dead-end street on the edge of downtown Los Angeles amid nothing but empty warehouses and a seedy strip club. One Yelp reviewer called it "the corner of Crack and Murder."

Ori: There were needles and condoms and cans of overflowing garbage in the street. It was horrible. But for some reason, the first time I walked through the alley toward the giant, corrugated-steel building, I was blind to all of it. I literally just didn't see it.

Genevieve: It's the newborn-baby syndrome. When you first lay eyes on your newborn child, you don't notice that it's covered in goop and its head is shaped like a cone. No, in that moment, they're literally the most beautiful thing you've ever seen.

Ori: That's how it was for me with Saffron, our daughter, and that's how it was with Bestia. I walked through the door, and even though it was all under construction and still broken up into three different apartments, I saw the potential in all of the metal, the exposed ceiling, the bones. It was beautiful and ugly all at the same time—just cool. And then I walked out into the courtyard with fig trees and cactus and the sound of fountains and stillness. I got back in my car, called Genevieve, and said, "I found it."

Genevieve: "Are you sure?" I asked him. Ori is a workaholic, and I knew how antsy he was to just find a place and get back into the kitchen. But then he said, "There's a courtyard." He knows me, I'm a sucker for stuff like that—anything that breaks the mold of a one-dimensional box. So I said, "OK, let me see it."

Ori: I drove home, picked her up, and took her back to the space. She immediately loved it too. This was our restaurant.

Genevieve: We were so confident about the location, but for no reason at all. The logical thing to do would have been to consider things like how many people will walk by, or what other businesses are around it. But no. None of this affected our conviction that this hidden industrial ruin on a dead-end street was the perfect spot for Bestia. Like everything else we do, we went entirely with our hearts.

Ori: Even more than the location, I was confident about the food. The menu would be Italian, but different from what I'd cooked before—more amplified, less traditional, and authentically mine. I knew we'd have handmade pastas and pizzas, but with an added focus on meat. I wanted to serve off-cuts like pan-seared chicken gizzards with beets and grilled beef heart, while also bringing in whole animals for house-cured salumi and steaks grilled over a wood fire.

Genevieve: The investors who tried Ori's food loved it, too. But even then, many of them pulled out when they saw the space. It's funny, we still didn't get the hint that our location could be an issue. The investors who stuck around were mostly friends who were either not in it for the money, or who'd scraped together whatever little money they had just because they wanted to help us fulfill our dream.

Ori: We basically had to build the restaurant out of nothing. But Genevieve had a friend who became our restaurant designer and gave us a great deal. Our contractor gave us a great deal. Our landlord gave us a great deal. Almost everything you see inside Bestia today was either built by friends or found at a swap meet. In the end, we put the entire restaurant together for less than $1 million.

Genevieve: It was all falling into place. But then two weeks before we opened, Ori's mom came to visit from Israel.

Ori: She saw the building and said, "Why did you do this?! There's nobody here? Why aren't you opening in an area where there's foot traffic?!" I told her to chill out and took her to nearby Urth Caffé to show her the crowds. But something about what she said flipped a switch in my head. Suddenly I saw it all—the neighborhood, the trash, everything. I hadn't even realized before that there was a strip club—and not even a classy one—just down the street. I panicked. I left one night after a long day of curing meats and called Genevieve. I told her we had made a big mistake.

Genevieve: He said, "Genevieve, I walked around. I'm seeing used condoms and needles all over the ground. It's disgusting. What did we do?" I thought it was just preopening anxiety. Again, like that moment right before you have a baby—you're like, "We're not ready!" I told him to calm down, but he continued to freak out. Finally I said, "Well, it's too late now. We're opening in two weeks. Let's just do this."

Ori: I made her promise, "If this doesn't work, we're moving to Israel. You agree?"

Genevieve: I said yes, but I was lying.

Ori: "Because if this doesn't work," I said, "it's our last chance. The only place we could build up something like this again is Israel. We aren't going to be able to do this one more time because nobody's going to trust us."

Genevieve: Especially since we picked this crazy location, they're all going to think we're insane. Which we sort of were. But finally, we decided okay, let's just see how it turns out. We planned to open the day after Thanksgiving, which is traditionally a dead day. Ori said, "It's great—we'll have maybe forty or fifty people tops, it'll be fine." I was nervous. This was my first real day as a professional pastry chef, and I didn't want a huge crowd.

But then the time came to open the doors, and I see a line of thirty people already waiting outside. How did this happen? There'd been barely any press. We were unknowns. The neighborhood was downright dangerous. The restaurant was really hard to find. But still, our customers found us. This is what I mean when I say that this restaurant shouldn't have worked. Against all odds, we ended up serving a hundred twenty people that opening night, and there has continued to be a line outside of Bestia at opening time every night for the past five years. We're eternally grateful for it.

Ori: Over the last half decade the restaurant has evolved. It had to in order to accommodate what's grown to a reliable crowd of five hundred or so covers a night. We doubled our kitchen's square footage, built an entire alcove in the back dedicated to butchery, and added more seating. But I've also changed the menu, incorporating more produce and seafood to balance all of the heavy meat dishes.

Genevieve: The neighborhood has changed a lot as well. The Arts District today is unrecognizable from what it once was—now it's full of pricey lofts, cafés, and shops. When I walk through our now-bustling alley each morning, it's easy to forget what all of this once looked like and how far we've come. We hope this book will serve as a lasting document of the past five years and a celebration of the restaurant that, against all odds, we built together.

OUR FOOD

Ori: I can't really explain it, but Italian food has always had a hold on me. I'm not Italian, but I've long identified with the festive, loud, communal style of eating that's particular to the Italian table. And since my earliest days as a chef, I've somehow had an instinctual understanding of how to work with Italian flavors. They just feel familiar. Not that I haven't wanted to try other things. During the ten years I spent working in Italian restaurants, I had many opportunities to cook with acclaimed chefs from France and Japan. But somehow, in every case, Italian food drew me back in and it has never let me go.

Bestia's food has its roots in the flavors of Italy. Most of our dishes draw inspiration from some traditional recipe, and we share the very Italian approach of showcasing the best of what's local, fresh, and seasonal. From there, though, the Italian influence stops. Instead, we look beyond any formal culinary style—to our own life experiences, our travels, and daily influences—to create dishes that are wholly original and wholly us.

For example, the Pineapple Mostarda (page 26) alongside our Grilled Pork Porterhouse (page 232) is a salute to the *al pastor* trucks cruising LA after midnight. Our Charred Shishito Peppers with Squid Ink Aioli (page 142) derives its flavor profile from Spain, one of our favorite places to travel. If you pick up the aroma of fig leaves in our lamb ragu (see page 215), look to the giant fig tree shading Bestia's front patio to know why. And the base of creamy yogurt beneath our lamb belly confit (see page 114) reminds me a little of the kebabs I grew up eating in Israel. More than any geographic region or culinary canon, the foods of Bestia are a reflection of our combined life experiences and, more important, our desire to extract the most flavor we can from the highest-quality ingredients.

Everything we serve at Bestia is designed to achieve maximum "craveability." I want you to take one bite of a dish and then feel compelled to have another one. And then another one. I think, "How can I make you to want to taste this again and again and again, no matter how full you are?" It's the same kind of trick that MSG pulls on your brain, but I achieve it organically, through building layer upon layer of natural umami. That's the reason behind our emphasis on dehydrated ingredients (see page 15), reduced sauces, cured meats, and aged cheeses. Processes like smoking, dehydrating, aging, and fermenting all bring out an ingredient's inherent savoriness. Put one or two—or even five—elements like that into a dish and you can create something that's completely addictive.

Genevieve: Our pastry program has the same goal. It's why I love to add savory ingredients like saffron and bay leaves and herbs and cheeses to my desserts. A generous use of salt and bitter elements further help to round out the flavor profile, creating something that's balanced, delicious, and so much more than "just sweet."

But as much as we're about enhancing flavors, we don't want to amplify every ingredient or dish; that can become too much. Instead, we pick one or two key elements to highlight—just enough to intrigue the palate but not exhaust it. In the end, it's all about extracting the very best flavor from the very best ingredients. If you want something that's chocolatey, it should be the creamiest chocolatey flavor. Strawberry ice cream should taste like real strawberries.

Ori: People always ask us, "What kind of food is Bestia?" But it's so much more about our philosophy and our approach to flavor than any particular style of cooking. We think our recipes included here reflect that.

HOW TO USE THIS BOOK

We've said it before, but it's important to note: neither of us went to culinary school. Everything we know today we learned through years of hard work and experimentation. As self-taught chefs, we're of the belief that anyone is capable of cooking great food, and our goal with this book is to share with you some of the knowledge that took years and a lot of painful hard work to acquire.

But to do that, we've fought hard to keep our recipes as true to the versions at the restaurant as possible. We didn't want to dumb them down or provide a "home cook" interpretation of the Bestia experience. As a result, the recipes in this book feature all of the authentic techniques and ingredients we employ night after night to make food that's as flavorful and balanced as possible.

Our hope is that by passing along this knowledge not only can anyone get a taste of Bestia—whether or not they ever make it to Los Angeles—but they can take what they read here and adapt it to their own cooking. We always say that the ultimate satisfaction will be when, ten years from now, we're eating at the restaurant of one of our former cooks and see something that we taught them on the plate. Our goal with this book is the same: we encourage you to make the recipes, then use what you learn from them to enhance your own cooking.

But first, some things to know that will help you get acclimated to some of the basic operations and go-to tools of our kitchen.

Weights and Measures

At the restaurant, we measure by weight almost exclusively. It's the most accurate form of measuring ingredients and allows for that most coveted of qualities in a restaurant kitchen: consistency. In this book, we provide cup and tablespoon options for most recipes, but we still encourage you to invest in a small digital kitchen scale. For our bread, pizza, charcuterie, and pastry recipes, however, a scale is absolutely imperative, both for the recipes to work properly and—in the case of charcuterie—health and safety.

Ingredients

MEAT AND FISH

This goes for every ingredient you work with, but particularly with meat and fish: freshness and quality are everything. A good butcher and fishmonger are some of the best friends you can have, and if there's a local shop or grocery in your area that specializes in fresh, high-quality meat or seafood, we recommend you buy there as often as possible. Even better, become as friendly as possible with the staff so they save you the good stuff. However, depending on where you live, some better supermarkets also feature specialty counters with an array of well-sourced proteins. Wherever you're buying, do your best to touch, smell, and, if possible, taste your product before purchasing.

PRODUCE

When the seasons change, so does our menu. We would never serve grilled corn or our tomato and burrata salad (page 100) in February, nor would we bake our Rhubarb-Raspberry Crostata (page 255) in October. The recipes in this book depend on you using ingredients that are at their peak, so shop locally and taste whenever possible. Because even when they're in season, not all fruits and vegetables are created equal.

SALT

All of the recipes in this book call for kosher salt. It's less processed and cleaner tasting than iodized or sea salt and has the proper salinity and sodium content for all of our ratios. You'll also see we frequently finish dishes with Maldon salt, a light, flaky sea salt that's readily available at most grocery stores.

Equipment

There's nothing in this book that (with the proper work-around) can't be prepared in a standard home kitchen with even the most basic equipment. That said, there are a few hardworking tools and more specialized items that we use all the time and which will make executing our recipes even easier. As always, the right tool for the right job makes every process easier and more effective.

CHINOIS, CHINA CAP, OR EXTRA-FINE-MESH STRAINER

The finer the strainer, the more thoroughly you'll be able to eliminate any larger, grainy particles that could otherwise affect the texture of your food. A chinois has an incredibly fine metal mesh that keeps all solids—no matter how small—from passing through. A China cap is similar to a chinois but has larger holes and creates a coarser purée.

FOOD DEHYDRATOR

We rely heavily on dehydrated ingredients in our cooking. Dehydrating concentrates foods' flavors and, by changing their texture, can transform them into potent flavor enhancers, whether stirred into a mix, crumbled on top to finish a dish, or as part of an assembly, where they also add visual appeal. While not essential for this book, a simple countertop food dehydrator is a powerful kitchen tool. For a guide to preparation, temperatures, and times for some candidates for dehydrating, see page 15.

SCALE

See Weights and Measures on the facing page. For more insight into how using a kitchen scale is even easier than cups and tablespoons, see Genevieve's explanation on page 247 in the Desserts chapter.

SCRAPER

This simple sliver of steel or plastic with a handle along the top edge (also called a bench scraper, scraper-chopper, or pastry scraper) is one of the most versatile tools in the kitchen. It functions as a dough scraper, a kneader, a scooper, a smasher—there is an endless array of tasks that are made simpler by the use of a scraper. The metal ones also offer a good cutting blade; the flexible plastic ones are for everything else.

VERY SHARP KNIVES

A sharp knife is the most important tool in the kitchen, for both savory and sweet ingredients. It's very important that your knives are sharpened regularly by a professional. The steel that comes with the knives is fine for daily use, but a more thorough sharpening is necessary at least once a month.

TAMIS

A tamis, which has a round, drum-like shape, is a great tool for getting a supersmooth texture in preparations like purées or pâtés. Using a tamis and a bench scraper, you can process a lot of an ingredient or perfect the texture of the final dish very quickly. An incredibly easy tool to use, a tamis can work wonders for mashed potatoes, bread crumbs, and even for sifting flour (see also page 246).

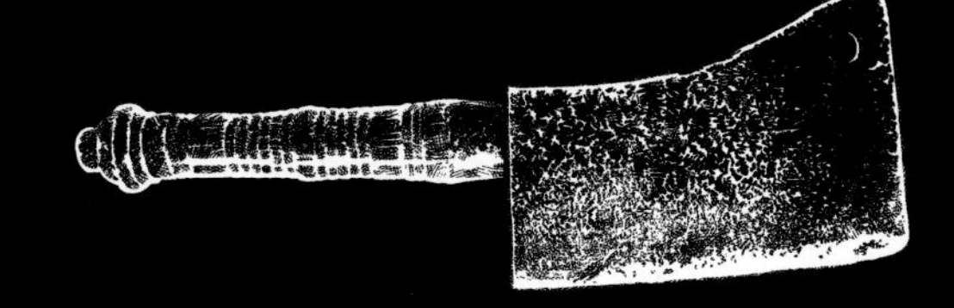

GINO ANGELINI

I first met the man who would become my mentor on my twenty-second birthday. We were celebrating with dinner at his Beverly Boulevard restaurant, Angelini Osteria, and it was nothing short of a transformative experience. After dinner I asked to meet the chef. I told him, "I don't care. I'll be a dishwasher. I'll do anything you want. I just have to work in your kitchen." He didn't have space at the time, but nine months later, Gino hired me for his new restaurant, La Terza. We clicked instantly, working eighteen-hour days side by side, discussing the finer points of food and life and everything in between.

Over the next five years, I learned a lot from Gino. He taught me how to cook Italian food like an Italian, with emotion and soul and simplicity. "One ingredient less" was his mantra. He beat into me that a hot plate is more important than a pretty plate, and that a chef's place is in the kitchen, not in the dining room. But most important, Gino Angelini taught me what it means to be a real chef—someone who cares about all of the people around him the most and himself the least. He was my mentor, yes, but more than that Gino is my friend. Without him, this book, these recipes, and possibly this restaurant wouldn't exist—at least not in the way it does now. For that, I thank him.

—ORI

PANTRY

FLAVOR BUILDING

The pantry is the heart of what makes Bestia, Bestia. People often wonder what it is about restaurant food that makes it taste so much better than what they cook at home; for the most part, we think the difference is attributable to these unromantic fundamentals. Hidden in the back—stacked in plastic tubs and deli cups—our basic building blocks of housemade stocks, sauces, vinaigrettes, pickles, preserves, dehydrated ingredients, compound butters, bread crumbs, and a few secret ingredients such as anchovies and bottarga for a touch of transforming umami are the workhorses of the Bestia kitchen and the secret to coaxing maximum flavor out of every dish.

But bountiful as it is, our pantry is also a function of always striving to eliminate food waste. Many of the recipes in this chapter came about as we looked for ways to use all of the scraps and surplus ingredients that would otherwise get thrown away—shallot tops, herb stems, and orange rinds. Once we began fermenting, pickling, and smoking these extras and adding them to our recipes, we noticed that the dishes tasted even better than before.

None of the recipes in this chapter are very long or complex, and many of them keep for months or more. Once you put in the work and have an array of these staples on hand, it becomes easy to quickly make something simple that tastes special.

Pantry Tools and Techniques

AIRTIGHT CONTAINERS

At the restaurant, we go through things so quickly that storage isn't a huge concern. But a supply of sturdy, good-quality glass storage containers, in a range of sizes and with airtight seals, is a worthwhile investment for safe and effective storage. Our pickling recipes call for glass mason jars, but anything with a tight-fitting lid will do (we always choose glass when we can).

COLD-SMOKING

A few recipes in this book use cold-smoking as a way of adding deep smoky flavor to an ingredient without cooking it, including our Pickled Smoked Shiitake Mushrooms (page 20), Smoked Dried Anchovies (page 50), and Smoked Egg Yolk Bottarga (page 53). Cold-smoking is a technique used specifically for flavoring the meat with smoke. The temperature of what you are smoking will never reach above 86°F. (Hot-smoking is used to cook at a low temperature while also infusing smoke flavor into the product. The temperature is always above 140°F, but should never go higher than 250°F.)

The technique is relatively simple and doesn't require much special equipment. At the restaurant, I use a perforated steam pan inside of a rectangular hotel pan, but if you have a grill, that's probably the best home tool for the job.

At home, I like to use the grill as the smoking chamber. It's outside of the house, which is safer and keeps me out of trouble with Genevieve. To set up the smoker, I use a small, inexpensive pellet tube smoker, available online for around $25. There are a variety of cold-smoker tools on the market—basically just simple perforated metal containers to hold pellets or wood chips. Just follow the manufacturer's instructions to start smoking.

To set up a grill for cold-smoking, fill your smoker tube with pellets or wood chips. (We like to use a variety of woods at Bestia: oak, almond, apple, cherry, or mesquite.) Light the smoker tube on one end and set it on the side of the grill opposite of where you will be placing the item you will be smoking. Close the lid of the grill and make sure the grill vent is left open to allow oxygen to flow so the pellets don't extinguish.

FOOD DEHYDRATOR GUIDE

A standard countertop food dehydrator can transform almost any produce into a potent flavor enhancer. By eliminating the moisture from an ingredient, its natural flavors are concentrated and intensified. Dehydration is also a great way to preserve the best of the season, allowing us to use certain ingredients year-round.

Here are some of our favorite dehydrated foods, which find their way into many of the recipes in this book.

Food Dehydrator

Dehydrating is an easy way to achieve the purest concentration of flavor possible. In many cases, a very low oven will work as a substitute, but if you want to make the bottargas in this chapter (pages 51 to 53), you will need an actual food dehydrator. It's a small investment and one of the most important tools in my kitchen.

INGREDIENT	PREPARATION	TIME (AT 110°F)
Anchovies	Smoke first (see page 50) and lay flat. After drying, grind into a powder.	36 hours
Cherry tomatoes	Cut in half and place skin-side down.	48 hours
Egg Yolk Bottarga	Refer to page 53.	24 hours
Fresno chiles	Halve lengthwise, with stems intact. Place skin-side down. After drying, grind into a powder.	72 hours
Olives	Remove pits, if necessary, and smash to flatten. Place skin-side down. Roughly chop before using.	36 hours
Pistachios	Remove shells.	24 hours
Shallots	Julienne. After drying, grind into a powder.	72 hours
Squid Ink Bottarga	Refer to page 53.	24 hours
Zucchini	Slice paper-thin and lay flat.	12 hours
Zucchini Flowers	Lay flat.	12 hours

Pickled Asian Pear 2-11
Pickled Sunchokes 9-9
Pickled Almonds 8-17
6 qt.
Pickled Fennel 9-12
Smoked Pickled shiitake
8/23
PICKLED LEMON

PICKLES AND PRESERVES

We make a ton of pickles at Bestia, but we don't have a pickle plate on the menu. Instead, we use pickled elements as ingredients, incorporating them into different dishes to add balance. Some of these pickles are on the sweeter side and mild enough to eat on their own, like the Pickled Fennel (page 18) and Pickled Baby Carrots (page 19). Others, like Pickled Smoked Shiitake Mushrooms (page 20), are extremely intense, meant to add another layer of flavor, but too assertive to eat on their own. These pickles have become an indispensable part of our cooking at the restaurant. Play around with them and you'll find many ways to incorporate them into your own daily cooking.

PICKLED SHALLOTS

MAKES ABOUT 2 CUPS

5 large shallots, thinly sliced
½ cup champagne vinegar
½ cup white wine vinegar
2½ tablespoons sugar
1 tablespoon kosher salt
1 sprig thyme
10 black peppercorns

Place the sliced shallots in a 1-quart mason jar or other airtight glass container.

In a small saucepan, combine both vinegars, the sugar, salt, thyme, and peppercorns and bring to a boil over medium-high heat. Pour the hot mixture into the mason jar. Press down to make sure all the shallots are submerged. Cover the jar tightly with the lid and let sit at room temperature until cooled, then refrigerate for 24 hours to allow the flavors to develop before serving. Store tightly covered in the refrigerator for up to 3 months.

PICKLED FRESNO CHILES

MAKES ABOUT 2 CUPS

15 Fresno chiles, stemmed, as many seeds removed as possible, sliced crosswise into about ⅛-inch-thick rings
1½ tablespoons kosher salt
1 tablespoon sugar
¾ cup red wine vinegar
¼ cup extra-virgin olive oil

In a bowl, combine the chiles, salt, and sugar. Toss to mix well. Transfer to a 1-quart mason jar or other airtight glass container. Cover the jar tightly with the lid and let sit at room temperature for 30 minutes. Open the jar and add the vinegar and olive oil. Re-cover the jar tightly and let sit at room temperature for 24 hours to allow the flavors to develop before serving. Store tightly covered in the refrigerator for up to 3 months.

QUICK PICKLED CUCUMBERS

MAKES ABOUT 2 CUPS

2 Persian or other thin-skinned cucumbers, halved lengthwise and sliced into ⅓-inch half-moons

1½ tablespoons kosher salt

1½ teaspoons sugar

¾ cup champagne vinegar

In a bowl, combine the cucumbers with the salt and sugar. Toss to mix well and let sit at room temperature for 30 minutes.

Add the vinegar and ¼ cup water and stir gently. Transfer the cucumbers and brine to a 1-quart mason jar or other airtight glass container, cover tightly, and let sit at room temperature for about 3 hours to allow the flavors to develop, then refrigerate until well chilled before serving. Store tightly covered in the refrigerator for up to 1 week.

PICKLED FENNEL

MAKES ABOUT 4 CUPS

12 baby fennel bulbs, halved lengthwise, cored, and sliced ¼ inch thick, or 3 regular fennel bulbs, cored and sliced ¼ inch thick

5 whole juniper berries, smashed

Pinch of fennel pollen (see Note)

2 teaspoons coriander seeds

1 teaspoon fennel seeds

2 whole star anise

⅓ cup champagne vinegar

⅓ cup apple cider vinegar

¼ cup honey

1 tablespoon plus 1 teaspoon kosher salt

Loosely pack a 1-quart mason jar or other airtight glass container with the fennel and top with the juniper berries and fennel pollen.

In a small saucepan over medium-low heat, combine the coriander seeds, fennel seeds, and star anise and toast, stirring occasionally, until fragrant, about 3 minutes. Transfer the spices to the jar with the fennel.

Combine both vinegars, the honey, salt, and 1½ cups water in the saucepan and bring to a boil over medium-high heat, stirring to help dissolve the honey. Pour the hot mixture into the mason jar, pressing down to make sure all of the fennel is submerged. Cover and let sit at room temperature for at least 2 days or up to 3 days to allow the flavors to develop, then refrigerate for another 2 days before serving. Store tightly covered in the refrigerator for up to 3 months.

NOTE

If you can't find fennel pollen at a specialty or health food store, it can be purchased online.

MAKES ABOUT 2 CUPS

PICKLED BABY CARROTS

1 pound baby carrots scrubbed and halved lengthwise

2 whole star anise

½ teaspoon fennel seeds

½ teaspoon caraway seeds

1 teaspoon ground turmeric

3 strips orange zest

⅓ cup golden balsamic vinegar (see Note)

⅓ cup champagne vinegar

2 tablespoons plus 2 teaspoons sugar

1 tablespoon plus 1 teaspoon kosher salt

Arrange the carrots in a 1-quart mason jar or other airtight glass container.

In a small saucepan over medium-low heat, combine the star anise, fennel seeds, and caraway seeds and toast, stirring occasionally, until fragrant, about 3 minutes. Transfer the spices to the jar with the carrots and add the turmeric and orange zest.

Combine both vinegars, the sugar, salt, and 1½ cups water in the saucepan and bring to a boil over medium-high heat. Pour the hot mixture into the mason jar, pressing down to make sure all of the carrots are submerged. Cover and let sit at room temperature for at least 2 days or up to 3 days to allow the flavors to develop, then refrigerate for another 2 days before serving. Store tightly covered in the refrigerator for up to 3 months.

NOTE

Golden balsamic has notes of caramelization with a touch more sweetness compared to white balsamic. You can substitute rice wine vinegar.

MAKES ABOUT 3 CUPS

PICKLED SMOKED SHIITAKE MUSHROOMS

14 shiitake mushrooms (about 10 ounces), stemmed

2 large stalks from the top of a fennel bulb, including fronds, cut into lengths to fit the canning jar

½ teaspoon coriander seeds

2 cloves garlic, halved

⅔ cup champagne vinegar

3 tablespoons sugar

1 tablespoon kosher salt

1 teaspoon red pepper flakes

SPECIAL EQUIPMENT

Cold smoker

Prepare a grill for cold-smoking (see page 14). Arrange the shiitake caps on the side of the grill grate opposite the smoker. Cover the grill and smoke for about 1 hour, venting as directed.

Tightly pack the fennel stalks and smoked shiitakes into a 1-quart mason jar or other airtight glass container.

In a small saucepan over medium-low heat, toast the coriander seeds until fragrant, about 3 minutes, then add them to the jar.

Combine the garlic, vinegar, sugar, salt, red pepper flakes, and 1½ cups water in the saucepan and bring to a boil over medium-high heat. Remove from the heat and let the mixture cool completely. Pour the mixture into the mason jar, pressing down to make sure all of the mushrooms are submerged. If any float, press a piece of plastic wrap on the surface to hold them down. Cover and let sit at room temperature for at least 2 days or up to 3 days to allow the flavors to develop, then refrigerate for 2 days longer before serving. Store tightly covered in the refrigerator for up to 3 months.

MAKES ABOUT 4 CUPS

PICKLED SUNCHOKES

5 sunchokes, sliced paperthin (see Note)
1 tablespoon fennel seeds
⅔ cup champagne vinegar
2 tablespoons sugar
1 tablespoon kosher salt
1 teaspoon ground turmeric

Tightly pack the sliced sunchokes into a 1-quart mason jar or other airtight glass container.

In a small saucepan over medium-low heat, toast the fennel seeds until fragrant, about 3 minutes, then add them to the jar.

Combine the vinegar, sugar, salt, turmeric, and 1½ cups water in the saucepan and bring to a boil over medium-high heat. Pour the hot mixture into the mason jar, pushing down to make sure all of the sunchokes are submerged. Cover and let sit at room temperature for 2 days to allow the flavors to develop, then refrigerate for 2 days longer before serving. Store tightly covered in the refrigerator for up to 3 months.

NOTE

A mandoline is ideal for cutting the translucently thin slices you want for these pickles. We use a Japanese Benriner model, available in cookware stores and online. Otherwise, use a very sharp chef's knife and a steady hand.

Preserved Myer

PRESERVED CITRUS

At Bestia, we're always looking for ways to use up the leftover peels from the citrus the bar uses for juice. Preserved citrus zest is a great solution. It's an amazing umami builder (umami, described as brothy, savory, meaty, and otherwise, is the fifth and most elusive category of taste, along with sweet, sour, salty, and bitter), and it provides a boost of salt and intensity—almost like an olive or a caper but with a rounder, brighter flavor. Famously, and so you may have heard, the traditional process of making preserved citrus from start to finish normally uses whole fruit and takes two months or more, depending on the temperature and the time of year. Following are quick preservation methods for lemon and orange zest. Once preserved, these preparations technically don't have an expiration date; they can be counted on to last as long as you are willing to store them.

While less common, you can use preserved orange zest in pretty much any of the same contexts preserved lemon is called for. However, keep in mind that the flavor is just a bit more delicate and floral. I use preserved orange wherever lemon might be too sharp, as with our Squid Ink Aioli (page 47) or Steamed Mussels and Clams with 'Nduja, Preserved Citrus, Fennel Pollen, and Grilled Bread (page 134).

PRESERVED LEMON

MAKES ABOUT 1 CUP

8 large lemons

½ cup kosher salt

3 tablespoons plus 1 teaspoon superfine sugar

2 sprigs thyme

15 black peppercorns

Using a sturdy, sharp vegetable peeler, peel the colorful zest from the lemons in approximately 1-inch-wide strips, being careful to avoid the bitter white pith beneath. Squeeze the juice from 3 of the lemons into a small cup or bowl and set aside.

Put the zest in a small saucepan. Add water just to cover and bring to a boil over high heat. As soon as the water reaches a boil, drain the zest in a colander and return it to the saucepan. Again add water to cover and repeat the boiling and draining process once or twice, until the lemon peels are pliable and no longer bitter.

continued

In a bowl, combine the cooked zest, salt, and sugar and toss to coat. Add the thyme and peppercorns and toss to mix well. Add the reserved lemon juice and stir gently. Transfer the mixture to a ½-pint mason jar or other airtight glass container. Press down gently to make sure all of the lemon peel is submerged in the liquid. Cover tightly and let sit at room temperature until the zest is slightly translucent, about 24 hours.

Store tightly covered at room temperature for up to 1 month or in the refrigerator pretty much forever. Always rinse before use.

PRESERVED ORANGE

MAKES ABOUT 1 CUP

6 large oranges

½ cup kosher salt

3 tablespoons plus 1 teaspoon superfine sugar

2 sprigs thyme

3 fresh bay leaves or 1 dried, torn

15 black peppercorns

Using a sturdy, sharp vegetable peeler, peel the colorful zest from the oranges in approximately 1-inch-wide strips, being careful to avoid the bitter white pith beneath. Squeeze the juice from 2 of the oranges into a small cup or bowl and set aside.

Put the zest in a small saucepan. Add water just to cover and bring to a boil over high heat. As soon as the water reaches a boil, drain the zest in a colander and return it to the saucepan. Again add water to cover and repeat the boiling and draining process once or twice, until the orange peels are pliable and no longer bitter.

In a bowl, combine the cooked zest, salt, and sugar and toss to coat. Add the thyme, bay leaves, and peppercorns and toss to mix well. Add the reserved orange juice and stir gently. Transfer the mixture to a ½-pint mason jar or other airtight glass container. Press down gently to make sure all of the orange peel is submerged in the liquid. Cover tightly and let sit at room temperature until the zest is slightly translucent, about 24 hours.

Store tightly covered at room temperature for up to 1 month or in the refrigerator pretty much forever. Always rinse before use.

PRESERVED
MEYER LEMON
Preserved Blod
15L
PRESERVED

MOSTARDA DI FRUTTA

In northern Italy, there is a tradition of candying fruit and combining it with a spicy mustard-infused syrup. Called *mostarda di frutta*, it's traditionally served alongside platters of boiled meats like *bollito misto*, which are pretty flavorless on their own, so these sweet condiments are a way to add flavor. At Bestia, I do something similar, infusing different kinds of candied fruit with mustard but adding chiles for some extra heat. My goal is to create a *mostarda* with a perfect mix of sweet, sour, and spicy, to help balance some of our saltier, heavier meat dishes. Citric acid is used here to both preserve and add acidity to balance the sweetness. You can apply this method to almost any fruit you like. The yields are higher in these recipes so as not to waste any of the pineapple and because it's worth making a large batch when strawberries are at their peak.

PINEAPPLE MOSTARDA

MAKES ABOUT 2 QUARTS

1 pineapple (2½ to 3 pounds)
1¾ cups sugar
1 tablespoon red pepper flakes
2 teaspoons brown mustard seeds
2 teaspoons yellow mustard seeds
½ teaspoon citric acid

Peel and core the pineapple and cut the flesh into ½-inch cubes.

In a large, heatproof airtight container, combine the pineapple with the sugar and toss to coat well. Cover tightly and let sit in a dark, cool place for 24 hours.

Strain the liquid that accumulated in the airtight container into a saucepan, leaving the pineapple in the container. Bring the liquid to a boil over medium-high heat. Pour the hot liquid back into the container over the pineapple and let cool to room temperature. Cover and refrigerate for 24 hours. Repeat the process two more times, refrigerating another 24 hours after the third boil. The pineapple will be translucent and reduced by about one-quarter of the original size.

To finish, combine the pineapple, juices, red pepper flakes, mustard seeds, and citric acid in a large saucepan and bring to a boil. Remove from the heat and let cool. The mostarda should have a slight chew, similar to gummy candy. If it doesn't, repeat the boiling and cooling until you reach the desired texture.

Use immediately, or store the mostarda, with all its juices, in an airtight container in the refrigerator for up to 3 months.

MAKES ABOUT 2 QUARTS

STRAWBERRY MOSTARDA

1½ pounds fresh strawberries, hulled and quartered

1 cup sugar

1 teaspoon citric acid

In a large, heatproof airtight container, combine the strawberries with the sugar and toss to coat well. Cover tightly and let sit in a dark, cool place for 24 hours.

Strain the liquid that accumulated in the airtight container into a saucepan, leaving the strawberries in the container. Bring the liquid to a boil over medium-high heat. Pour the hot liquid back into the container over the strawberries and let cool to room temperature. Cover and refrigerate for 24 hours. Repeat the process two more times, refrigerating another 24 hours after the third boil. The fruit should look translucent.

To finish, combine the strawberries, juices, and citric acid in a large saucepan and bring to a boil. Remove from the heat and let cool. The mostarda should have a slight chew, similar to gummy candy. If it doesn't, repeat the boiling and cooling until you reach the desired texture.

Use immediately, or store the mostarda, with all its juices, in an airtight container in the refrigerator for up to 3 months.

MAKES ABOUT 2 QUARTS

FERMENTED BLACKBERRY JAM

2½ pounds fresh blackberries

2¼ cups plus 2 tablespoons sugar

¾ cup Lambrusco wine

Small pinch of citric acid, or 1 teaspoon freshly squeezed lemon juice

Put the blackberries and sugar in a large, heatproof airtight container and toss to combine. Cover the container tightly and let the berries sit at room temperature (the warmer the room, the faster the fermentation process), tossing twice each day, until they smell slightly alcoholic and taste strongly fermented, at least 3 days or up to 5 days. If you see any berries beginning to mold, just remove them and discard.

Once fermented, strain the juices that accumulated in the airtight container into a saucepan, leaving the berries in the container. Bring the liquid to a boil over medium-high heat. Pour the hot liquid back into the container over the berries and let cool to room temperature. Cover and refrigerate for 24 hours. Repeat the process once a day for 5 days, until the berries are mostly cooked through and slightly candied.

On the fifth day, drain the berries once more, reserving the juices, and set the berries aside. Add the juices to a saucepan along with the Lambrusco. (If substituting lemon juice for the citric acid, stir in the lemon juice now.) Bring to a boil and simmer gently until the liquid becomes thick and syrupy and has reduced by one-third, about 10 minutes. Add the reserved blackberries to the thickened syrup and continue to boil for about 5 minutes longer, until the berries are just starting to soften but still remain whole fruit, then remove from the heat. Stir in the citric acid now, if using, and transfer the jam to an airtight container.

Use immediately, or press a piece of plastic wrap on the surface of the jam, making sure all of the berries are submerged, and store in the airtight container in the refrigerator for up to 3 months.

MAKES ABOUT 1 CUP

CANDIED BLOOD-ORANGE PEEL

20 blood oranges, halved and juiced (drink the juice or save for another use), rinds reserved

8 cups sugar, plus more for coating

½ cup light corn syrup

Bring a large pot of water to a boil and add the orange rinds. Boil until the rinds are easily pierced with a fork but not falling apart, about 5 minutes. Drain and let cool completely. Use a spoon to scoop out all of the remaining flesh and membranes but leaving the skin and the pith. Cut the cleaned peels into long slices about ¼ inch wide.

Combine the sugar, corn syrup, and 2 cups water in a large saucepan and bring to a boil. Add the orange peel strips. Lower the heat to a simmer, cover, and cook until the peels turn slightly translucent, about 30 minutes. Uncover and continue to simmer until the peels are fully translucent and the syrup begins to thicken, about 30 minutes longer. Drain the orange peels, reserving the syrup for other uses, if desired. Set the candied peels aside on a baking sheet to cool. When cool enough to handle, sprinkle the peels with a few tablespoons of sugar and toss to coat well. Store in an airtight container in the refrigerator for up to 6 months.

Tumeric 9-22
lemon chili 9-22
chopped 9-22
Walnuts
Red Whine 9-22
lemon Thime 9-2
Apple 9-22

VINAIGRETTES

You have to be confident when you're dressing a salad. The ingredients are raw and fragile and every time you toss them, you're risking their integrity. I always tell my kitchen staff that if you have to adjust the dressing more than once, throw it away.

Most of my vinaigrettes are one part vinegar to two parts oil, and you'll notice that I don't include a ton of salt. Most of the actual seasoning goes into the salad itself. A salty dressing will wilt your lettuces much faster, so by adding the salt to the greens at the end you increase the shelf life of your salad. All of these dressings will keep, stored tightly covered in the refrigerator, for up to 5 days.

APPLE CIDER VINAIGRETTE

MAKES ABOUT ¾ CUP

2 tablespoons apple cider vinegar
2 tablespoons red wine vinegar
1 teaspoon minced shallot
½ teaspoon kosher salt
5 grinds of black pepper
½ cup extra-virgin olive oil

In a bowl, combine both vinegars and the shallot and set aside for 10 minutes. Add the salt and pepper, then slowly drizzle in the olive oil while whisking until the dressing is combined and emulsified.

CINNAMON VINAIGRETTE

MAKES ABOUT ¾ CUP

¼ cup champagne vinegar
1 teaspoon minced shallot
½ teaspoon kosher salt
5 grinds of black pepper
½ teaspoon ground cinnamon
½ cup extra-virgin olive oil
1 teaspoon packed chopped fresh thyme

In a bowl, combine the vinegar and shallot and set aside for 10 minutes. Add the salt, pepper, and cinnamon, then slowly drizzle in the olive oil while whisking until the dressing is combined and emulsified. Add the thyme and give the dressing a few final whisks.

LEMON VINAIGRETTE

MAKES ABOUT ¾ CUP

- ¼ cup freshly squeezed lemon juice
- 1 teaspoon minced shallot
- ½ teaspoon kosher salt
- 5 grinds of black pepper
- ½ cup extra-virgin olive oil

In a bowl, combine the lemon juice and shallot and set aside for 10 minutes. Add the salt and pepper, then slowly drizzle in the olive oil while whisking until the dressing is combined and emulsified.

VARIATIONS

For Lemon-Thyme Vinaigrette, add 1 teaspoon chopped fresh thyme.

For Lemon-Chile Vinaigrette, add ½ teaspoon ground red pepper flakes and omit the black pepper.

POMEGRANATE VINAIGRETTE

MAKES ABOUT ¾ CUP

- 2 tablespoons champagne vinegar
- 2 tablespoons freshly squeezed lemon juice
- 1 tablespoon pomegranate molasses
- 1 teaspoon minced shallot
- ½ teaspoon kosher salt
- 5 grinds of black pepper
- ½ cup extra-virgin olive oil

In a bowl, combine the vinegar, lemon juice, and pomegranate molasses and whisk to mix. Add the shallot and set aside for 10 minutes. Add the salt and pepper, then slowly drizzle in the olive oil while whisking until the dressing is combined and emulsified.

RED WINE VINAIGRETTE

MAKES ABOUT ¾ CUP

- ¼ cup red wine vinegar
- 1 teaspoon minced shallot
- ½ teaspoon kosher salt
- 5 grinds of black pepper
- ½ cup extra-virgin olive oil

In a bowl, combine the vinegar and shallot and set aside for 10 minutes. Add the salt and pepper, then slowly drizzle in the olive oil while whisking until the dressing is combined and emulsified.

TURMERIC VINAIGRETTE

MAKES ABOUT ¾ CUP

- 2 tablespoons freshly squeezed lemon juice
- 2 tablespoons champagne vinegar
- 1 tablespoon calamansi vinegar
- 1 teaspoon minced shallot
- ½ teaspoon kosher salt
- ½ teaspoon ground turmeric
- ½ teaspoon grated fresh turmeric, or ½ teaspoon plus ⅛ teaspoon ground turmeric
- ½ cup extra-virgin olive oil

In a bowl, combine the lemon juice, both vinegars, and the shallot and set aside for 10 minutes. Add the salt and ground and fresh turmeric, then slowly drizzle in the olive oil while whisking until the dressing is combined and emulsified.

WALNUT VINAIGRETTE

MAKES ABOUT ¾ CUP

- 2 tablespoons freshly squeezed lemon juice
- 2 tablespoons champagne vinegar
- 1 teaspoon whole-grain mustard
- ½ teaspoon kosher salt
- 5 grinds of black pepper
- ¼ cup grapeseed oil
- ¼ cup walnut oil

In a bowl, combine the lemon juice, vinegar, mustard, salt, and pepper. Slowly drizzle in both oils while whisking until the dressing is combined and emulsified.

FISH SAUCE VINAIGRETTE

MAKES ABOUT ¾ CUP

- ¼ cup freshly squeezed lemon juice
- 1 teaspoon minced shallot
- 1 tablespoon plus 1 teaspoon fish sauce
- ½ teaspoon red pepper flakes
- ¼ cup extra-virgin olive oil
- ¼ cup grapeseed oil

In a bowl, combine the lemon juice and shallot and set aside for 10 minutes. Add the fish sauce and red pepper flakes, then slowly drizzle in both oils while whisking until the dressing is combined and emulsified.

VEG
LOBSTER

STOCKS AND BASES

Stock is basically flavored water. These heady, almost magical liquids add an intensity to dishes that you can't get using plain water, and which stock you choose from the wide array of possibilities depends on which particular flavor you want to enhance: earthiness with mushroom stock, oceanic sweetness with lobster stock, a rich meatiness with lamb, veal, beef, or chicken stock. Take the time to make your own stock instead of buying it from the store and whatever you cook will taste like your grandmother made it. If you have to use store-bought, make sure it's the best quality, preferably low sodium. There are easy basic stock recipes everywhere; you likely already have your own go-tos. We have included just a few of our favorites here, starting with a classic vegetable stock that is fairly neutral but adds great depth of flavor to sauces and soups.

VEGETABLE STOCK

MAKES ABOUT 2 QUARTS

¼ cup grapeseed oil

2 large yellow onions, chopped

2 large carrots, peeled and chopped

2 celery stalks, trimmed and chopped

5 fresh bay leaves or 2 dried

15 black peppercorns

3 stems flat-leaf parsley

1 whole head garlic, halved crosswise

2 sprigs thyme

Preheat a large stockpot over low heat, then pour in the grapeseed oil and increase the heat to high. Add the onions, carrots, and celery and let them sear, stirring occasionally, for about 2 minutes. Add the bay leaves and peppercorns to the pot and cook until the vegetables are lightly caramelized and golden brown but not burned, about 10 minutes. Add the parsley and 3 quarts water. Cover the pot and bring to a boil. Once boiling, remove the lid and add the garlic halves. Turn the heat to low and simmer gently, uncovered, until the liquid has reduced by one-third, about 1½ hours.

Remove the pot from the heat. Add the thyme and let sit for 10 minutes. Using a chinois or extra-fine-mesh strainer, strain the stock into an airtight container or containers. Discard the solids. Use immediately, or cover tightly and refrigerate for up to 5 days or freeze for up to 3 months.

MAKES ABOUT 2 QUARTS

MUSHROOM STOCK

6 tablespoons grapeseed oil

8 ounces fresh mushroom stems and scraps or whole mushrooms, chopped

2 large yellow onions, chopped

2 large carrots, peeled and chopped

2 celery stalks, trimmed and chopped

5 fresh bay leaves or 2 dried

15 black peppercorns

1 whole head garlic, halved crosswise

3 stems flat-leaf parsley

2 sprigs thyme

¼ ounce dried porcini or shiitake mushrooms

Preheat a large stockpot over high heat. When very hot, add 3 tablespoons of the grapeseed oil and the fresh mushrooms and sauté until the mushrooms begin to caramelize and smell fragrant, about 3 minutes. Using a slotted spoon, transfer the mushrooms to a bowl and set aside.

Add the remaining 3 tablespoons grapeseed oil to the pot. Add half each of the onions, carrots, and celery along with the bay leaves and peppercorns and cook, stirring occasionally, until the vegetables golden brown and well caramelized but not too dark, about 10 minutes.

Return the cooked mushrooms to the pot along with the remaining onions, carrots, and celery; the garlic; parsley; and 3 quarts water. Cover the pot and bring to a boil, then uncover, turn the heat to low and simmer gently, until the liquid has reduced by about one-third, 1 to 1½ hours.

Remove the pot from the heat. Add the thyme and dried mushrooms and let sit for 10 minutes. Using a chinois or extra-fine-mesh strainer, strain the stock into an airtight container or containers. Discard the solids. Use immediately, or cover tightly and refrigerate for up to 5 days or freeze for up to 3 months.

MAKES ABOUT 4 CUPS

LOBSTER STOCK

1 whole lobster, about 1 pound (see Note)

6 tablespoons grapeseed oil

¼ cup Cognac

1 large yellow onion, chopped

1 large carrot, peeled and chopped

1 celery stalk, trimmed and chopped

3 fresh bay leaves or 1 dried

15 black peppercorns

Juice from 1 (28-ounce) can San Marzano whole peeled tomatoes (save the tomatoes for another use)

1 whole head garlic, halved crosswise

½ teaspoon kosher salt

4 sprigs thyme

SPECIAL EQUIPMENT

China cap

Bring a saucepan of water to a boil over high heat. Have ready a large bowl filled with ice and water.

Meanwhile, separate the lobster into parts for stock by using a sharp knife to cut the lobster head in half lengthwise to swiftly kill it. Sever the head from the body and clean the guts out of the head pieces. Set the head pieces aside.

Twist the tail and claws off and add to the boiling water. Cook until shocked but not fully cooked, until the color of the shell changes from a brick red to more of a shade of orange, about 1½ minutes for the tail and 3½ minutes for the claws. Using tongs, transfer the parts to the ice bath to stop the cooking process. Remove the meat from the tail and claws, set the shells aside, and save the meat for another dish. (Store in an airtight container in the refrigerator for up to 3 days.)

Preheat a large stockpot over high heat and add 2 tablespoons of the grapeseed oil. When the oil is hot, add the lobster head and shells and cook, tossing occasionally, until golden brown, about 5 minutes.

Remove the pot from the heat, add the Cognac, and return to the stove for another minute. Transfer the shells to a bowl and set aside.

Lower the heat to medium and add the remaining 4 tablespoons grapeseed oil to the pot. Add the onion, carrot, and celery and let caramelize, stirring only occasionally, until the vegetables begin to brown, about 2 minutes. Add the bay leaves and peppercorns and continue to sauté the vegetables until they're just golden brown, about 10 minutes longer.

Lower the lobster shells to the pot and, using sharp tongs or a spatula, gently break up the shells into smaller pieces. Increase the heat to high and add the tomato juice. Cook, stirring occasionally, until the juice becomes thick and paste-like, about 5 minutes. Add the garlic, salt, and 6 cups water and bring to a boil. Turn the heat to low and simmer gently, uncovered, until reduced by half or the consistency of the stock has thickened, 1 to 1½ hours.

Remove the pot from the heat. Add the thyme and let sit for 10 minutes. Using a China cap (which has larger holes than a chinois) or a medium-mesh strainer, strain the stock into an airtight container or containers, pressing down on the solids to extract as much liquid as possible. (In this case, you want some of the solids to push through the strainer as well because that's where all of the flavor lives.) Use immediately, or cover tightly and refrigerate for up to 2 days or freeze for up to 1 month.

NOTE

This recipe calls for a whole lobster for the purpose of making stock, but whenever you're preparing lobsters for a meal (the Lobster Crostini on page 110, for example), whether boiled or grilled tails or using the meat for a bisque, always keep in mind that you can save the pieces that are usually discarded for a luxurious homemade stock.

SOFFRITOS

Soffrittos are slow-cooked reductions of vegetables in olive oil, and act as the base for ragus, stews, and sauces. Simply an assortment of vegetables confited in lots of olive oil, the result is a powerful concentrate that adds deep flavor to just about anything. We probably go through a hundred pounds of raw vegetables every week just to make the soffrittos for our kitchen.

Don't throw out the oil after you drain the soffritto. That oil is now infused with huge amounts of caramelized vegetable flavor. Use it as you would any other infused oil.

VEGETABLE SOFFRITTO

MAKES ABOUT 2 CUPS

1 large yellow onion, diced
2 carrots, peeled and diced
2 celery stalks, trimmed and diced
1½ to 2 cups extra-virgin olive oil

Put the onion, carrots, and celery in a saucepan. Add enough olive oil to half submerge the vegetables. (As the vegetables start to cook, they will shrink and become fully submerged.) Cook over high heat until the vegetables begin to sizzle, about 5 minutes, then turn the heat to low and simmer, stirring occasionally, until the vegetables are a deep golden brown and very sweet, about 1 hour.

Strain the soffritto, reserving the oil for another use. Store the soffritto and the oil in separate airtight containers in the refrigerator for up to 1 week.

FENNEL SOFFRITTO

MAKES ABOUT 2¾ CUPS

2 large fennel bulbs, cored and diced
1 large yellow onion, diced
2 carrots, peeled and diced
2 celery stalks, trimmed and diced
3½ to 4½ cups extra-virgin olive oil

Put the fennel, onion, carrots, and celery in a saucepan. Add enough olive oil to half submerge the vegetables. (As the vegetables start to cook, they will shrink and become fully submerged.) Cook over high heat until the vegetables begin to sizzle, about 5 minutes, then turn the heat to low and simmer, stirring occasionally, until the vegetables are a deep golden brown and very sweet, about 1 hour.

Strain the soffritto, reserving the oil for another use. Store the soffritto and the oil in separate airtight containers in the refrigerator for up to 1 week.

BASIC POLENTA

MAKES ABOUT 4 CUPS

- 2 to 2½ cups whole milk
- ½ small russet potato (about 4 ounces), peeled
- 1 cup stone-ground polenta
- 5 to 6 tablespoons unsalted butter
- ½ yellow onion, thinly sliced
- ¾ cup freshly grated Parmesan cheese
- 1 tablespoon kosher salt

Combine 2 cups of the milk and 2 cups water in a large saucepan. Using a Microplane, grate the potato into the saucepan, then place over high heat and bring to a boil. Turn the heat to very low and slowly add the polenta while whisking vigorously. Continue to cook, whisking about every 5 minutes, until the polenta is super-creamy but the grains still have a little texture; the timing depends on the package directions.

Meanwhile, combine 5 tablespoons of the butter and the onion in a small saucepan over very low heat. Cover and cook, stirring often, until the butter has melted and the onions are translucent, about 20 minutes.

When the polenta is done, stir in the onion and butter, then add the Parmesan and salt and whisk to combine. If the texture seems too thick, add up to another 1 tablespoon butter and up to ½ cup warm milk or water to thin.

Serve immediately, or press a piece of plastic wrap on the surface of the polenta, nestle the saucepan in a bowl or larger saucepan of warm water, and hold for up to 2 hours.

BASIC LENTILS

MAKES ABOUT 4 CUPS

- 2 cups lentils, picked over for stones and grit, rinsed
- ½ large yellow onion, halved
- 1 carrot, peeled and cut into 4 chunks
- 1 celery stalk, trimmed and halved crosswise
- 1 whole head garlic, halved crosswise
- 1 Fresno chile, stemmed and halved lengthwise, with seeds
- 4 fresh bay leaves or 2 dried
- 1 cup dry white wine
- 2 tablespoons kosher salt

Put the lentils in a bowl and add water to cover by 2 inches. Soak for 8 hours or up to overnight.

When you're ready to cook, drain the lentils and set aside. Preheat a cast-iron frying pan over high heat. Place the onion, carrot, celery, garlic, chile, and bay leaves in the hot pan (cut-side down, for those ingredients that have cut sides) and let them char a bit before flipping. Continue to cook, turning occasionally, until the vegetables and aromatics are evenly charred on all sides, 5 to 8 minutes. Remove the pan from the heat and set aside.

Preheat a stockpot over high heat. Add the wine and cook until reduced by three-fourths, about 4 minutes. Drain the lentils. Add the charred vegetables to the pot along with the lentils and 2 quarts water. Bring to a boil, turn the heat to low, and simmer gently, uncovered, until the lentils are almost fully cooked but still have a little bit of bite, 15 to 22 minutes. Pick out the vegetables, garlic, chile, and bay leaves and discard. Stir in the salt.

Use immediately, or store the lentils in the liquid in an airtight container in the refrigerator for up to 3 days.

CREAMY RICOTTA

MAKES ABOUT 3 CUPS

4 cups whole milk
2 cups heavy cream
1 cup buttermilk
2½ teaspoons kosher salt

SPECIAL EQUIPMENT

Candy thermometer
Cheesecloth

Combine the milk, cream, and buttermilk in a saucepan and whisk gently a few times just to blend. Place over very low heat and warm gently, scraping the bottom of the pan with a spatula every 5 minutes or so, until a thick skin forms on top, the solids (the cheese) start separating from the liquid (the whey), and a candy thermometer reads 208°F, about 30 minutes. Do not let the mixture boil. Remove the pan from the heat, cover tightly with plastic wrap to trap in all of the moisture so the cheese (solids) will settle, and let sit for 30 minutes.

Cut a large piece of cheesecloth and fold it to make a piece four layers thick and large enough to cover a large fine-mesh strainer. Line the strainer with the cloth and place it over a large pot or bowl. Pour the cheese into the cheesecloth and loosely tie the ends of the cheesecloth over the top to cover. Let the cheese drain for about 4 hours, until it's reached a nice firm consistency. Transfer the cheese from the cheesecloth to a large bowl. Add the salt and mix until it is evenly distributed. Use immediately, or store in an airtight container in the refrigerator for up to 4 days.

NOTE

Save the whey (the liquid that drains from the cheese) for adding a bit of silky sweetness to homemade pasta dough (see Strozzapreti, page 180) or for adding more liquid to your ricotta cheese to reach a desired consistency.

Tonato
9-22
Squid Aioli
9-22

SAUCES

When I was a kid, my dad would always say, "You know why they have that sauce and that lemon with the fish? It's because the fish isn't fresh." Whenever he cooked fish, he would go into the Old City in Jaffa and buy the freshest fish that was caught that day. If we reached for a lemon wedge, he would scold us, saying, "No, no, you'll ruin it. It doesn't need anything." And he was right. Sauces were made to cover something up. I'm all about enhancing ingredients' natural qualities, not hiding them. So, the few sauces we do have at Bestia are all about helping that fish, that tomato, that corn, or that endive taste more like the best version of itself, with a couple elements of umami to give it a little boost.

TOMATO SAUCE

MAKES ABOUT 2 CUPS

1 (28-ounce) can whole peeled San Marzano tomatoes

4 tablespoons reserved vegetable soffritto oil (see page 38) or extra-virgin olive oil

5 cloves garlic, thinly sliced

½ cup packed Vegetable Soffritto (page 38)

2½ teaspoons kosher salt

Pinch of freshly ground black pepper

3 large fresh basil leaves, torn into small pieces

Strain the tomatoes, reserving the juices. Set the tomatoes and juices aside separately.

Preheat a large saucepan over high heat. When the pan is hot, add 2 tablespoons of the soffritto oil. When the oil is hot, add the tomatoes and move them gently until they're soft and starting to brown, about 5 minutes. With a wooden spoon or spatula, begin to gently break up the tomatoes as they cook, being careful not to let them burn. Turn the heat to medium and continue cooking, stirring occasionally, until the tomatoes are golden and have emulsified with the oil and almost formed a paste, about 8 minutes longer.

Meanwhile, in a small saucepan over medium heat, combine the garlic and the remaining 2 tablespoons soffritto oil. Cook, stirring, until the garlic just begins to brown around the edges, 2 to 3 minutes, then turn the heat to low. Add the soffritto and stir until it's warmed through, then remove from the heat.

Return the heat under the tomatoes to high. Add the reserved tomato juices, salt, and pepper and bring to a simmer. Cook gently for 2 minutes, stirring occasionally. Add the soffritto-garlic mixture and basil and stir well.

Remove the pan from the heat and let cool slightly, then pass the sauce through a ricer or transfer to a food processor and pulse until the mixture is smooth but still contains visible chunks of tomato. Use immediately, or refrigerate in an airtight container for up to 3 days or freeze for up to 2 months.

PESTO

MAKES ABOUT 1 CUP

¾ cup packed fresh basil leaves
½ cup extra-virgin olive oil
1 clove garlic
1 tablespoon freshly grated Parmesan cheese
1 tablespoon toasted pine nuts
Pinch of kosher salt
¼ teaspoon freshly ground black pepper

Combine all of the ingredients in a food processor and process until well combined, stopping the machine and scraping down the sides of the bowl as needed. Use immediately, or refrigerate in an airtight container for up to 3 days.

SALSA VERDE

MAKES ABOUT 2 CUPS

½ cup extra-virgin olive oil
2 cups packed chopped fresh flat-leaf parsley
1 tablespoon freshly squeezed lemon juice
1 large clove garlic, grated on a Microplane or very finely minced
2 teaspoons capers, strained and coarsely chopped, plus ¼ teaspoon caper brine
1 teaspoon anchovy paste, homemade (page 50) or store-bought, or 2 anchovy fillets packed in oil, chopped
1 teaspoon rinsed and finely chopped Preserved Lemon (page 23)
1 teaspoon red wine vinegar
1 teaspoon chopped Pickled Shallots (page 17) or jarred cocktail onions
½ teaspoon kosher salt
½ teaspoon freshly ground black pepper

Combine all of the ingredients and ¼ cup water in a bowl and stir until evenly mixed, pressing lightly on the anchovy paste with the back of the spoon to help incorporate it into the oil. Use immediately, or refrigerate in an airtight container for up to 3 days.

MAKES ABOUT 2 CUPS

PAPRIKA SALSA VERDE

¼ cup dehydrated cherry tomatoes (see page 15) or chopped sun-dried tomatoes

½ cup roughly chopped fresh mint

½ cup roughly chopped fresh flat-leaf parsley

2 tablespoons extra-virgin olive oil

1 tablespoon plus 2 teaspoons freshly squeezed lemon juice

1 tablespoon plus 1 teaspoon paprika

1 tablespoon capers, strained and chopped, plus ½ teaspoon caper brine

1 tablespoon tomato juice from canned tomatoes, or 1 teaspoon tomato paste

2 teaspoons rinsed and finely chopped Preserved Lemon (page 23)

2 cloves garlic, minced

2 teaspoons Smoked Dried Anchovies (page 50) or chopped drained oil-packed anchovies (the flavor won't be as smoky)

2 teaspoons white wine vinegar

¼ teaspoon ground red pepper flakes

In a small bowl, soak the cherry tomatoes in hot water until soft, about 5 minutes. Strain, reserving the liquid. Chop the cherry tomatoes.

In a large bowl, combine the cherry tomatoes with all of the remaining ingredients. Add 2 teaspoons of the tomato-soaking liquid and stir to mix well. Use immediately, or cover tightly and refrigerate for up to 3 days.

MAKES ABOUT 2 CUPS

MINT AND FENNEL SALSA VERDE

½ cup minced fresh flat-leaf parsley

½ cup minced fresh mint

2 tablespoons extra-virgin olive oil

2 tablespoons freshly squeezed lemon juice

2 tablespoons freshly squeezed orange juice

1 tablespoon finely minced serrano chile

1 tablespoon toasted fennel seeds

2 cloves garlic, grated on a Microplane or very finely minced

2 teaspoons fish sauce

1½ teaspoons rinsed and minced Preserved Lemon (page 23)

6 grinds of black pepper

¼ teaspoon ground star anise

Combine all of the ingredients in a bowl and stir until evenly mixed. Use immediately, or cover tightly and refrigerate for up to 3 days.

AIOLIS

The aioli below becomes the base for the two aiolis that we use in the restaurant. Because it is a base, there is no salt in it. From there, we develop two aiolis that are super-flavorful and versatile: one is Squid Ink Aioli and the other is Paprika Aioli. The Squid Ink Aioli is used for our Lobster Crostini (page 110) and our charred shishito peppers (see page 142). The Paprika Aioli is used for our roasted cauliflower (see page 149). Either of these two can be used for anything that needs added flavor.

Use the aioli immediately, or cover tightly and refrigerate for up to 1 week.

BASE AIOLI

MAKES ABOUT 2 CUPS

1 tablespoon plus 1 teaspoon boiling water

¼ teaspoon packed saffron threads

2 large egg yolks

2 tablespoons freshly squeezed lemon juice

2 cloves garlic, grated on a Microplane or very finely minced

1½ cups canola oil

¼ cup extra-virgin olive oil

In a small heatproof cup or bowl, pour the boiling water over the saffron. Stir to help steep and let sit for 10 minutes, then stir again.

In a food processor, combine the egg yolks, lemon juice, and garlic and process until well blended. Add half of the saffron water and pulse to mix.

With the food processor running, slowly add the canola oil and olive oil, stopping to add the rest of the saffron water when the mixture begins to thicken. Process until the aioli is smooth and fully emulsified.

MAKES ABOUT 2 CUPS

SQUID INK AIOLI

2 tablespoons squid ink (see Note)

1 tablespoon plus 1 teaspoon fish sauce

1 tablespoon packed chopped fresh flat-leaf parsley

2 teaspoons rinsed and finely minced Preserved Orange (page 24)

¾ teaspoon ground red pepper flakes

Pinch of kosher salt

2 cups Base Aioli (facing page)

In a bowl, combine the squid ink, fish sauce, parsley, preserved orange, red pepper flakes, and salt and stir to combine. Fold in the aioli until well blended and smooth.

NOTE

Squid ink can be purchased online or at a specialty store or seafood market.

MAKES ABOUT 2 CUPS

PAPRIKA AIOLI

1 tablespoon plus 1 teaspoon paprika

1 tablespoon fish sauce

2 teaspoons freshly squeezed lemon juice

2 teaspoons rinsed and finely chopped Preserved Lemon (page 23)

1 teaspoon red wine vinegar

1 small clove garlic, grated on a Microplane or very finely minced

1 teaspoon chile powder, preferably Fresno

1 teaspoon kosher salt

½ teaspoon ground red pepper flakes

½ teaspoon superfine sugar

2 cups Base Aioli (facing page)

In a bowl, combine the paprika, fish sauce, lemon juice, preserved lemon, vinegar, garlic, chile powder, salt, red pepper flakes, and sugar and stir to combine. Fold in the aioli until well blended and smooth.

TONNATO SAUCE

MAKES ABOUT 2 CUPS

¼ cup dry white wine

1 tablespoon plus ½ teaspoon freshly squeezed lemon juice

1 tablespoon capers, drained and chopped, plus ¾ teaspoon caper brine (from above)

2 cloves garlic, grated on a Microplane or very finely minced

1½ teaspoons Smoked Dried Anchovies (page 50), or 1 teaspoon anchovy paste, homemade (page 50) or store-bought

5 grinds of black pepper

1 large egg yolk

1 cup canola oil

1 tablespoon chopped fresh flat-leaf parsley

¼ cup extra-virgin olive oil

1 (5-ounce) can oil-packed tuna

1 teaspoon kosher salt

In a small saucepan over high heat, bring the wine to a boil. Turn the heat to medium and simmer until reduced by two-thirds, or about 1 teaspoon. Remove from the heat and set aside.

In a food processor, combine the reduced white wine, lemon juice, capers and brine, garlic, anchovies, and pepper and process until combined. Add the egg yolk and then, with the food processor running, slowly drizzle in the canola oil until the mixture just lightens in color and turns thick, stopping the machine and scraping down the sides of the bowl as needed. Add the parsley and 2 tablespoons water and process until combined.

Again with the machine running, slowly drizzle in the olive oil. Add the tuna and salt and blend for 5 to 10 seconds more. Do not overmix the tuna or the texture will become gritty. Use immediately, or refrigerate in an airtight container for up to 5 days.

BLACK BUTTER

MAKES 1 POUND

1 pound unsalted butter

Melt the butter in a sauté pan over high heat. Once melted, turn the heat to the lowest setting and let cook, undisturbed, until the solids have settled to the bottom of the pan and blackened and the butter turns a dark amber color, about 30 minutes. Let cool, then transfer to an airtight container and refrigerate for up to 1 month.

BB 9/19

THINGS I CAN'T COOK WITHOUT

These are some of my go-to items to enhance flavor or add texture to dishes. Some of these preparations take time, but are worth the wait.

SMOKED DRIED ANCHOVIES

MAKES ABOUT 5 OUNCES

1 (28-ounce) can salt-packed anchovies

SPECIAL EQUIPMENT

Cold smoker
Food dehydrator

Rinse the anchovies under water to remove the salt. Using the tip of a small knife, remove the spine to separate the fish into fillets.

Prepare a grill for cold-smoking (see page 14). Arrange the anchovies on the side of the grill grate opposite the smoker. Cover the grill and smoke for 1 hour, venting as directed.

Remove the anchovies from the smoker, transfer to a tray, and place in the food dehydrator. Dehydrate at 110°F for 24 hours. Once dry, chop the fillets with a knife into a coarse powder. Use immediately, or store in an airtight container in the refrigerator for up to 3 months.

ANCHOVY PASTE

MAKE ABOUT 1½ CUPS

1 (3½-ounce) jar anchovy fillets, packed in oil

1 Fresno chile, seeds and membranes removed, diced

15 cloves garlic, peeled and trimmed

2 tablespoons packed fresh marjoram leaves

1 teaspoon fresh thyme leaves

Zest of ½ lemon, in large strips

1 cup extra-virgin olive oil

Drain the anchovy fillets and put them in a small saucepan along with the chile, garlic, marjoram, thyme, lemon zest, and olive oil. Place the pan over high heat and cook until the ingredients begin to sizzle, then turn the heat to low and gently simmer, stirring occasionally so they don't stick to the pan, until the garlic cloves are very tender, about 1 hour.

While it's still hot, purée the mixture in a blender or mash with a fork until smooth. Transfer the paste to an airtight container and let cool. Use immediately, or cover and refrigerate for up to 3 months.

BOTTARGAS

Bottarga is poor man's caviar. Made from preserved fish eggs, it's one of those ingredients that, with just a small amount, can take something from being just good to being really good. Like MSG—but natural. Back in Israel, my dad would make his own, old-school style, hanging the fish eggs in nets and drying them in the sun. As kids, we would eat the bottarga plain with some tomatoes, bread, and olive oil.

I developed a version for the restaurant made with cured egg yolks as the base. In these versions, the fishy flavor comes from either sea urchin, fish sauce, or squid ink. It's our play on a traditional bottarga, and I grate it like cheese over any dish that needs a salty, fishy, umami boost.

EGG YOLK BOTTARGA

MAKES 6 PIECES

1⅔ cups superfine sugar
1¼ cups kosher salt
6 large egg yolks, at room temperature

SPECIAL EQUIPMENT
Food dehydrator

In a bowl, whisk together the sugar and salt. Spread half of the salt-sugar mixture in a layer about ¼ inch thick in the center of a plate or small rimmed baking sheet. Using your fingers, make six small, evenly spaced hollows in the mixture. Gently slip an egg yolk from your hand into each hollow without breaking the yolk. Cover with the remaining mixture, then cover the whole assembly tightly with plastic wrap. Refrigerate for 24 to 48 hours, until the yolks are firm to the touch.

Once firm, unwrap the baking sheet and rinse the yolks under lukewarm running water until the curing mixture has completely washed off. If not rinsed well, the product will be too salty. Transfer to a dehydrator tray lined with a nonstick silicone mat. Dehydrate at 110°F until very firm, about 24 hours. Store in an airtight container in the refrigerator for up to 3 months.

SMOKED EGG YOLK BOTTARGA

MAKES 6 PIECES

6 egg yolks from Egg Yolk Bottarga (page 51), prepared through the rinsing step.

½ cup fish sauce

SPECIAL EQUIPMENT

Food dehydrator
Cold smoker

Place the 6 cured egg yolks in a sealable plastic bag and add the fish sauce. Seal the bag, submerging the yolks in the fish sauce, and refrigerate for 24 hours.

Remove the yolks from the fish sauce. Transfer to a dehydrator tray lined with a nonstick silicone mat. Dehydrate at 110°F until very firm, about 24 hours.

Prepare a grill for cold-smoking (see page 14). Arrange the egg yolks on the side of the grill grate opposite the smoker. Cover the grill and smoke for about 2 hours, venting as directed. Store in an airtight container in the refrigerator up to 3 months.

SQUID INK BOTTARGA

MAKES 6 PIECES

6 large egg yolks

1 teaspoon squid ink (see Note, page 47)

1⅔ cups superfine sugar

1¼ cups kosher salt

SPECIAL EQUIPMENT

Food dehydrator

In a bowl, whisk together the egg yolks and squid ink until thoroughly mixed. Pour a ½-inch layer into six of the compartments of an ice-cube tray and freeze until solid, about 8 hours.

In a bowl, whisk together the sugar and salt. Spread half of the salt-sugar mixture in a layer about ¼ inch thick in the center of a plate or small rimmed baking sheet.

Dip the base of the ice-cube tray quickly under warm running water. Unmold the bottarga cubes and place them on top of the salt-sugar mixture, spacing them evenly about 2 inches apart. Cover with the remaining mixture, then cover the whole assembly tightly with plastic wrap. Return to the freezer for another 72 hours.

One at a time, remove the cubes from the mixture and rinse under cold running water until the curing mixture has completely washed off. Transfer to a dehydrator tray lined with a nonstick silicone mat. Dehydrate at 110°F until very firm, about 36 hours. Wrap in plastic wrap and store in the refrigerator for up to 3 months.

FRIED LENTILS

MAKES ABOUT 1 CUP

Canola oil for frying

1 cup Basic Lentils (page 39), drained and dried thoroughly

Kosher salt

Red pepper flakes

SPECIAL EQUIPMENT

Deep-frying thermometer

Pour canola oil into a small saucepan to a depth of 2 inches and place over medium heat until the oil reaches 375°F on a deep-frying thermometer.

In ¼-cup batches, drop the cooked lentils into the oil and fry until crispy, about 90 seconds. Using a spider or slotted spoon, transfer each batch to paper towels to drain.

Sprinkle the lentils lightly with salt and ground red pepper flakes while still warm and toss to coat. Use immediately.

PARSLEY BREAD CRUMBS

MAKES ABOUT 1 CUP

- 1 cup panko bread crumbs
- ½ cup chopped fresh flat-leaf parsley
- 1 tablespoon extra-virgin olive oil
- 1 clove garlic, grated on a Microplane or very finely minced
- 1 teaspoon kosher salt

Combine all of the ingredients in a food processor and pulse until they are well incorporated. Transfer the bread-crumb mixture to a nonstick sauté pan over low heat and toast for 3 to 5 minutes, until evenly golden brown. Remove from the heat and let cool. Use immediately, or store in an airtight container in the refrigerator for up to 5 days.

THE HUDDLE

Ten minutes before the doors to the restaurant open every night, we stop what we're doing and take a pause. Everyone puts down their knives, turns the stoves down to low, and gathers in the kitchen for the pre-service huddle. It will be the only moment of stillness in the kitchen for the next seven hours, and the only time we really get to speak and listen to one another. Each night, one member of the staff—often it's me, but it could be anybody—does the talking. We might announce an exciting chef who's coming in for dinner; we might talk about a last-minute adjustment that needs to be made. But most of the time, we talk about life. It's a time to acknowledge both weaknesses and strengths. And talk about why we love what we do, and why we do it day in and day out—because in this career, no one's in it for the money. We talk about personal hurdles that we've overcome or that we hope to someday, and make goals for the future. But whatever the subject matter, we do it with fire in our eyes and our hearts, and commit to making the night a success. Because it has to be. At 4:59 we break, the doors open, and it's on.

—**ORI**

COCKTAILS

At Bestia, the kitchen rules. Yes, guests stream into our dining room night after night because of the drinks, the service, and the ambience; but above all else, it's the food. Nevertheless, our cocktail program is a point of pride, and we make a concerted effort to incorporate as many culinary aspects of Bestia as possible. Whether it's infusing bourbon with smoked pork fat from our butcher, Mario, to create an old fashioned (see page 63), or using leftover strawberry water from a Strawberry Mostarda (page 27) for Chef Ori's Slow-Roasted Suckling Pig (page 239), the bar team works together with the kitchen to feature as many of its unique ingredients as possible. In that way, our cocktails truly complement and play off of the flavors on the menu, and also inspire us to find creative use for product that would otherwise go to waste.

The bar team at Bestia is a family all its own, and throughout the years we've worked together to create a constantly changing, original, seasonal cocktail menu that represents the playful spirit of the restaurant. This selection of recipes reflects some of Bestia's most popular and well-known cocktails from over the years, and serves as an homage to the passion and creativity of some of our previous bar directors. Cheers!

—Victoria Rau, bar director

LEAH BUNCH

Leah's background is in teaching, not restaurants. But when we met her, she had this incredible intelligence and demeanor; so despite her inexperience, we hired her as our assistant manager. When less than a year in we suddenly found ourselves without a GM, we thought of Leah, though we feared we might be setting her up for failure. When we asked her, she responded with such passion and conviction that she could do it, we gave her the job.

Since then, Leah has not only risen to the occasion but exceeded it. She may look dainty, but believe us, nobody messes with her. Leah is also amazingly calm and warm, a tone that permeates the entire restaurant. And when Saffron skips in the door, Leah is always the first person she runs to.

—GENEVIEVE

CHEF'S OLD FASHIONED

SERVES 1

This is our smoky, savory, pork-infused version of a classic old fashioned and a house favorite of a lot of our guests.

- 2½ ounces Smoked Pork–Infused Bourbon (recipe follows)
- 3 dashes of Angostura bitters
- 1 strip orange zest

Pour the bourbon into a mixing glass filled with ice. Add the bitters and stir to mix well and chill.

Put a fresh ice cube or two (the bigger the cube, the better, so it doesn't melt and dilute the cocktail) in a double old-fashioned glass and strain the drink into the glass. Garnish with the orange zest and serve.

SMOKED PORK–INFUSED BOURBON

MAKES ENOUGH FOR 5 COCKTAILS

- 1 cup plus 3 tablespoons bourbon
- 2 tablespoons Smoked Pork Fat (see right)
- 2 tablespoons plus 1½ teaspoons Simple Syrup (see right)

In a sealable plastic bag, combine the bourbon and pork fat and seal, then cook sous-vide at 131°F for 1 hour. (Alternatively, submerge the bag of bourbon and pork fat in a pot of water and bring to 131°F. Continue to cook for 1 hour.) Transfer the bag to the freezer for 8 hours or overnight, then strain to remove all of the solidified pork fat.

Transfer to an airtight container and then stir in the simple syrup. Store in the refrigerator for up to 1 week.

SMOKED PORK FAT

MAKES ABOUT 1 POUND

- 1 cup applewood chips
- 1 pound pork back fat

Soak the wood chips in water to cover for at least 30 minutes or up to 45 minutes. When ready to cook, drain the chips thoroughly.

Set up a grill for cold-smoking (see page 14). Place the pork fat on the side of the grill grate opposite the smoker and fill your smoking apparatus with the drained applewood chips or pile the chips on the fire. Cover the grill and smoke for 1 hour.

Grind the pork fat through a meat grinder. Place the fat in a small saucepan and melt over low heat, then strain through a fine-mesh strainer and refrigerate until solid. Store in an airtight container in the refrigerator for up to 1 month.

SIMPLE SYRUP

MAKES ABOUT 1 CUP

- 1 cup sugar
- 1 cup water

In a saucepan over medium heat, combine the sugar and the water and warm gently, stirring to help dissolve the sugar. When the sugar is completely dissolved, remove from the heat and let cool.

Transfer to a bottle or jar, cap or cover tightly, and store in the refrigerator for up to 1 month.

WHITE NEGRONI

SERVES 1

A riff on one of the Campari classics, using a clear bitter liqueur instead to give it a completely different look (pictured opposite).

1½ ounces high-quality gin

¾ ounce Kina L'Avion d'Or or other white aperitif wine

½ ounce Suze or other bitter gentian liqueur

1 strip grapefruit zest

Combine the gin, wine, and liqueur in a mixing glass and stir. Add about 6 medium ice cubes and stir to dilute, about 30 complete stirs. Pour over fresh ice in a double old-fashioned glass. Garnish with the grapefruit zest and serve.

PERAZZI

SERVES 1

Inspired by bubbly Italian favorite the Aperol spritz, our Perazzi has no soda water and adds amaro to give the drink an extra layer of depth and flavor.

¾ ounce Amaro Cia Ciaro, Averna, or Meletti Amaro

¾ ounce Aperol

½ ounce freshly squeezed lemon juice

2 ounces prosecco

1 strip orange zest

Combine the amaro, Aperol, and lemon juice in a cocktail shaker and shake with ice. Double-strain into a coupe glass and top with the prosecco. Garnish with the orange zest and serve.

5TH & ADAMS

SERVES 1

An ode to an intersection in Los Angeles, the 5th & Adams is a spicy and fruity mescal cocktail everyone can get behind.

1½ ounces high-quality mescal
1 ounce pineapple juice
¾ ounce Ginger Syrup (see right)
½ ounce freshly squeezed lemon juice
2 dashes of Peychaud's bitters
1 pineapple spear

Combine the mescal, pineapple juice, ginger syrup, lemon juice, and bitters in a cocktail shaker and shake with ice. Double-strain into a coupe glass. Garnish with the pineapple spear and serve.

GINGER SYRUP

MAKES ABOUT ¼ CUP

¼ cup sugar
2 tablespoons fresh ginger juice

Combine the sugar, ginger juice, and 1 tablespoon water in a blender and process until completely smooth and emulsified; it may take as long as 10 minutes. Use immediately.

BESTIA COLA

SERVES 1

What is the world's most popular drink with food? A Coca-Cola. This cocktail was made to look and taste like Coca-Cola without actually using any of the soda, making it the perfect pairing for almost every dish.

- **1 ounce freshly squeezed grapefruit juice**
- **¾ ounce Punt E Mes**
- **¾ ounce Cappelletti**
- **½ ounce freshly squeezed lemon juice**
- **½ ounce honey**
- **¼ ounce aged balsamic vinegar**
- **¼ ounce maraschino cherry liquid, plus 1 high-quality maraschino cherry**
- **2 ounces club soda**
- **1 lemon wedge**

In a cocktail shaker filled with ice, combine the grapefruit juice, Punt E Mes, Cappelletti, lemon juice, honey, vinegar, and cherry liquid. Shake to mix well, then add the club soda. Fill a Collins glass with ice. Strain the cocktail into the Collins glass, garnish with the lemon wedge and maraschino cherry, and serve.

HAPPY TALK

SERVES 1

Everyone loves the look of a tiki drink, but sometimes the sweetness can be overwhelming. Happy Talk (pictured opposite) was our way of creating a fun tiki-style drink that's still balanced and can be sipped with food without overpowering it.

- **1½ ounces dark Jamaican rum**
- **¾ ounce freshly squeezed lime juice**
- **½ ounce dry curaçao**
- **½ ounce fresh pineapple juice**
- **⅓ ounce Velvet falernum**
- **¼ ounce yellow Chartreuse**
- **2 dashes of aromatic bitters**
- **1 orange slice**
- **1 high-quality maraschino cherry**
- **1 small sprig mint**

In a cocktail shaker filled with ice, combine the rum, lime juice, curaçao, pineapple juice, Velvet falernum, Chartreuse, and bitters and shake to mix well. Strain into a tulip glass. Add crushed ice to cover. Garnish with the orange slice, cherry, and mint and serve.

CHARCUTERIE

Spicy coppa
7.22
pepper
10.21

I've been obsessed with cured meats since way back at my first real kitchen job. The chef there was curing pork jowls, which we would then use in a multitude of dishes, like spaghetti carbonara and bucatini all'amatriciana. I had never seen curing in action before, and immediately I was hooked. The impact was incredible. I couldn't believe how this ancient, seemingly simple technique could completely transform a piece of meat into a powerful tool for umami. That first cure was the beginning of what's now become one of my life's passions.

Today at Bestia, cured meats are the cornerstone of the menu. Almost every dish features something that went through a fermentation and aging process, which ultimately gives it a soulful depth of flavor. But I didn't get here overnight. There were years of trial and error, extensive reading, and experimentation. I've now been curing meats for more than a decade, and I still feel like there's more to learn. But it's exactly this complexity that drives me.

As much as I have learned about the science behind meat curing, to me it's still a magical process. You cure something, then age it for months. When you finally get a taste, it can be exhilarating or painful, depending on the result. After all, you've invested tons of time into each piece. So, when tasting each new morsel, if you're lucky, you think, "This is incredible"; or, if it isn't, you have to think, "What am I going to do to make it better?" My goal with this chapter is to share the lessons I've learned, and hopefully allow you the thrill of perfect results on the first try. But whatever the turnout, don't be discouraged if something fails. We all learn through failure.

A note for the home cook: I've gone into a lot of detail in these recipes, but this chapter is aimed at advanced cooks who may have experimented with meat curing before, or perhaps work in a professional kitchen and possess a relatively advanced level of culinary skill. That's not to say you shouldn't attempt these if you're a charcuterie novice, but I also want to be up front that the equipment, time, technique, and resources necessary for safe fermentation and aging are not insignificant.

KEYS TO SUCCESSFUL MEAT CURING

Sourcing

Most people think that salami is made up of leftovers and nasty bits, but that's not the general truth, and certainly not the case for us. At Bestia, we use the highest-quality, freshest, most flavorful pork we can find—non-GMO, pasture-raised, heritage-breed pigs from Marin Sun Farms. We're in love with this product, and you should be able to find the same or similar quality from a local farm or quality butcher shops. Anything less and you'll taste the difference in the end. And make sure the animal is mature and heavy; if the muscles aren't large or fatty enough, you can end up with a small, dry end product.

Butchering, Dicing, and Grinding

Sharp tools and near-freezing temperatures are the keys to efficient, safe, and uniform butchering, skinning, dicing, and grinding. The low temperature will also help prevent smear—a fatty paste—during grinding, which can happen when the meat and fat are too warm, or your grinder blades are too dull. This will result in dry, brittle salami.

All of our salamis are made of both diced and ground meat. This is for the visual effect as well as binding and texture. The smaller the salami, the smaller the dice must be, but for larger salamis, you can play around with the size of the dice to achieve the look and texture you want.

Salt and Sugar

KOSHER SALT

The most important ingredient in the curing process is salt. It preserves the meat by dehydrating it and decreases the possibility of bacteria growth. These recipes all call for kosher salt (we like Diamond brand), but you can substitute sea salt if you like. Just be sure *not* to use iodized salt of any kind. The chemicals in iodized salt will poorly affect the end product.

CURING SALT

Sodium nitrite, also called Instacure #1, is a curing salt used for short cures that will in the end be cooked. Sodium nitrate, also called Instacure #2, is a curing salt used for long cures that don't get cooked. Sodium nitrites are crucial to prevent bacteria from growing during the curing process, and they also help preserve color and keep fat from tasting rancid. Nitrates, another chemical compound, act more like a time-release nitrite. Over time, nitrates become nitrites during the longer cures. Nitrites and nitrates together are essential for the curing process for the looks, safety, and the longevity of the product.

SUGAR

Granulated sugar or dextrose are added to balance the salt in cured meats, but, most important, sugar acts a food source for fermentation (see following).

Stuffing and Pricking

Any freestanding sausage stuffer should work for these recipes. Slide the open end of the casing onto the tube end of the stuffer, then turn the crank while lightly holding the casing onto the stuffer and releasing slowly as the meat is fed into the casing. The proper pressure will take some getting used to, but don't be discouraged; it takes a lot of practice. It's important to pack the meat as tightly as possible. Any air within the sausage can cause spoilage and a rancid flavor. Prick the sausages while stuffing to release any visible air pockets, then thoroughly prick again all over after tying. As the meat starts to dry and shrink, the casing will do the same. If not, there will be a gap between the meat and the casing in the end product.

Fermentation

Fermentation is an agent of preservation, providing the acidity and sourness necessary to balance the meat's richness. By lowering pH levels and developing lactic acid, fermentation creates a harsh environment for harmful bacteria, which results in an edible-safe product. Cooked-fermented sausages use high temperatures for a short period of time to create this acidic character, while dry-cured meats ferment at lower temperatures for a longer period of time.

There are two types of cultures that we use to ferment:

CHR Hansen F-RM-52 is used for fast acidification and should be fermented between 70° and 90°F.

CHR Hansen T-SPX is milder in acidity and should be fermented between 65° and 80°F.

We get ours from butcher-packer.com.

Keep both cultures frozen to preserve freshness, and each will need to bloom in distilled water for 10 to 30 minutes before using.

To ferment, you need to hang your sausage or other meat in a fermentation chamber—which is essentially any enclosed space that has between 80 and 90 percent humidity and is set to the temperature outlined in each recipe—until the pH drops below 5.3 (see following).

MEASURING PH

At the restaurant, we use an electronic meter to measure the pH of the meat throughout the fermentation process. These meters are expensive, but the process can be done at home using Hydrion MicroFine testing strips, which use color comparison to give you a close reading of the pH. While these aren't as precise as the electronic meter, they're accurate enough. The strips come in two ranges, 3.9 to 5.7 pH and 4.9 to 6.9 pH; most salami products will be in the range of 4.6 to 5.3 pH. To test, purée 1 part chopped meat with 2 parts distilled water in a blender. Dip 1 inch of the testing strip into the meat solution and match the results to the color on the chart.

GOOD MOLD

Developing the right exterior mold will help prevent the salami from drying out and add a nice aroma to the finished product. At Bestia, we use Bactoferm Mold-600. To use, in a spray bottle, mix 2.5 grams of mold culture into 1 liter of distilled water and spray the salami with the solution during the first 48 hours of fermentation.

Storing

Each recipe includes storing instructions. For longer-term storing, vacuum-sealed charcuterie will keep for up to 3 months in a cool, dark spot.

The Curing Cellar

At Bestia, we have a cellar for curing our meats, which I keep at between 53°F and 55°F and at 75 percent humidity. Less than 75 percent humidity might dry out your product on the outside, but not the inside, while too much humidity (anything more than 80 percent) can cause rot and unwanted mold growth. Our curing cellars are specifically designed for this purpose, but at home you could use a wine cellar or even a basement conditioned to the stated temperature and humidity ranges to create that type of environment, or close to it. There are several resources online to research the best way to create a curing cellar at home.

Equipment

Not all of the equipment at right is necessary for each of the recipes that follows, but every item is called for at some point in the chapter. Sausagemaker.com or butcher-packer.com are great sources for these specialty tools needed to make cured meats.

EQUIPMENT

Butcher's Twine: For tying casings and trussing cured meats

Food Processor: For emulsifying mortadella

Instant-Read Thermometer: To read temperatures of all cooked meats accurately

Meat Grinder with Blades: For all sausages and salamis. One with a strong grinding motor is best

Meat Saw: For butchering

pH Meter: To measure pH during fermentation

Plastic Containers with Lids: For storing seasoned meat overnight or the larger muscles for longer periods of time

Sausage Casings: All of these recipes call for natural casings, either beef bung, beef middles (cow intestines), or hog casings (pig intestines)

Sausage Mixer: To knead the meat and achieve an even distribution of the ingredients (optional; you can also mix by hand)

Sausage Prickers: To remove any air pockets and prevent the casing from separating from the meat

Sausage Stuffer with Tube Attachments: For any stuffed sausages

Scale: To accurately measure all weights

Sharp Knife: For uniform cutting and dicing; a sharp blade makes the job quicker and more efficient

Spice Grinder: For freshly ground spices for seasoning

Steamer: To steam the semicured meats that you won't want to poach

Vacuum Sealer: For poaching meat without water diluting the flavor, or storing cured meat; just peel off the skin, seal, and store for 3 months.

THE LIFE CYCLE OF A PIG AT BESTIA

Every Friday morning, two whole 220-pound, pasture-raised, non-GMO Red Wattle pigs arrive at the restaurant. With bone saws, knives, and cleavers lined up like surgical tools, Mario goes to work methodically dissecting each pig into its various parts. It's strenuous work, and I don't have to get my pork this way, but I want to. As a hunter, I feel the need to use every part of every animal I kill. If I didn't, the sport wouldn't be fun for me. The same goes for the restaurant; I force myself to find ways to utilize every piece of every animal. Trust me, it'd be so easy to throw away all of the skin every time we butcher a pig. We'd have a ton more space in our walk-in if we did. But I like to use it anyway, smoking it to infuse into stocks and add flavor to our pork ragu. Following is a basic breakdown of how every bit of the 440 pounds of pig we go through each week makes its way onto the Bestia menu.

THE BREAKDOWN

Back Fat: Salami, 'Nduja

Belly: Pork Belly

Bones: Roasted for stock

Chops: Tomahawk Chop

Ears: Pig Ear Salad

Head: Coppa di Testa

Leg: Culatello, Speck, Prosciutto

Porterhouse: Pork Porterhouse

Shank: Braised for Casuela special

Shoulders: Coppa, Norcina Sausage, Salami, 'Nduja, pork ragu, Coppa Steak

Skin: Pork ragu, pork broth

Trotters: Gelatin for terrine

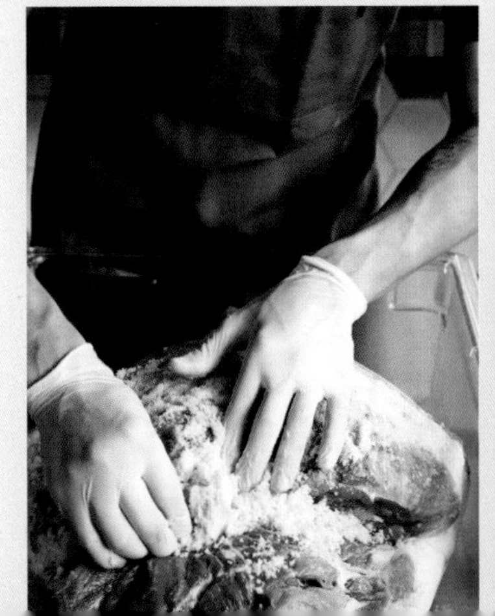

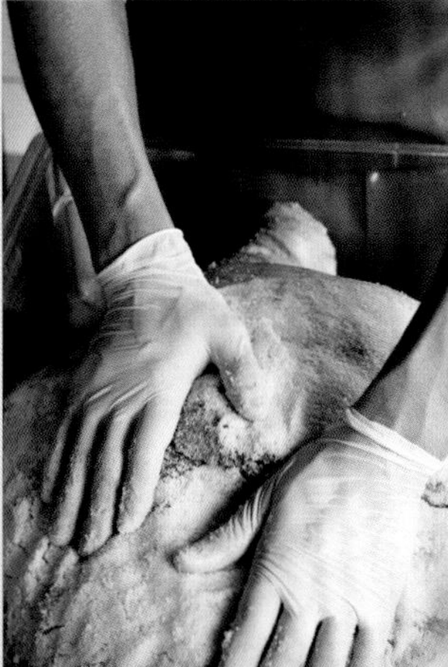

NORCINA SAUSAGE

MAKES 1 KILOGRAM/2¼ POUNDS

This simple, clean-tasting sausage is not infused with any specific spice—just salt, pepper, and garlic. That plainness is intentional, as it gets added into our Cavatelli alla Norcina (see Note), which already has a lot of flavor. This mixture also works as a general base recipe for other sausages: add some fennel seeds for fennel sausage, red pepper flakes and paprika for spicy Italian sausage, or rosemary and sugar for breakfast sausage.

---

750 grams lean pork shoulder

250 grams pork back fat

30 grams cold (about 39°F) distilled water

16.5 grams kosher salt

2.5 grams Instacure #1 (see page 74)

5 grams Microplaned or very finely minced garlic

4 grams freshly ground black pepper

2 grams dextrose

10 feet of hog casing (32 to 35 millimeters in diameter), or as needed

Cut all of the pork shoulder and pork back fat into 1-inch dice and place in a large bowl in the freezer—along with the grinder parts—until firm but not frozen, at least 30 minutes but no more than 45 minutes.

Grind the chilled meat and fat through a ¼-inch plate and return to the bowl. Add the cold distilled water, kosher salt, Instacure #1, garlic, black pepper, and dextrose, then knead the meat mixture for 2 to 3 minutes, until the meat firms and has a tacky texture and a small portion sticks to the underside of your palm without falling.

Set up the sausage stuffer and fill it with the meat mixture. Case the sausage in the hog casing to the desired length, making sure that you thoroughly prick the entire length of each sausage all over while you're stuffing to eliminate air pockets. Use immediately, or refrigerate in an airtight container for up to 3 days.

NOTE

At the restaurant, we do not case the sausage. Instead we panfry Ping-Pong-size balls, then halve them and add them to our Cavatelli alla Norcina, page 197.

LAMBRUSCO–BLACK PEPPER SALAMI

MAKES 665 GRAMS/1½ POUNDS

This salami and the one on page 80 are very simple and don't have a lot going on. It's not about how many ingredients we add to them, but rather the quality of the pork that we start with. As in most Italian food, less is more; and that's our approach.

- 750 grams lean pork shoulder
- 250 grams pork back fat
- 28 grams kosher salt
- 2.5 grams Instacure #2 (see page 74)
- 4.5 grams dextrose
- 4 grams Microplaned or very finely minced garlic
- 5 grams black peppercorns
- 25 grams Lambrusco wine
- 0.5 gram T-SPX starter culture (see page 75)
- 50 grams cold (about 39°F) distilled water
- 10 feet of beef middle casing (55 to 60 millimeters in diameter), or as needed
- Bactoferm Mold-600, in spray bottle (see page 75)

Cut all of the pork shoulder into 1-inch dice and place in a large bowl in the freezer—along with the grinder parts and the pork back fat—until the meat is firm but not frozen, at least 30 minutes but no more than 45 minutes.

Grind the chilled pork shoulder through a ¼-inch plate and return to the bowl. Cut the chilled pork back fat into ¼-inch dice and add to the bowl. Add the kosher salt, Instacure #2, dextrose, garlic, peppercorns, and Lambrusco to the meat and mix well by hand, then refrigerate.

In a small bowl, dissolve the starter culture in the cold distilled water and let it sit and bloom for 10 minutes. When the starter is ready, add to the meat mixture and knead for 2 to 3 minutes, until the meat firms and has a tacky texture and a small portion sticks to the underside of your palm without falling.

Set up the sausage stuffer and fill it with the meat mixture. Tie one end of the casing with enough twine to form a loop for hanging the sausage. Stuff the casing as tightly as possible, pricking anywhere you see potential air pockets. When you reach 12 inches, tie the other end like you did the first but without the loop. Process the rest of the meat the same way. Prick the sausages again, this time all over, to release any air between the meat and the casing.

At this point you'll have leftover sausage mix. Wrap it in plastic wrap as close as possible to the same shape and size as the cased product; this is what you'll be testing for pH during fermentation. Ferment in a cool, dark place between 65°F and 80°F at 80 to 90 percent humidity, checking the pH repeatedly, until the pH drops under 5.3; this will take close to 48 hours. Spray the salami with the mold culture during this phase of fermentation. After fermentation, transfer the salami to the curing cellar to hang at 53°F to 55°F and at 75 percent humidity until it has lost one-third of its initial weight.

Store the salami on a paper towel in the refrigerator for up to 2 weeks.

FENNEL POLLEN SALAMI

MAKES 665 GRAMS/1½ POUNDS

750 grams lean pork shoulder

250 grams pork back fat

28 grams kosher salt

2.5 grams Instacure #2 (see page 74)

4.5 grams dextrose

4.5 grams Microplaned or very finely minced garlic

4 grams fennel pollen (see Note, page 18)

4 grams cracked black pepper

0.5 gram T-SPX starter culture, (see page 75)

50 grams cold (about 39°F) distilled water

10 feet of beef middle casing (55 to 60 millimeters in diameter), or as needed

Bactoferm Mold-600, in spray bottle (see page 75)

Cut all of the pork shoulder into 1- inch dice and place in a large bowl in the freezer—along with the grinder parts and the pork back fat—until the meat is firm but not frozen, at least 30 minutes but no more than 45 minutes.

Grind the chilled pork shoulder through a ¼-inch plate and return to the bowl. Cut the chilled pork back fat into a ¼-inch dice and add to the bowl. Add the kosher salt, Instacure #2, dextrose, garlic, fennel pollen, and black pepper to the meat and mix well by hand, then refrigerate.

In a small bowl, dissolve the starter culture in the cold distilled water and let it sit and bloom for 10 minutes. When the starter is ready, add to the meat mixture and knead for 2 to 3 minutes, until the meat firms and has a tacky texture and a small portion sticks to the underside of your palm without falling.

Set up the sausage stuffer and fill it with the meat mixture. Tie one end of the casing with enough twine to form a loop for hanging the sausage. Stuff the casing as tightly as possible, pricking anywhere you see potential air pockets. When you reach 12 inches, tie the other end like you did the first but without the loop. Process the rest of the meat the same way. Prick the sausages again, this time all over, to release any air between the meat and the casing.

At this point you'll have leftover sausage mix. Wrap it in plastic wrap as close as possible to the same shape and size as the cased product; this is what you'll be testing for pH during fermentation. Ferment in a cool, dark place between 65°F and 80°F at 80 to 90 percent humidity, checking the pH repeatedly, until the pH drops under 5.3; this will take close to 48 hours. Spray the salami with the mold culture during this phase of fermentation. After fermentation, transfer the salami to the curing cellar to hang at 53°F to 55°F and at 75 percent humidity until it has lost one-third of its initial weight.

Store the salami on a paper towel in the refrigerator for up to 2 weeks.

'NDUJA

MAKES 950 GRAMS/2 POUNDS

'Nduja is a spicy, spreadable pork sausage from Calabria, typically made from off-cuts and Calabrian chiles. At the restaurant, we actually case both our 'Nduja and White 'Nduja (page 84) in a beef bung, but here we use beef middles because the quantity is much smaller. If you like, you can make bigger batches and case them in a beef bung like we do. We like the way the spiciness complements our steamed mussels and clams (see page 134) and our 'Nduja Pizza (page 164).

- **750 grams pork back fat**
- **250 grams lean pork shoulder**
- **26 grams kosher salt**
- **2.5 grams Instacure #2 (see page 74)**
- **5 grams Microplaned or very finely minced garlic**
- **33 grams ground red pepper flakes**
- **30 grams paprika**
- **5 grams dextrose**
- **3 grams ground fennel seeds**
- **0.5 gram T-SPX starter culture (see page 75)**
- **50 grams cold (about 39°F) distilled water**
- **10 feet of beef middle casing (60 to 65 millimeters in diameter), or as needed**

Cut all of the pork back fat and pork shoulder into 1-inch dice and place in a large bowl in the freezer—along with the grinder parts—until firm but not frozen, at least 30 minutes but no more than 45 minutes.

When the fat and meat are chilled, add the kosher salt, Instacure #2, garlic, red pepper flakes, paprika, dextrose, and ground fennel seeds and mix well by hand. Grind the mixture through a ¼-inch plate and refrigerate.

In a small bowl, dissolve the starter culture in the cold distilled water and let it sit and bloom for 10 minutes. When the starter is ready, add to the meat mixture and knead for 2 to 3 minutes, until the meat firms and has a tacky texture and a small portion sticks to the underside of your palm without falling.

Set up the sausage stuffer and fill it with the meat mixture. Tie one end of the casing with enough twine to form a loop for hanging the sausage. Stuff the casing as tightly as possible, pricking anywhere you see potential air pockets. When you reach 12 inches, tie the other end like you did the first but without the loop. Process the rest of the meat the same way. Prick the sausages again, this time all over, to release any air between the meat and the casing.

At this point you'll have leftover sausage mix. Wrap it in plastic wrap as close as possible to the same shape and size as the cased product; this is what you'll be testing for pH during fermentation. Ferment in a cool, dark place between 65°F and 80°F at 80 to 90 percent humidity, checking the pH repeatedly, until the pH drops under 5.3; this will take close to 48 hours. After fermentation, transfer the 'nduja to the curing cellar to hang at 53°F to 55°F and at 75 percent humidity for 1 month.

Store in the refrigerator for up to 2 weeks.

NORCINA SAUSAGE

LAMBRUSCO–BLACK PEPPER SALAMI AND FENNEL POLLEN SALAMI

'NDUJA

WHITE 'NDUJA

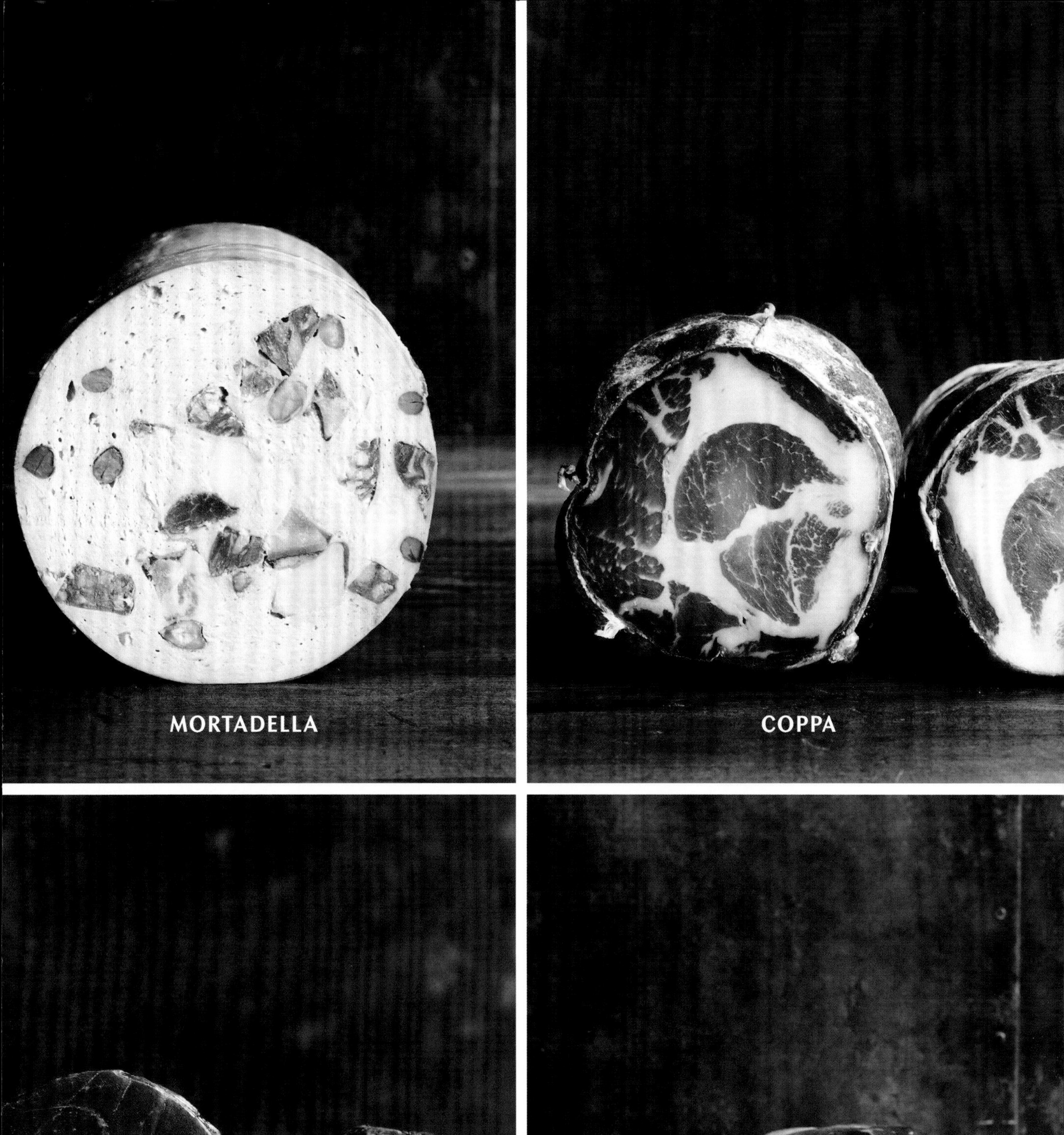
MORTADELLA
COPPA

BRESAOLA

PROSCIUTTO

WHITE 'NDUJA

MAKES 950 GRAMS/2 POUNDS

This white version of our 'Nduja (page 81) is reminiscent of a whipped *lardo*. We call it 'nduja because the method is very similar, but it has no spice—so technically it's not 'nduja at all. At the restaurant, we spread it on toast with date purée for a sweet and salty addition to our *salumi* board.

---

5 grams fennel pollen (see Note, page 18)

3 grams ground fennel seeds

3 grams freshly ground black pepper

750 grams pork back fat

250 grams lean pork shoulder

25 grams kosher salt

2.5 grams Instacure #2 (see page 74)

5 grams Microplaned or very finely minced garlic

5 grams dextrose

0.5 gram T-SPX starter culture (see page 75)

50 grams cold (about 39°F) distilled water

10 feet of beef middle casing (60 to 65 millimeters in diameter), or as needed

In a small saucepan over medium-low heat, combine the fennel pollen, fennel seeds, and black pepper and toast, stirring occasionally, until fragrant, about 3 minutes. Set aside to cool.

Cut all of the pork back fat and pork shoulder into 1-inch dice and place in a large bowl in the freezer—along with the grinder parts—until firm but not frozen, at least 30 minutes but no more than 45 minutes.

When the fat and meat are chilled, add the kosher salt, Instacure #2, garlic, dextrose, fennel pollen, fennel seeds, and black pepper and mix well by hand. Grind the mixture through a ¼-inch plate and refrigerate.

In a small bowl, dissolve the starter culture in the cold distilled water and let it sit and bloom for 10 minutes. When the starter is ready, add it to the meat mixture and knead for 2 to 3 minutes, until the meat firms and has a tacky texture and a small portion sticks to the underside of your palm without falling.

Set up the sausage stuffer and fill it with the meat mixture. Tie one end of the casing with enough twine to form a loop for hanging the sausage. Stuff the casing as tightly as possible, pricking anywhere you see potential air pockets. When you reach 12 inches, tie the other end like you did the first but without the loop. Process the rest of the meat the same way. Prick the sausages again, this time all over, to release any air between the meat and the casing.

At this point you'll have leftover sausage mix. Wrap it in plastic wrap as close as possible to the same shape and size as the cased product; this is what you'll be testing for pH during fermentation. Ferment in a cool, dark place between 65°F and 80°F at 80 to 90 percent humidity, checking the pH repeatedly, until the pH drops under 5.3; this will take close to 48 hours. After fermentation, transfer the 'nduja to the curing cellar to hang at 53°F to 55°F and at 75 percent humidity for 1 month.

Store in the refrigerator for up to 2 weeks.

MORTADELLA

MAKES 3 KILOGRAMS/6⅔ POUNDS

For years, I've been trying to find ways to use the leftover ends of the cured meats we can't slice at the restaurant. I finally decided to put them into my mortadella. Most mortadella recipes you see in cookbooks are very complicated. Mine is relatively simple, but it's also exactly the version we use at the restaurant. The only difference is that we steam our mortadella instead of simmering it, and the batch here is much smaller than what we make at the restaurant.

PART 1

1.6 kilograms lean pork shoulder

900 grams pork back fat

39 grams kosher salt

6.25 grams Instacure #1 (see page 74)

30 grams sugar

20 grams Microplaned or very finely minced garlic

5 grams ground coriander

5 grams celery salt

5 grams shallot powder or onion powder

5 grams dry mustard

2 grams ground mace

2 grams ground cinnamon

0.5 gram freshly grated nutmeg

625 grams crushed ice

PART 2

500 grams cured meat scraps (or use any scraps from recipes in this chapter or from store-bought cured meat), cut into ½-inch dice (optional)

150 grams pork back fat, cut into ½-inch dice, boiled for 4 minutes, then shocked in ice water

60 grams whole pistachios

5 grams black peppercorns

1 large beef bung casing (5 inches or more in diameter)

For Part 1, cut the pork shoulder and back fat into 1-inch dice and place in a large bowl in the freezer—along with the grinder parts—until firm but not frozen, at least 30 minutes but no more than 45 minutes.

Grind the chilled meat and fat through a ¼-inch plate and return to the bowl. Add all of the remaining ingredients in Part 1, and knead well to combine.

Working in batches, transfer the meat mixture to a food processor and purée into a paste. Transfer to a large bowl as you work and keep the mixture in the refrigerator before and after puréeing; check the temperature throughout this process to make sure it doesn't get warmer than 55°F.

For Part 2, when all of the meat is puréed, fold in the meat scraps, pork fat, pistachios, and black peppercorns and knead the meat for 2 to 3 minutes.

Set up the sausage stuffer and fill it with the meat mixture. Tie one end of the casing with enough twine to form a loop for hanging the sausage. Stuff the casing as tightly as possible. When you reach your desired length, tie the other end like you did the first but without the loop.

Transfer the mortadella to a large pot and add water to cover. Warm over low heat until the water reaches 160°F, then cook until the mortadella reaches an internal temperature of 155°F. This will take 2½ to 4 hours, depending on the size of the beef bung. (Alternatively, cook sous-vide at 160°F until it reaches an internal temperature of 155°F.) Transfer the mortadella to an ice bath and chill to 40°F, then wrap in plastic wrap and refrigerate for 2 days before slicing. Store, cut-end wrapped, in the refrigerator for up to 2 weeks.

COPPA

MAKES 700 GRAMS/1½ POUNDS

Coppa is a muscle that runs from the neck of the pig to the fourth and fifth rib of the shoulder. It is featured two different ways in this book. In the recipe on page 225, it is marinated and grilled. Here, it is cured in the traditional style and coated with a nice amount of spice to cut the richness of the meat, making it perfect for a charcuterie board.

37.5 grams kosher salt
2.5 grams Instacure #2 (see page 74)
4.5 grams sugar
1 kilogram coppa
12 grams Microplaned or very finely minced garlic
20 grams cracked black peppercorns
6 bay leaves, torn
1 gram whole red pepper flakes
8 juniper berries, smashed
28 grams dry red wine
5 grams paprika
5 grams ground red pepper flakes
5 grams Aleppo pepper
3 grams shallot power
1 beef bung casing (large enough for the diameter of the coppa)

NOTE

Here, all of the ingredient amounts are scaled to a 1-kilogram coppa; you will have to adjust the quantities depending on the weight of the coppa. For example, if your coppa is 1.6 kilograms, multiply all of the other ingredients by 1.6. Refrigerate the curing meat for 2 days per every 500 grams of meat, at no colder than 35°F.

In a small bowl, whisk together the kosher salt, Instacure #2, and sugar. Place the coppa in a plastic container large enough to hold it without crowding and rub the curing mixture all over and into the meat, distributing it as evenly as possible.

Add the garlic, black peppercorns, bay leaves, whole red pepper flakes, and juniper berries to the meat and turn to coat. Cover and refrigerate for 24 hours. Flip the coppa and continue to refrigerate based on the weight-determined curing time (see Note), flipping again once a day to redistribute the cure. When finished curing, the coppa should feel firm to the touch.

Remove the coppa from the cure and rinse it under cold water for 2 to 3 minutes. Return the coppa to the plastic container, massage it with the red wine, and return to the refrigerator, uncovered, for 24 hours.

In a small bowl, whisk together the paprika, ground red pepper flakes, Aleppo pepper, and shallot powder and rub all over the coppa.

Tie one end of the beef bung casing with enough twine to form a loop for hanging the coppa. Stuff the chile-rubbed coppa into the beef bung by hand as tightly as possible, then tie the other end like you did the first end but without the loop. Thoroughly prick the entire length of the coppa all over to eliminate any air pockets.

Truss the casing as tightly as possible, as you would a large roast. (The Internet has many good resources with details on how to truss.) Transfer the coppa to the curing cellar and age at 53°F to 55°F and at 75 percent humidity until it has lost one-third of its initial weight. This will take 3 months or more, depending on the size of the coppa.

Store on a paper towel in the refrigerator for up to 2 weeks.

BRESAOLA

MAKES 750 GRAMS/1¾ POUNDS

I like to age bresaola for less time than I do any other whole-muscle pork cure. When it's dried completely, it becomes too dry. When it still has a little bit of moisture and give, it melts in your mouth. If you can catch it at exactly the right moment, it will be the best bresaola you've ever had.

- 30 grams kosher salt
- 2.5 grams Instacure #2 (see page 74)
- 4.5 grams sugar
- 1 kilogram beef top round
- 16 grams garlic, smashed
- 2 grams freshly grated orange zest
- 2 grams red pepper flakes
- 5 juniper berries, smashed
- 3 sprigs thyme
- 1 small sprig rosemary
- 40 grams dry red wine
- 1 beef bung casing (large enough for the diameter of the bresaola)

NOTE

Here, all of the ingredient amounts are scaled to a 1-kilogram bresaola (beef top round); you will have to adjust the quantities depending on the weight of the bresaola. For example, if your bresaola is 1.6 kilograms, multiply all of the other ingredients by 1.6. Refrigerate the curing meat for 2 days per every 500 grams of meat, at no colder than 35°F.

In a small bowl, whisk together the kosher salt, Instacure #2, and sugar. Place the top round in a plastic container large enough to hold it without crowding and rub the curing mixture all over and into the meat, distributing it as evenly as possible.

Add the garlic, orange zest, red pepper flakes, juniper berries, thyme, rosemary, and wine to the meat and turn to coat. Cover and refrigerate for 24 hours. Flip the top round and continue to refrigerate based on the weight-determined curing time (see Note), flipping again once a day to redistribute the cure. When finished curing, the meat should feel firm to the touch.

Remove the top round from the cure and rinse it under cold water for 2 to 3 minutes. Return the top round to the plastic container and refrigerate, uncovered, for 2 hours. Tie one end of the beef bung casing with enough twine to form a loop for hanging the bresaola. Stuff the bresaola into the beef bung by hand as tightly as possible and prick all over, then tie the other end like you did the first end but without the loop. Thoroughly prick the entire length of the bresaola all over to eliminate any air pockets.

Truss the casing as tightly as possible, as you would a large roast. (The Internet has many good resources with details on how to truss.) Transfer the bresaola to the curing cellar and age at 53°F to 55°F and at 75 percent humidity until it has lost one-fourth of its initial weight. This will take 1½ to 2 months, depending on the size of the bresaola. (Again, I like to serve bresaola when it's not too dry.)

Store in the refrigerator for up to 2 weeks.

PROSCIUTTO

MAKES 600 GRAMS/1⅓ POUNDS

The first time I ever made prosciutto, I eyeballed it. I didn't weigh the salt or the meat, and yet somehow it turned out amazing. When the prosciutto was finally ready, Gino had a party at his house, and we decided to make piadine and stuff them with the finished product. I put a meat slicer in my car and drove it to his house. Gino was toasting the piadine and stuffing them with burrata and greens and I was slicing the prosciutto—it was just incredible. We all felt so proud celebrating with something that we made, aged, and waited almost a year to taste. We knew after the first bite that it was perfect. Still, that was the last time I ever eyeballed it. I now have a ratio that lets me reliably capture the same experience time and time again. You should be able to source the pig leg from a specialty butcher.

PART 1

1-kilogram bone-in pig leg

56 grams kosher salt

4.5 grams brown sugar

2.5 grams Instacure #2 (see page 74)

PART 2

100 grams leaf lard (see Note)

10 grams rice flour

1 gram freshly ground black pepper

NOTES

Here, all the ingredient amounts in Part 1 are scaled to a 1-kilogram bone-in pig leg; you will have to adjust the quantities depending on the weight of the leg. For example, if your pig leg is 10 kilograms, multiply all of the other Part 1 ingredients by 10.

Leaf lard is the pliable fat that you pull off the inner cavity area of the pig. You can purchase it at a specialty butcher shop.

For Part 1, place the pig leg on a cutting board, skin-side up, and smack it with a mallet all over to soften the muscle. Flip the leg and massage with your thumbs, pushing toward the exposed side to force out any remaining blood. This will decrease the possibility of spoilage. Place the leg in a plastic container large enough to hold it without crowding.

In a small bowl, whisk together the kosher salt, brown sugar, and Instacure #2. Stir a little bit of water into the salt mixture, just until loose enough to help it stick to the pork. First, rub the skin side of the leg with the curing mixture, then flip and coat the exposed meat and (most important) the shank and knee. Cover and refrigerate at a temperature no colder than 35°F. After 24 hours, the leg will release a lot of liquid. Drain by tilting the container over a sink, then return to the refrigerator. Repeat the draining process after 4 or 5 days more, or whenever the leg has released a sufficient quantity of liquid.

Continue to refrigerate the salted leg for 1½ days per 500 grams, typically between 35 and 45 days. When finished curing, the meat should feel firm and dense to the touch. Hang the prosciutto by the foot in a refrigerator at 39°F and 85 percent humidity for 4 to 6 months.

For Part 2, after hanging the leg for 4 to 6 months, it will have lost about one-third of its original weight. At this point, trim a ⅛-inch-thick layer from the exposed meat to get rid of the aged trimmings. Whip the leaf lard in a food processor until smooth and pasty, then add the rice flour and black pepper and blend to combine. Spread the exposed part of the leg with a layer of the whipped fat mixture to cover thoroughly.

Transfer the prosciutto to the curing cellar and hang it from the foot at 53°F to 55°F and at 75 percent humidity. Age for as long as desired before slicing—the longer you age, the more flavor it will develop. At Bestia, I age our prosciutto between 12 and 18 months.

Store in the refrigerator, with the exposed part wrapped in plastic, for up to 3 months. When ready to serve, trim and discard the first piece you slice, then continue slicing.

MARIO BRAVO

When we first opened Bestia, the only butcher we had on staff was me. I was always stuck at the restaurant after service until 3 a.m. butchering whole pigs, lambs, and beef. It was killing me. Around that time, Mario had just been promoted from dishwasher to prep cook, and I remember looking at him and thinking, "This is a guy who likes to cut stuff up."

It sounds weird, but there's a personality for the butchery trade, and Mario has it. He's not afraid of blood, and he's physically and mentally strong. So, I began training him. We'd break down animals together, and I'd explain everything about sanitation, fermentation, salting, curing, and aging. He just got it—like I said, he's a natural.

Mario has an edge that makes him the perfect butcher. He's systematic and orderly, which you need to be when you're butchering five hundred pounds of pork. On top of breaking down four animals every week for four years, in his downtime he takes a variety of butchery courses, and he has started a side business sharpening knives—a perfect edge for $10 a blade. He has dedicated himself to learning the craft at the highest level.

—ORI

SALADS

GENEVIEVE'S LITTLE GEM SALAD

SERVES 4

When Genevieve was pregnant with our daughter, Saffron, I was obsessed with her. When she would walk into the restaurant, waddling with her belly, it was like a ray of sunshine was beaming directly down on her. I couldn't believe how cute she was. So I felt compelled to name a dish after her, and this is the kind of salad she loves—very simple, with a lot of greens. On the whole, the salad is nicely acidic, which makes it good to serve alongside anything on the richer side. Or you can eat it like Genevieve does—on its own, with her fingers.

---

2 large or 4 small heads Little Gem lettuce, cored, leaves left whole

½ cup loosely packed fresh flat-leaf parsley leaves

¼ cup roughly chopped fresh dill

3 large radishes, very thinly sliced

2 tablespoons minced shallot

8 fresh chives, cut into 1-inch pieces

½ cup walnuts, toasted and chopped

3 to 4 tablespoons Walnut Vinaigrette (page 33)

Kosher salt and freshly ground black pepper

1 ounce ricotta salata cheese

½ teaspoon walnut oil

In a large bowl, combine the lettuce, parsley, dill, radishes, shallot, chives, and walnuts and toss gently to mix.

Dress the greens with 3 tablespoons of the vinaigrette and toss quickly, then season with salt and pepper and toss again, making sure each leaf is evenly coated with the dressing.

Transfer the salad to a large serving platter. Using a vegetable peeler, shave strips of ricotta salata over the top. Finish with the small drizzle of walnut oil. Taste and adjust the vinaigrette and salt if needed and serve.

CUCUMBER, PLUM, AND GORGONZOLA SALAD

SERVES 4

This salad came about because I love dill pickles. The celery, dill, and turmeric are a play on classic pickling spices, and the Gorgonzola has the same effect as the blue cheese dip that sometimes accompanies Southern-fried pickles. In summertime, the markets here have a huge variety of cucumbers, and we use a mix of different kinds to add complexity to the salad—each has its own characteristics. Whatever kind you choose, just make sure your cucumbers were grown in the dirt, not a hothouse, and choose plums with a nice amount of acidity; if they're too sweet they'll overwhelm the cucumbers.

---

1 ear sweet corn, husk and silk removed

2 Persian or other thin-skinned cucumbers, halved lengthwise and sliced into half-moons about ¼ inch thick

2 ounces fresh purslane leaves

3 tablespoons Turmeric Vinaigrette (page 33)

Kosher salt and freshly ground black pepper

1 cup packed watercress, tough stems removed

1 ripe plum, halved, pitted, and cut into 16 thin wedges

Maldon or other flaky sea salt

2 tablespoons crème fraîche, at room temperature

1 ounce Gorgonzola cheese, preferably Gorgonzola Dolce, frozen for at least 3 hours

Celery leaves and small dill sprigs for garnish

Pinch of dill or fennel pollen (see Note, page 18; optional)

Preheat a cast-iron frying pan over high heat. Place the corn directly on the pan and let sear, turning as needed, until evenly charred on all sides. Transfer to a cutting board and let sit until cool enough to handle, then cut off the kernels with a knife.

In a large bowl, combine the cucumbers, corn, and purslane and toss by hand to combine. Add 2 tablespoons of the vinaigrette, season with kosher salt and pepper, and toss. Taste and adjust the seasoning as necessary.

In a separate large bowl, lightly dress the watercress with the remaining 1 tablespoon vinaigrette. Season with kosher salt and pepper and toss well.

Pile the cucumber salad in a large shallow serving bowl or on a platter and top it with the dressed watercress. Season the plum slices with Maldon salt and arrange on top of the salad. Whisk the crème fraîche with a fork a little to loosen the consistency and drizzle on top. Grate the frozen Gorgonzola over everything until the entire salad is fully coated. Garnish with the celery leaves, dill, and a pinch of dill pollen, if desired, and serve.

CORALINE AND CITRUS SALAD WITH MASCARPONE YOGURT, RADISH, AND CELERY

SERVES 4

Coraline is new variety of chicory related to endive, radicchio, and dandelion. It looks like a combination of Belgian endive and frisée, and the leaves have some bitterness, which works with this salad's sweet, sour, and spicy notes. The citrus adds a lot of acidity to the salad, so be careful not to overdress. When I first made this salad, Genevieve took one look and asked, "Is that yogurt in there? Isn't that going to be too bitter and sour?" I told her to taste it, but she had already made up her mind. "I guess it's OK," she said. "I don't really like it." I told her, "I don't care, I'm putting it on the menu." A few days later, I caught her eating an entire salad by herself alone in the office. We looked at each other; she shrugged her shoulders. "It's pretty delicious after all," she admitted. "You know better than to listen to me anyway, so get that smirk off your face."

¼ cup plain whole-milk Greek yogurt

3 tablespoons mascarpone

4 heads Coraline chicory or Belgian endive, cored, leaves separated, and cut into 2-inch pieces

1 celery stalk, trimmed and cut into ¼-inch dice

3 radishes, thinly sliced

2 tablespoons roughly chopped wild fennel fronds (see Note), regular fennel fronds, or fresh dill

3 tablespoons Pomegranate Vinaigrette (page 32)

Kosher salt and freshly ground black pepper

¼ teaspoon toasted black sesame seeds

¼ teaspoon fennel pollen (see Note, page 18)

¼ pomelo or sweet grapefruit such as Oro Blanco, supremed (see Note)

¾ blood orange, supremed

1 mandarin orange, supremed

Ground red pepper flakes

Maldon or other flaky sea salt for sprinkling

In a small bowl, stir together the yogurt and mascarpone. Set aside.

In a large bowl, combine the Coraline, celery, radishes, fennel fronds, and vinaigrette and toss by hand, gently massaging each leaf to make sure they are evenly coated with the dressing. Season with kosher salt and black pepper and toss again, then loosely pile the salad onto a large serving platter and sprinkle with the sesame seeds and fennel pollen.

Cut all of the citrus sections crosswise into thirds and scatter evenly over the top of the salad, followed by dollops of the yogurt-mascarpone mixture. Sprinkle with a pinch each of red pepper flakes and Maldon salt and serve.

NOTES

Wild fennel can be found in fields and on hillsides and ocean cliffs. You may be able to find it at your farmers' market. It has a fuller flavor than store-bought fennel.

To supreme citrus, cut off the ends and carefully carve away the peel and pith without cutting into the citrus flesh. Cut out the segments by following the membranes of the citrus.

CHOPPED SALAD WITH BRUSSELS SPROUTS, FENNEL POLLEN SALAMI, FRIED LENTILS, AND FRESH OREGANO

SERVES 4

Salads don't typically have much umami, but this type of salad always does. We use housemade salami, toasted nuts, and golden raisins to give this chopped salad a great texture and balance. The dressing reminds me of the intense savoriness of a larb.

---

2 large Brussels sprouts, trimmed and thinly sliced

2½ ounces baby kale or curly kale leaves, tough stems removed, julienned

3 tablespoons golden raisins, large ones halved

3 tablespoons roasted almonds, halved

15 fresh mint leaves

2 ounces Fennel Pollen Salami (page 80), thinly sliced and cut into 1½-inch matchsticks

2 tablespoons plus 1½ teaspoons Fish Sauce Vinaigrette (page 33)

Kosher salt

1 lemon wedge (optional)

1 tablespoon Fried Lentils (page 54)

15 fresh oregano leaves

Pinch of red pepper flakes

In a large bowl, combine the Brussels sprouts, kale, raisins, almonds, mint, and salami. Add the vinaigrette and toss well. Taste and adjust the seasoning with salt, toss again, and pile the salad onto a serving platter. Taste again, and if it needs more acidity, squeeze the lemon wedge to add a couple of drops of lemon juice. Garnish with the lentils, oregano, and red pepper flakes and serve.

ARUGULA AND OPAL BASIL SALAD

SERVES 4

Throughout the week, the menu at Bestia alternates between different large-format pork dishes, like the tomahawk chop and the porterhouse. This simple green salad is what I like to serve with these larger proteins. It's clean and aromatic, and the opal basil goes really well with pork. Opal basil, which is milder in flavor than regular basil, can be found at farmers' markets.

---

4 ounces arugula, tough stems removed, or baby arugula

15 small fresh opal basil leaves or 7 or 8 small regular basil leaves

Kosher salt and freshly ground black pepper

2 tablespoons Lemon-Chile Vinaigrette (see page 32)

In a large bowl, combine the arugula and basil and toss gently. Season with salt and pepper. Add the vinaigrette, toss well, and serve.

ARUGULA, RADISH, AND TARRAGON SALAD

SERVES 4

This simple salad works really well with the recipe for coppa steak on page 225. It might seem like the tarragon in the salad and the pickled mushrooms that accompany the steak would not be the best combination, but they actually complement each other, and mixing all of the elements together creates the perfect bite.

---

4 ounces arugula, tough stems removed, or baby arugula

2 radishes, sliced paper-thin

Leaves from 2 sprigs tarragon

Kosher salt and freshly ground black pepper

2 tablespoons Apple Cider Vinaigrette (page 31)

In a large bowl, combine the arugula, radishes, and tarragon and toss gently. Season with salt and pepper. Add the vinaigrette, toss well, and serve.

TOMATO AND BURRATA WITH SMOKED BOTTARGA, FINGER LIME, TOASTED BUCKWHEAT, AND MARJORAM

SERVES 4

This is my take on the seasonal favorite tomato and burrata salad. Using cinnamon in the vinaigrette brings out the inherent warmth that tomatoes capture while ripening in the sun. The finger lime and toasted buckwheat add texture and help tone down a dish that traditionally registers as sweet, while the bottarga and marjoram finish it with a much-needed savoriness.

1½ teaspoons buckwheat

1 pound heirloom tomatoes, any seasonal mixture, small ones halved, larger ones cut into bite-size wedges

2 tablespoons Cinnamon Vinaigrette (page 31)

6 ounces burrata cheese, broken into 1-inch pieces

Maldon or other flaky sea salt and freshly ground black pepper

Pearls of 1 whole finger lime (see Note), or ⅛ teaspoon freshly grated lemon zest

Leaves from 2 sprigs marjoram

¼ piece Smoked Egg Yolk Bottarga (page 53) or store-bought bottarga

In a small saucepan over high heat, toast the buckwheat, tossing frequently, until the kernels start to brown but do not burn. Remove from the heat and toss to help cool quickly. Set aside.

In a bowl, toss the tomatoes in the vinaigrette. Arrange the tomatoes in a single layer on a serving platter. Place the burrata among the tomatoes, then evenly top the salad with the toasted buckwheat and season with salt and pepper. Place the finger lime pearls evenly on top of each of the burrata pieces, then garnish the plate with the marjoram leaves. Finish by grating the bottarga over the top and serve.

NOTE

Finger limes are in season mid-July through January. They can be found at farmers' markets, specialty stores, or online.

THREE FARRO SALADS

In Israel, we have a lot of salads that are based around grains. I chose to do something similar with farro, which is nutty, firm, and fits better with the style of our restaurant. But due to a lot of mediocre deli-case versions, farro has gotten a bad reputation, so it's a challenge to make it interesting. I would never put a farro salad on the menu, nor put it in this book, if the flavor combinations weren't complex and a little out of the ordinary. We use cooked farro infused with aromatics (see below) as the base for salads that change year-round depending on what produce is in season, with enough refreshing elements—herbs and a cool, creamy base that helps bind ingredients together—so that it still feels like you just ate a salad along with the heartiness of the grain, but not in a dorky quinoa kind of way.

Following are three seasonal variations.

COOKED FARRO

MAKES ABOUT 4 CUPS

- 2 cups farro
- ½ yellow onion, quartered
- 1 celery stalk, trimmed and halved crosswise
- 1 small carrot, peeled and halved crosswise
- 3 fresh bay leaves or 1 dried
- 1 Fresno chile, halved lengthwise
- 2 tablespoons kosher salt
- 2 tablespoons extra-virgin olive oil

In a saucepan over medium-high heat, combine the farro, onion, celery, carrot, bay leaves, chile, salt, and 2 quarts water and bring to a boil. Lower the heat to maintain a gentle simmer and cook, uncovered, until the farro has a firm, chewy texture, about 40 minutes.

Remove the pan from the heat and let sit for 10 minutes, then drain.

Line a baking sheet with parchment paper.

Pour the drained farro onto the prepared baking sheet and spread into an even layer. Pick out all of the vegetables and aromatics and discard. Transfer the farro to a bowl, add the olive oil, and toss to coat the grains.

Use immediately, or refrigerate in an airtight container for up to 3 days.

FARRO SALAD WITH POMEGRANATE AND WALNUTS

SERVES 4

- 2 cups cooked farro (see facing page)
- ½ cup pomegranate seeds (see Note)
- ½ cup roughly chopped toasted walnuts
- ¼ cup roughly chopped fresh mint
- 2 tablespoons finely diced red onion
- 8 fresh basil leaves, torn into small pieces
- Kosher salt and freshly ground black pepper
- ¼ cup Red Wine Vinaigrette (page 32)
- ¼ cup crème fraîche
- ½ clove garlic, Microplaned or finely minced
- ½ serrano chile, seeded and Microplaned or finely minced
- 2 tablespoons minced fresh dill
- ½ teaspoon pomegranate molasses

In a large bowl, combine the farro, pomegranate seeds, walnuts, mint, red onion, and basil. Season with salt and pepper. Add the vinaigrette and toss until just incorporated, but don't overmix. Taste and adjust the salt as needed.

In a small bowl, stir together the crème fraîche, garlic, chile, and dill.

Spread the dill crème fraîche around the base of a serving platter or large, shallow bowl, pile the salad on top. Finish with a drizzle of the pomegranate molasses and a pinch more pepper and serve.

NOTE

There are a few tricks to cleaning pomegranate seeds; here's the one we like. Cut a pomegranate in half. Then, holding it cut-side down over a bowl, firmly and repeatedly hit the outside of the pomegranate with the back of a large chef's knife so the seeds fall into the bowl. Pour a little water into the bowl and the remaining pith should rise to the surface. Skim off the pith and drain the seeds.

FARRO SALAD WITH SUNCHOKES AND SNAP PEAS

SERVES 4

2 cups cooked farro (see page 102)

1 cup snap peas, trimmed and strings removed, cut into 1-inch pieces

3 tablespoons chopped pistachios

2 tablespoons finely diced red onion

2 tablespoons minced Pickled Sunchokes (page 21) or Pickled Baby Carrots (page 19)

8 fresh basil leaves, torn into small pieces

¼ cup roughly chopped fresh mint

Kosher salt and freshly ground black pepper

¼ cup Red Wine Vinaigrette (page 32)

¼ cup crème fraîche

½ teaspoon nigella seeds

In a large bowl, combine the farro, snap peas, pistachios, onion, sunchokes, basil, and mint and toss well. Season with salt and pepper. Add the vinaigrette and toss until just incorporated, but don't overmix. Taste and adjust the salt as needed.

Spread the crème fraîche on the base of a serving platter or large, shallow bowl, pile the salad on top. Finish with the nigella seeds and a pinch more pepper and serve.

FARRO SALAD WITH CAULIFLOWER AND AVOCADO CREAM

SERVES 4

AVOCADO CREAM

1 avocado, halved, pitted, and flesh scooped from peel

3 tablespoons extra-virgin olive oil

2 teaspoons champagne vinegar

2 teaspoons toasted pine nuts

1 teaspoon fish sauce

½ teaspoon kosher salt

½ cup chopped fresh flat-leaf parsley

1 clove garlic, Microplaned or very finely minced

1 teaspoon freshly squeezed lemon juice

2 cups cooked farro (see page 102)

¼ cup toasted pine nuts

2 tablespoons finely diced red onion

¼ cup roughly chopped fresh mint leaves, plus 12 small leaves

2 tablespoons roughly chopped fresh flat-leaf parsley

Kosher salt and freshly ground black pepper

¼ cup Red Wine Vinaigrette (page 32)

¼ small cauliflower, very thinly sliced on a mandoline

16 slices Pickled Fresno Chiles (page 17)

1 ounce Montasio or aged goat cheese, shaved

To make the avocado cream, combine all of the ingredients in a blender and purée until smooth, adding 1 to 2 tablespoons water as needed for a good consistency.

In a bowl, combine the farro, pine nuts, onion, chopped mint, and parsley and toss well. Season with salt and pepper. Add the vinaigrette and toss until just incorporated; do not overmix. Taste and adjust the salt as needed. Transfer to a serving platter or large, shallow bowl.

In a separate bowl, toss together the cauliflower and avocado cream and season with salt. Pile the cauliflower on top of the farro salad. Garnish with the mint leaves, pickled chile, and shaved Montasio and serve.

CALAMARI A LA PLANCHA WITH CHICORY, WATERCRESS, OYSTER MUSHROOMS, PINE NUTS, AND CHILE OIL

SERVES 4

When properly cooked, calamari has an amazing texture; but even then, the flavor is pretty one-dimensional. The mushrooms in this dish mimic the texture of the calamari while providing much-needed umami.

---

5 tablespoons grapeseed oil

1 sprig thyme

3 cloves garlic; 2 halved, 1 whole

3 oyster mushrooms (about 2 ounces total weight), cut into 1-inch pieces

Kosher salt and freshly ground black pepper

1 tablespoon extra-virgin olive oil

Heaping 1 tablespoon 'Nduja, (see page 81)

1 sprig rosemary

1 teaspoon paprika

2 large calamari or squid (about 8 ounces total weight)

¼ teaspoon ground red pepper flakes

4 teaspoons unsalted butter

2 large heads Coraline chicory (see headnote, page 97) or Belgian endive, cored and leaves separated

1 ounce watercress, tough stems removed

1 teaspoon toasted pine nuts

2 large fresh basil leaves, torn into small pieces

⅛ teaspoon toasted black sesame seeds

2 tablespoons Lemon-Thyme Vinaigrette (see page 32)

¼ teaspoon aged balsamic vinegar

⅛ teaspoon freshly squeezed lemon juice

¼ teaspoon chopped fresh chives

In a small frying pan over medium heat, combine 3 tablespoons of the grapeseed oil, the thyme, and the halved garlic cloves and cook until the garlic begins to smell fragrant, about 1 minute. Discard the garlic and thyme, then turn the heat to low and add the mushrooms. Season with salt and black pepper and cook, stirring often, until the mushrooms are just browned, 1 to 2 minutes. Taste and adjust the seasoning. Transfer the mushrooms to a plate and set aside.

Wipe the pan clean and return it to medium heat. Add the olive oil, 'nduja, rosemary, paprika, and whole garlic clove, and cook, stirring occasionally, until the 'nduja is melted and all of the fat has rendered, about 2 minutes. Remove from the heat and discard the garlic and rosemary. Set aside.

Pull off and discard the head and innards from each calamari, then cut off the tentacles, rinse them and set aside. Butterfly the bodies so they lie flat, rinse well, then lightly score the inside with a crosshatch pattern. Generously season the calamari with salt and the ground red pepper flakes.

Preheat a cast-iron frying pan over high heat. Add 1 tablespoon grapeseed oil and, when smoking, add a butterflied calamari, scored-side down, and its tentacles. Sear for 30 seconds, then add 2 teaspoons of the butter. When the butter is melted and bubbling, use a pair of tongs to slowly curl the calamari body in on itself. Cook until the calamari body and tentacles begin to brown on the edges. Transfer to a cutting board and repeat the process with the second calamari and remaining tentacles, the remaining 1 tablespoon grapeseed oil, and the remaining 2 teaspoons butter. Cut the calamari bodies into ¼-inch-wide strips and quarter the tentacles. Cover to keep warm while you assemble the salad.

Combine the Coraline, watercress, mushrooms, pine nuts, basil, sesame seeds, and vinaigrette in a large bowl. Season with salt and pepper and toss to mix and coat well. Pile the salad onto a large serving platter and top with the warm calamari, 'nduja oil, balsamic vinegar, and lemon juice. Garnish with the chives and serve.

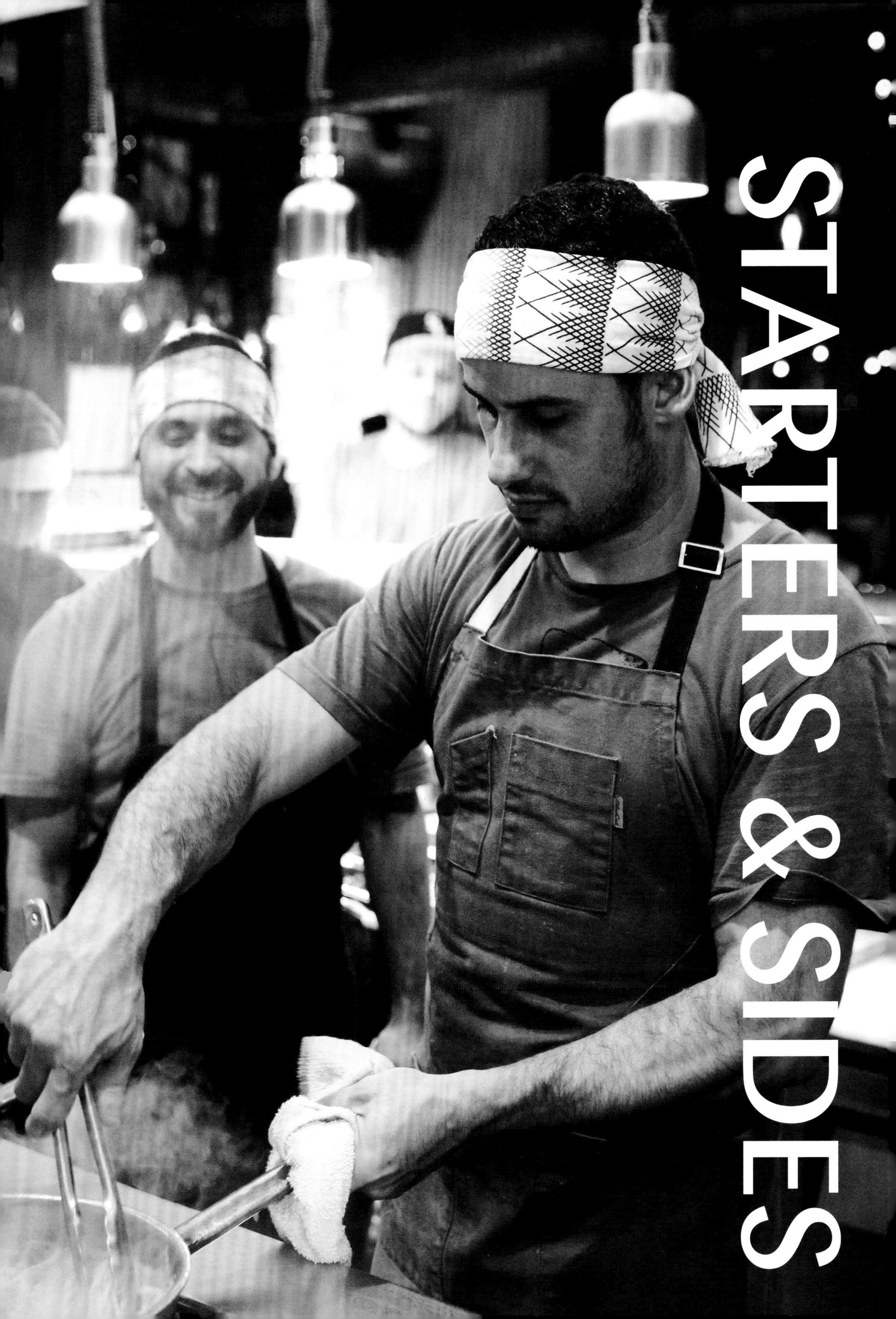

STARTERS & SIDES

LOBSTER CROSTINI

SERVES 2 AS A STARTER

I love it when people begin their meal with this crostini. It's filling enough to take the edge off your initial hunger, but it is also bright and full of acid—exactly what you want in your first bite. Also, the Squid Ink Aioli (page 47) is the best aioli on the planet. Period.

5 ounces prepared lobster meat (see below), cut into ½-inch pieces

1 teaspoon freshly squeezed lemon juice

1 teaspoon olive oil, plus more for brushing

Kosher salt

2 thick slices country bread, homemade (page 153) or crusty, rustic store-bought

Freshly ground black pepper

1 clove garlic

2 tablespoons Squid Ink Aioli (page 47)

Pickled Fresno Chiles (page 17) for serving

10 small fresh Thai basil leaves

10 small fresh opal basil leaves

½ teaspoon freshly grated lemon zest

Maldon or other flaky sea salt

In a bowl, combine the lobster, lemon juice, olive oil, and ½ teaspoon kosher salt and stir gently until the lobster meat is evenly coated. Set aside.

Preheat a cast-iron frying pan or grill pan over high heat.

Brush the tops of the bread slices with olive oil and season lightly with salt and pepper. Arrange the bread slices, oil-side down, in the hot pan and grill, turning once, until lightly charred on both sides, about 1 minute per side. Remove from the heat. Cut the garlic clove in half lengthwise and rub the cut sides all over the oiled side of the grilled bread slices, then spread a thin layer of the aioli on top.

Pile the lobster meat on top of the aioli on each slice of grilled bread, dividing it evenly. Garnish with the chiles, basil leaves, lemon zest, and a pinch of Maldon salt and serve.

PREPARED LOBSTER

1 small yellow onion, cut into chunks

1 celery stalk, trimmed and cut into chunks

1 carrot, peeled and cut into chunks

1 whole head garlic, halved crosswise

1 sprig thyme

2 juniper berries, smashed

20 black peppercorns

5 fresh bay leaves or 2 dried

1 tablespoon kosher salt

3 tablespoons white wine vinegar

1 live lobster, about 1 pound

In a saucepan, combine all of the ingredients except the lobster with 6 cups water and bring to a rolling boil. Meanwhile, fill a large bowl with water and ice.

Using a sharp knife, cut the head lengthwise to kill the lobster, then twist to remove the tail and claws. (Reserve the head for stock.) Drop the tail in the boiling liquid for 45 seconds, then transfer to the ice bath. Next, boil the claws for 3 minutes, then transfer to the ice bath. Chill for 10 minutes.

Wrap the tail in a kitchen towel, roll it onto its side, and press down until it cracks. Unwrap, turn belly up, crack the shell apart, remove the meat (it will still be mostly raw), split lengthwise, and remove the center vein. Wrap the claws in a kitchen towel, strike them firmly with the back of a knife where the pincers attach to the base, unwrap, bend the pincers back, and slide out the meat. Cover and chill for up to 24 hours.

SCALLOP CRUDO WITH CITRUS AND DRIED OLIVES

SERVES 4 AS A STARTER

Sicilians make a great winter salad that mixes blood oranges with red onions, black olives, and fresh herbs. It's salty and sweet and a delicious way to showcase the best of the season. This simple scallop crudo plays off of just that—using a mix of lemons, limes, and oranges to highlight fresh raw scallops. Don't worry about mimicking the exact varieties of citrus listed here—we change ours throughout the season. If you don't have Meyer lemon, decrease the amount of lemon juice and increase the orange juice to help balance the acidity.

¼ cup freshly squeezed orange juice

¼ cup freshly squeezed blood orange or mandarin orange juice

¼ cup freshly squeezed Meyer lemon juice, plus freshly grated Meyer lemon zest for sprinkling

2 tablespoons freshly squeezed lime juice

4 large sushi-grade scallops

Maldon salt or fleur de sel

4 small strawberries, hulled and quartered

1 blood orange, supremed (see Note, page 97)

6 small fresh mint leaves, torn into small pieces

2 fresh opal basil leaves, torn into small pieces

1 tablespoon meaty black olives such as Kalamata or Taggiasche, dehydrated (see page 15) and chopped

2 teaspoons extra-virgin olive oil

In a small bowl, whisk together all of the citrus juices. Set aside.

With a sharp knife, cut the scallops crosswise into halves, then cut each half into quarters. Place the scallop pieces in the middle of a shallow serving bowl and spoon 6 tablespoons of the citrus juice mixture over the top (reserve the remaining juice mixture for another use).

Season the scallops with a large pinch each of salt and lemon zest, then top with the strawberries, blood orange sections, mint, and basil. Sprinkle the crudo with the olives, drizzle with the olive oil and serve.

NOTE

It's important to have the fresh ingredients of this salad well chilled beforehand and keep them as cold as possible while you work.

LAMB BELLY CONFIT WITH LIME YOGURT AND GRAPEFRUIT, MINT, AND PEA TENDRIL SALAD

SERVES 4 AS A STARTER

Every time I put this dish on the menu, Genevieve yells at me: "This is not our Middle Eastern restaurant! This is our Italian restaurant, remember?" She's right—lamb with yogurt is something you would find in Israel, not Italy. But every once in a while, my roots sneak their way onto the plates at Bestia. We make our own yogurt at the restaurant, but you can use store-bought full-fat Greek yogurt for the same effect.

2½ teaspoons kosher salt

¾ teaspoon Instacure #1 (see page 74)

¾ teaspoon freshly ground black pepper

1 lamb belly (about 2 pounds)

1 whole head garlic, halved crosswise

1 fresh fig leaf

10 sprigs thyme

5 sprigs marjoram

2 sprigs sage, or about 10 fresh leaves

3 fresh bay leaves or 1 dried

4½ cups duck fat

1½ cups lamb fat or duck fat

½ cup plain whole-milk Greek yogurt

Freshly grated zest of 1 lime

Grapefruit, Mint, and Pea Tendril Salad (recipe follows) for serving

SPECIAL EQUIPMENT

Cheesecloth

In a small bowl, mix together the kosher salt, Instacure #1, and pepper. Place the lamb belly in a roasting pan and season thoroughly with all of the salt mixture, going a little heavier on the thicker parts of the meat.

Cut a 10-inch square of cheesecloth and place the garlic halves, fig leaf, thyme, marjoram, sage, and bay leaves in the middle. Wrap them tightly in the cheesecloth, then tie the neck of the bundle with kitchen string several times to form a tight sachet. Using the heel of your knife or a heavy pan, pound the sachet a few times to help crush the herbs and release their aromas, then place it in the roasting pan beside the lamb belly. Cover and refrigerate for 24 hours.

Preheat the oven to 350°F.

In a large saucepan over low heat, melt the duck fat and lamb fat, then set aside to let cool just slightly. Remove the chilled lamb belly from the refrigerator and pour the melted fat into the roasting pan. Cover the pan with a layer of oven-safe plastic wrap, followed by a layer of aluminum foil.

Transfer the roasting pan to the oven and lower the temperature to 250°F. Bake until the lamb belly is fully soft all the way through (a fork should slide in easily), about 7 hours. Remove the lamb belly from the oven and let cool in the pan to room temperature, then transfer to the refrigerator for 24 hours.

When ready to cook, preheat the oven to 300°F. Place the roasting pan in the oven, then turn the oven off and use the residual heat to reliquefy the fat, about 20 minutes. Remove the lamb belly from the fat, place it on a plate, and refrigerate for 30 minutes.

Preheat a large cast-iron frying pan over medium-low heat. Place the lamb belly in the pan and sear on one side until crispy, about 5 minutes. Turn and sear on the other side until crispy, 2 to 3 minutes longer. Transfer the lamb belly to a cutting board and cut into 1½-inch-thick slices.

Meanwhile, in a small bowl, stir together the yogurt and lime zest.

Spoon a heaping 1 tablespoon of the lime yogurt onto each of four individual plates and top with slices of lamb belly, dividing them evenly. Pile a handful of the salad on top of each plate and serve.

GRAPEFRUIT, MINT, AND PEA TENDRIL SALAD

2 tablespoons Pickled Shallots (page 17)

¼ teaspoon ground red pepper flakes

8 ounces pea tendrils, tough stems removed

1 grapefruit, supremed (see Note, page 97) and sections cut into thirds

¼ cup fresh mint leaves

1½ tablespoons Lemon-Chile Vinaigrette (see page 32)

Kosher salt

In a small bowl, combine the shallots and red pepper flakes and stir to mix well.

In a large bowl, combine the pea tendrils, grapefruit sections, mint, and shallot mixture. Drizzle with the vinaigrette, season with salt, and toss well before serving.

VEAL TARTARE CROSTINI

SERVES 2 AS A STARTER

This is a play on the traditional Piedmontese dish *vitello tonnato*, which pairs thin slices of leftover cooked veal with a tuna-based sauce. Our version is in the form of a delicate, clean tartare, lightly coated in a tuna-anchovy aioli. We always get amused when customers order it without the understanding that *tonnato* means tuna sauce, and then comment to their server, "You know, it was delicious, but it tasted a little fishy."

---

4 ounces veal fillet, finely diced

1 tablespoon finely diced Fresno chile, seeds and membranes removed

2 teaspoons finely diced shallot

2 teaspoons extra-virgin olive oil, plus more for brushing and drizzling

1½ teaspoons freshly squeezed lemon juice

Kosher salt and freshly ground black pepper

2 thick slices country bread, homemade (page 153) or crusty, rustic store-bought

1 clove garlic

2 tablespoons Tonnato Sauce (page 48)

1 teaspoon chopped fresh flat-leaf parsley

Maldon or other flaky sea salt

In a bowl, combine the veal, chile, shallot, and olive oil and stir until thoroughly mixed and the veal is evenly coated with oil. Add the lemon juice, ½ teaspoon kosher salt, and a pinch of pepper and stir gently to mix. Set aside.

Preheat a cast-iron frying pan or grill pan over high heat.

Brush the tops of the bread slices with olive oil and season lightly with salt and pepper. Arrange the bread slices, oil-side down, in the hot pan and grill, turning once, until lightly charred on both sides, about 1 minute per side. Remove from the heat. Cut the garlic clove in half lengthwise and rub the cut sides all over the oiled side of the grilled bread slices.

Spread the grilled bread slices with a ¼-inch layer of the veal tartare, followed by a thin layer of the tonnato sauce. Drizzle lightly with olive oil and finish with the parsley, Maldon salt, and more pepper before serving.

CHICKEN LIVERS

We do chicken liver two ways at Bestia, and they are completely opposite. The pâté is delicate and creamy, with the liver notes toned down and softened, almost like a foie gras. The chopped livers, on the other hand, are old-world: rustic and liver-forward, with a multitude of pungent ingredients to balance the liver notes. We have devotees for each version, and I get complaints from customers whenever I swap one version for the other on the menu. I don't even know which one I like more—it really depends on the day. The divergent spirit of these two dishes is not a coincidence. This kind of duality runs through the veins of everything you see and taste at Bestia.

CHICKEN LIVER PÂTÉ WITH DATE VINEGAR, TARRAGON, AND PRESERVED LEMON

SERVES 4 AS A STARTER

1½ cups port

½ shallot, chopped

1 sprig rosemary

1 sprig sage

1 sprig marjoram

5 black peppercorns

5 juniper berries, smashed

Zest of ½ orange, in strips

10 ounces chicken livers, cleaned (see Note)

¾ cup duck fat or unsalted butter, melted and returned to room temperature

2 teaspoons kosher salt

¾ teaspoon Instacure #1 (see page 74)

4 large whole eggs plus 1 large egg yolk

1 cup heavy cream

1 tablespoon aged date vinegar, aged balsamic vinegar, or saba

2 strips Preserved Lemon (page 23), rinsed and cut into chiffonade

¼ teaspoon fresh tarragon leaves

A few fresh flat-leaf parsley leaves

Thick slices of country bread, homemade (page 153) or crusty, rustic store-bought, toasted or grilled, to serve

½ teaspoon smoked salt, Maldon salt, or other flaky sea salt (but the smoky flavor is preferable here)

SPECIAL EQUIPMENT

Vacuum sealer (optional)

To make the pâté, preheat the oven to 350°F.

In a small saucepan over medium-high heat, combine the port, shallot, rosemary, sage, marjoram, peppercorns, juniper berries, and orange zest. Bring to a simmer, then turn the heat to low and simmer gently until the liquid has reduced to about 2 tablespoons. Strain through a fine-mesh strainer or chinois into a small bowl and set aside.

In a blender, combine the chicken livers, duck fat, kosher salt, Instacure #1, whole eggs, egg yolk, and port reduction. Blend on high speed to a smooth purée, then add the cream and

continued

blend once more quickly just to combine. Do not overmix to avoid whipping in too much air. Strain the mixture through an extra-fine-mesh strainer or chinois into a standard (9-by-5-inch) loaf pan. Tightly cover with oven-safe plastic wrap and then a layer of aluminum foil, then set aside.

Create a bain-marie (water bath) by bringing a kettle of water to a boil. Set the covered loaf pan in the center of any larger oven-safe vessel, like a 9-by-13-inch baking dish or roasting pan. Pour the boiling water into the larger pan until it reaches halfway up the sides of the loaf pan.

Lower the oven temperature to 275°F and place the entire bain-marie assembly in the oven. Bake until the pâté is just set and a knife inserted into the center comes out clean, 60 to 80 minutes. Let the pâté cool completely at room temperature for 1 hour, then refrigerate until well chilled, at least 2 hours or up to 24 hours.

Once the pâté is chilled, scrape off the top browned layer with a spoon and discard. Scoop out the pâté and, using a rubber spatula or scraper, press the entire batch through a tamis or extra-fine-mesh strainer into an airtight container. Pound the container firmly on the countertop a few times to remove any air bubbles. (Alternatively, if you have a vacuum sealer, spoon the mixture into a bag and vacuum seal to remove the air.) Use immediately, or refrigerate for up to 3 days.

Spread the pâté evenly around the sides of a shallow bowl, leaving a well in the center. Pour the vinegar into the well and garnish with the lemon chiffonade and herbs. Serve with the toasted bread and pass the smoked salt at the table for sprinkling.

NOTE

To clean chicken livers, trim off the connective tissue from the livers with a sharp knife.

CHOPPED CHICKEN LIVERS WITH AGED BALSAMIC, ROSEMARY, CHILES, AND GARLIC

SERVES 4 AS A STARTER

10 ounces chicken livers, cleaned (see Note, facing page)

Kosher salt and freshly ground black pepper

2 tablespoons grapeseed oil

2 tablespoons unsalted butter

1 tablespoon finely chopped shallot

1 large clove garlic, finely chopped

1 teaspoon chopped jarred Calabrian chiles

2 tablespoons capers, drained and chopped

2 tablespoons packed chopped fresh flat-leaf parsley, plus more for garnish

1 teaspoon packed chopped fresh marjoram

1 teaspoon chopped fresh rosemary

¼ cup aged balsamic vinegar, plus more for garnish

2 teaspoons sugar

¼ cup extra-virgin olive oil

Thick slices of country bread, homemade (page 153) or crusty, rustic store-bought, toasted or grilled

Minced fresh chives for garnish

Maldon or other flaky sea salt for garnish

In a bowl, combine the chicken livers with 2 teaspoons kosher salt and ¼ teaspoon pepper and toss to coat well.

Preheat a frying pan over high heat until smoking. Add 1 tablespoon of the grapeseed oil, 1 tablespoon of the butter, and half of the chicken livers. Spread the chicken livers in the pan to make sure they're not crowded and will sear and not steam. Sear the livers on all sides, turning as needed, until nicely browned but still pink in the middle, 2 to 3 minutes. Using tongs, transfer the livers to a plate. Discard the oil, wipe the pan clean, and repeat with the remaining oil, butter, and chicken livers, but this time reserve all the juices in the pan after you've transferred the second batch of livers to the plate. Remove the pan from the heat.

When the pan stops smoking, add the shallot and garlic and sauté off the heat for about 1 minute, then add the chiles, capers, 1 tablespoon of the parsley, the marjoram, and the rosemary. Return the pan to low heat and sauté for 1 minute, then add the vinegar and the sugar and cook, stirring occasionally, until the sauce has reduced to a thick syrup, about 3 minutes. Remove from the heat and set aside.

Transfer the livers to a cutting board and chop finely. In a large bowl, combine the chopped livers, balsamic reduction, olive oil, and remaining 1 tablespoon parsley and stir to mix well. Cover and refrigerate for 20 minutes until completely cooled to stop the cooking process and to allow the flavors to develop.

Bring the chopped livers to room temperature. Pile them atop the toasted bread. Garnish with parsley and chives, a drizzle of aged balsamic, and a pinch of Maldon salt and serve.

STEAMED PORK BELLY WITH HERBED AND SPICED BROTH, PICKLED CUCUMBERS, AND MINT AND FENNEL SALSA VERDE

SERVES 4 AS A STARTER

With this dish, my goal was to create a pork belly dish that actually felt light and refined, and that's exactly what I think it achieves. I pair it with a delicate but flavorful broth that's redolent of spice and smoke, and a mint salsa verde with enough acidity to offset the belly's inherent richness.

BRINE

2 tablespoons fennel seeds

¾ cup kosher salt

⅓ cup sugar

1 whole head garlic, halved crosswise

1 lemon, juiced and zest cut in strips

3 fresh bay leaves or 1 dried

10 juniper berries, smashed

2 sprigs rosemary

3 sprigs thyme

20 black peppercorns

1 to 1½ pounds pork belly

Kosher salt and freshly ground black pepper

FOR STEAMING

1 large Fresno chile, halved lengthwise

1 whole head garlic, halved crosswise

1 fresh bay leaf or 1 dried

5 cups vegetable stock, homemade (page 35) or good-quality, low-sodium store-bought

½ cup white wine

4 sprigs thyme

1 Persian cucumber, sliced paper-thin

8 fresh mint leaves, roughly chopped

1 teaspoon extra-virgin olive oil

1 teaspoon freshly squeezed lemon juice

Kosher salt and freshly ground black pepper

20 slices Quick Pickled Cucumbers (page 18)

Mint and Fennel Salsa Verde (page 45)

SPECIAL EQUIPMENT

Oven-safe steamer, such as a hotel pan with steam-table insert or a roasting pan with a rack

---

To make the brine, in a small frying pan over medium heat, toast the fennel seeds, stirring often, until just fragrant, about 2 minutes. Remove from the heat and set aside.

In a large saucepan over high heat, combine the ¾ cup salt, sugar, and 2 quarts water and bring to a boil, stirring to help dissolve the salt and sugar. Once boiling, add the toasted fennel seeds, garlic, lemon juice and zest, bay leaves, juniper berries, rosemary, thyme, and peppercorns, then remove from the heat and let cool to room temperature.

Place the pork belly in a large container, add the brine, and cover the container. Refrigerate for at least 2 hours or up to 4 hours, but no longer or it will be too salty. Rinse the pork belly in cold water, then pat dry and transfer to a cutting board. Season the pork belly liberally on all sides with salt and pepper. Using a sharp knife, lightly score the skin side of the belly in a crosshatch pattern.

To steam the pork belly, preheat the oven to 350°F.

Meanwhile, preheat a dry cast-iron frying pan over high heat. Place the chile and garlic, cut-sides down, in the pan, then add the bay leaf. Char until the garlic and chile are black on the bottom and the bay leaf is starting to burn, 5 to 8 minutes. Transfer all of the aromatics to the base of a steamer tray or a roasting pan. Pour in the vegetable stock and wine and scatter in the thyme sprigs.

Place the pork belly in a steam-table insert in the steamer tray or on a rack in the roasting pan. Cover the assembly tightly with a layer of ovens-safe plastic wrap and then a layer of aluminum foil. Transfer to the oven and bake until a fork easily penetrates the thickest part of the meat with no resistance, about 3 hours.

Remove the pork belly from the oven and let cool slightly, then remove the meat from the steamer insert or roasting rack and wrap

in plastic wrap. Strain the leftover steaming broth into a bowl. Cover and refrigerate the meat until firm and the broth until well chilled, about 2 hours. After chilling, scrape off the layer of fat that has risen to the surface of the broth with a spoon and discard.

Transfer the broth to a small saucepan and warm over low heat, and preheat a cast-iron frying pan over medium heat. Slice the pork belly into slices about ¾ inch thick. Add the pork belly to the hot frying pan and sear on both sides (the skin side too) until very crispy, 1 to 2 minutes per side.

Meanwhile, in a small bowl, stir together the fresh cucumber slices, mint, olive oil, and lemon juice. Season with salt and pepper and toss to mix.

Place 5 slices of pickled cucumber on the base of four shallow serving bowls, pour ½ cup of the warm broth into each bowl, and place a slice of pork belly on top. (There will be leftover pork belly.) Spoon 2 teaspoons of salsa verde over each slab of pork belly, then pile the cucumber and mint salad on top and serve.

PAN-ROASTED CHICKEN GIZZARDS WITH BEETS AND ENDIVE

SERVES 4 AS A STARTER

I came up with this dish back when I was working at Angelini Osteria. The combination of sharp cheese with chicken gizzards is unusual, but when brought together with the endive and beets, they end up complementing each other beautifully. Apparently, Angelini just didn't have the right crowd; at the end of the night, we'd sold only one. I told myself then that if I ever had my own restaurant, I would put this on the menu.

And so I did. This starter was the very first dish on the Bestia menu, and today I go through about sixty pounds of chicken gizzards a week. That's why I love our diners so much—so many of them come here with an open mind.

---

8 ounces chicken gizzards, cleaned (see Note)

Pinch of Instacure #1 (see page 74)

Kosher salt and freshly ground black pepper

6 cups duck fat

4 strips orange peel

7 sprigs fresh thyme

1 Fresno chile, halved lengthwise

1 whole head garlic, halved crosswise

1½ pounds beets

1½ tablespoons olive oil

5 cloves garlic, peeled but left whole, plus 1 clove garlic, smashed

3 heads Belgian endive, cored and leaves separated

3 teaspoons packed chopped fresh chives

2 tablespoons Red Wine Vinaigrette (page 32)

1 tablespoon grapeseed oil

1 tablespoon unsalted butter

2 tablespoons beef or chicken stock

1 tablespoon aged balsamic vinegar

½ ounce aged goat cheese such as Capra Sarda

In a large metal bowl or other stainless-steel container, combine the gizzards, Instacure #1, 1 teaspoon salt, and ¼ teaspoon pepper and toss to coat. Cover and refrigerate for 2 hours.

Preheat the oven to 350°F.

In a large saucepan over low heat, melt the duck fat until fully liquefied. Transfer the chilled gizzards to a metal roasting pan and tuck the orange peel, 3 of the thyme sprigs, the chile, and the garlic halves around the pan. Pour in the melted duck fat and cover the roasting pan with a layer of oven-proof plastic wrap, followed by a layer of aluminum foil. Put the roasting pan in the oven and lower the temperature to 250°F degrees. Bake until the gizzards are very soft, fork-tender, and crush easily when compressed, about 6 hours. Remove the gizzards from the oven and let cool to room temperature, then transfer to the refrigerator for 24 hours.

A couple of hours before you're ready to serve, roast the beets. Preheat the oven to 375°F and line the bottom of a large roasting pan with aluminum foil.

In a large bowl, toss the beets with the olive oil, 3 thyme sprigs, and the 5 whole garlic cloves; season with salt and pepper. Transfer the beets to the foil-lined roasting pan along with ½ cup water. Cover the pan tightly with foil and bake until fork-tender but not mushy, 45 minutes to 1 hour. Remove from the oven and let cool. When cool enough to handle, use a paring knife to peel off the skins. Cut small beets into quarters, larger ones into six wedges.

continued

Lower the oven temperature to 300°F. Transfer the pan with the gizzards from the fridge to the oven, immediately turn off the oven, and use the residual heat to melt the fat again, about 20 minutes. Remove the gizzards from the fat, place them on a plate, and return to the refrigerator for 30 minutes to firm up.

Just before you're ready to serve, preheat a cast-iron frying pan over high heat.

In a bowl, combine the endive leaves, beets, and 2 teaspoons of the chives and stir gently to mix. Add the vinaigrette, season with salt and pepper, and toss well. Pile the salad onto a large platter and set aside.

Add the grapeseed oil to the hot frying pan. Add the smashed garlic clove and sauté until just fragrant, about 30 seconds. Discard the garlic. Add the chilled gizzards to the pan and top with the butter. Let the gizzards cook on one side, untouched, until they're dark brown and crispy on the bottom, about 1 minute. Remove the pan from the heat, flip the gizzards over, and season them with salt and pepper. Using tongs, arrange the gizzards on top of the salad.

Drain the fat from the pan and add the remaining thyme sprig, the stock, and balsamic. Place the pan over low heat and cook quickly until the sauce is reduced by half, about 1 minute. Taste and adjust the seasoning with salt, if necessary. Pour the sauce over the gizzards and garnish with the remaining 1 teaspoon chives. Using a vegetable peeler, shave strips of the goat cheese over the salad and serve.

NOTE

Make sure your gizzards are cleaned by your butcher.

GRILLED OCTOPUS WITH BLACK BRAISED GARBANZO BEANS AND PAPRIKA SALSA VERDE

SERVES 4 AS A STARTER

Properly cooked, octopus is almost like a steak. There's a common misconception that it should have the bouncy chew of calamari, but that's not true. There is, however, a fine line between octopus being too fibrous or too tough, and hitting the right texture feels like an achievement. Italians swear that cooking octopus with a wine cork helps to tenderize the meat. Nobody can really explain why, but I've cooked two versions side by side—one with a cork and one without—and the one without a cork was, in fact, not as tender. Thus it remains part of the equipment here.

The braised garbanzos, blackened from the addition of squid ink, make a nice, substantial base for the octopus but are also delicious on their own.

BLACK BRAISED GARBANZO BEANS

1 cup dried garbanzo beans, picked over for stones and grit, rinsed

2 teaspoons baking soda

2 tablespoons extra-virgin olive oil

2 cloves garlic, chopped

2 tablespoons finely minced shallot

1 teaspoon chopped Pickled Fresno Chiles (page 17)

1 tablespoon chopped fresh flat-leaf parsley

2 teaspoons tomato paste

¼ cup dry white wine

1 to 1½ teaspoons squid ink (see Note, page 47)

Kosher salt and freshly ground black pepper

OCTOPUS

1 cup dry red wine

1 yellow onion, halved

1 large carrot, peeled and cut into chunks

2 celery stalks, trimmed and cut into chunks

1 whole head garlic, halved crosswise

3 sprigs thyme

1 Fresno chile, halved lengthwise

2 fresh bay leaves or 1 dried

10 juniper berries, smashed

20 black peppercorns

Kosher salt

1 octopus (about 2 pounds)

1 teaspoon red pepper flakes

Freshly ground black pepper

Extra-virgin olive oil for drizzling

1 lemon, halved

Fresh mint and flat-leaf parsley leaves for garnish

Paprika Salsa Verde (page 45) for garnish

SPECIAL EQUIPMENT

1 wine cork

To make the garbanzo beans, place the beans in a large bowl and add water to cover by 2 inches. Add 1 teaspoon of the baking soda, stir to combine, and let soak for at least 8 hours or up to overnight.

Drain the beans in a colander placed over the sink. Rinse the beans under cold running water for 5 minutes.

Preheat a saucepan over high heat. Add the drained beans and the remaining 1 teaspoon baking soda and toast the beans in the dry pan for about 3 minutes. Add 3 cups water (more or less; make sure the beans are covered by about 1 inch) and bring to a boil, then lower the heat to maintain a gentle simmer and cook, skimming off any foam

continued

that rises to the top with a slotted spoon, until the beans are tender, 30 to 50 minutes.

Strain the beans well, reserving the cooking liquid. Transfer ½ cup of the cooked beans and 1 cup of the cooking liquid to a blender and blend to a smooth purée. Set aside.

To prepare the octopus, while the beans soak and cook, in a stockpot, combine the wine, onion, carrot, celery, garlic, thyme, chile, bay leaves, juniper berries, peppercorns, wine cork, and 5 quarts water. Place over high heat and bring to a boil.

Add ¼ cup salt to the boiling aromatic water, then, using tongs, carefully dip in the octopus, tentacles first, and quickly pull it back out. Repeat the dipping process about eight times, until the tentacles tighten and curl, then drop the whole octopus into the water—it should sink to the bottom of the pot. If it floats, repeat the dipping process a few more times.

Once the octopus has settled, add the red pepper flakes to the pot, adjust the heat to a simmer, and cover. Simmer the octopus until the tentacles have a little give, 40 to 50 minutes. Remove the pot from the heat, cover with plastic wrap, and let the octopus steam for 15 minutes.

Meanwhile, fill a large bowl with ice and water. Once the octopus has steamed, gently plunge it into the ice bath, being careful not to damage the skin. Let the octopus cool in the ice bath for 10 minutes, then drain thoroughly, arrange on a clean kitchen towel, and transfer to the refrigerator to air-dry, uncovered, for 1 hour.

Preheat a grill to high or a cast-iron frying pan over very high heat. Transfer the octopus to a cutting board. Using a large chef's knife, remove the head from the octopus and discard. Cut the tentacles from the body, season lightly with salt and black pepper, and drizzle with olive oil. Add the tentacles to the grill or hot pan and sear, flipping once, until crispy on all sides, 3 to 4 minutes total.

Meanwhile, finish the beans. In a saucepan over low heat, combine the olive oil, garlic, shallot, chiles, and parsley and cook, stirring often, until the garlic begins to turn golden, about 3 minutes. Add the tomato paste and continue to cook over low, stirring, for another 2 minutes, then stir in the white wine and cook until fully evaporated.

Add the reserved beans and bean purée to the saucepan and stir to combine. The consistency should be similar to a risotto. If it's too thick, add a little more of the reserved cooking liquid. Stir in the squid ink and cook for 2 minutes more. Season with salt and pepper.

Spoon ½ cup of the braised garbanzos on each of four serving plates and top with 2 octopus tentacles. Finish each plate with a squeeze of lemon, a few mint and parsley leaves, and 1 tablespoon salsa verde spooned over the octopus and serve.

MEATBALLS WITH CREAMY RICOTTA, TOMATO SAUCE, AND BRAISED GREENS WITH PRESERVED LEMON

MAKES 18 MEATBALLS; SERVES 6 AS A STARTER

I bought an entire half of a cow once, like an idiot. I butchered it and did my best to use all of the parts but still ended up with a lot of leftover trim cuts. I decided to run meatballs as a special, but after we sold through all of the extra beef, customers were still asking for them. The grill became constantly overcrowded with meatballs, and we didn't have any space to cook anything else, which forced us to take them off the menu anyway.

This recipe is for grilled meatballs, the way we make them at the restaurant. For a braised version, see page 133. In both cases, I serve them with wilted greens and fresh ricotta to lighten the dish.

MEATBALLS

¾ cup panko bread crumbs

1 cup whole milk

1¼ pounds ground beef chuck (80/20—that is, 80 percent lean and 20 percent fat—is a good choice here)

5 ounces ground pork fat

½ cup Creamy Ricotta (page 40), made without the salt, or store-bought whole-milk ricotta cheese

⅓ cup plus 1 tablespoon freshly grated Parmesan cheese

¼ cup packed chopped fresh flat-leaf parsley

3 cloves garlic, finely chopped

1½ teaspoons anchovy paste, homemade (page 50) or store-bought

1¾ teaspoons Fresno chile powder, or 1¼ teaspoons ground red pepper flakes

2¼ teaspoons toasted caraway seeds

1 tablespoon plus 1½ teaspoons ground fennel seeds

1 tablespoon kosher salt

1 teaspoon fish sauce

TOMATO SAUCE

1 cup dry white wine

3 tablespoons extra-virgin olive oil

10 cloves garlic, thinly sliced

1 cup Fennel Soffritto (page 38)

1 (28-ounce) can puréed San Marzano tomatoes

1 tablespoon Smoked Dried Anchovies (page 50), or 4 salt-packed anchovy fillets, rinsed and chopped

1 tablespoon kosher salt

BRAISED GREENS

¼ cup olive oil

4 cloves garlic, smashed

2 pounds leafy cooking greens such as beet greens, Swiss chard, or spinach, tough stems removed, roughly chopped

2 tablespoons rinsed and finely chopped Preserved Lemon (page 23)

1½ cups Creamy Ricotta (page 40), or store-bought whole-milk ricotta cheese for serving

Maldon salt, fennel pollen (see Note, page 18), dried oregano, and extra-virgin olive oil for garnish

To make the meatballs, in a small bowl, combine the bread crumbs and milk and let soak for 10 minutes. Drain the bread crumbs, squeezing to remove excess milk, then transfer to a food processor and process until smooth.

In a large bowl, combine the beef, pork fat, bread-crumb purée, ricotta, Parmesan, parsley, garlic, anchovy paste, chile powder, caraway seeds, ground fennel seeds, salt, and fish sauce. Mix thoroughly by hand, kneading until you have a smooth, even mixture. Roll the mixture in your hands to form 18 well-packed 2-ounce balls, roughly the size of golf balls, arranging them on a baking sheet as you work. Refrigerate until ready to cook.

continued

To make the tomato sauce, in a small saucepan over high heat, bring the wine to a boil and cook until reduced to 1 tablespoon, about 10 minutes. Remove from the heat and set aside.

In a medium saucepan over medium-low heat, warm the olive oil. Add the garlic and cook, stirring occasionally, until just beginning to brown around the edges, about 1 minute. Add the soffritto and cook, stirring occasionally, for 2 minutes. Add the reduced wine, the tomatoes, anchovies, salt, and 2 cups water. Increase the heat to high and bring to a simmer, then remove the sauce from the heat and set aside.

Meanwhile, take the meatballs out of the fridge and bring to room temperature while you build a medium fire in a charcoal grill or preheat a gas grill to medium. Brush the grill grate with olive oil. Arrange the meatballs on the grate over medium heat. Sear on one side until well grill-marked, about 5 minutes, being careful not to move them too much; turn and sear for another 5 minutes until fully cooked. Remove from the heat and cover to keep warm.

Just before you're ready to serve, make the braised greens. In a sauté pan over high heat, warm the olive oil. Add the garlic and sauté until just beginning to brown, about 1 minute. Add the greens to the pan in batches and sauté until wilted. Add the preserved lemon and ½ cup water and toss quickly until the water evaporates. Remove from the heat and set aside.

Place 3 meatballs in the center of each serving bowl. Ladle about ½ cup tomato sauce over the meatballs. (Store any extra tomato sauce in an airtight container in the refrigerator for up to 5 days or freeze for up to 1 month.) Top each serving with about ½ cup of the braised greens and ¼ cup of the ricotta. Garnish with a pinch of Maldon salt, a pinch of fennel pollen, a pinch of dried oregano, and a drizzle of olive oil and serve.

BRAISED MEATBALLS

To cook the meatballs in the tomato sauce instead of on the grill, once the sauce is simmering, turn the heat to low and add the meatballs. Simmer for about 10 minutes, until cooked through, turning the meatballs once after about 5 minutes. Remove from the heat, then cover and let rest for 5 minutes before serving. The braised meatballs can be made up to 2 days ahead and stored, covered, in the refrigerator; just rewarm in the sauce over low heat before serving.

STEAMED MUSSELS AND CLAMS WITH 'NDUJA, PRESERVED CITRUS, FENNEL POLLEN, AND GRILLED BREAD

SERVES 4 AS A STARTER

A lot of nights after service, I'll sit down with nothing but a plate of these mussels and clams. It reminds me why I love rustic cooking so much—you don't need anything more than this and some really good bread for an amazing meal. The broth is incredible. Genevieve is very sensitive to spice, but this broth is so good, even when she was pregnant and the heartburn was killing her, she couldn't withstand her cravings. She would eat an entire bowl and then come in the kitchen and start cussing about how much pain she was in.

- ¼ cup 'nduja, homemade (page 81) or store-bought
- 1 tablespoon chopped shallot
- 2 cloves garlic, roughly chopped
- 2 tablespoons chopped fresh flat-leaf parsley, plus whole leaves for garnish
- 1 teaspoon rinsed and chopped Preserved Lemon (page 23) or Preserved Orange (page 24)
- 1 teaspoon ground toasted fennel seeds
- 12 ounces mussels, scrubbed and debearded
- 12 ounces clams, scrubbed
- 2 lemon wedges
- ¼ cup dry white wine
- ¼ cup Lobster Stock (page 36) or store-bought fish stock
- ¼ cup vegetable stock, homemade (page 35) or good-quality, low-sodium store-bought, plus more as needed
- 1 tablespoon Tomato Sauce (page 43) or canned diced tomatoes
- Pinch of fennel pollen (see Note, page 18), or ½ teaspoon ground toasted fennel seeds for garnish
- Thick slices of country bread, homemade (page 153) or crusty, rustic store-bought, grilled and rubbed with garlic, for serving

In a large sauté pan over low heat, cook the 'nduja slowly until the fat has melted and the bits of meat have begun to brown, about 5 minutes. Add the shallot and garlic and sauté until they begin to sweat, about 1 minute, then stir in the chopped parsley, preserved lemon, and ground fennel.

Increase the heat to medium, add the mussels and clams, and toss well. Squeeze the juice from the lemon wedges over the shellfish, being careful to avoid adding seeds, and then add the wedges to the pan. Add the wine and stir for about 30 seconds to cook off the alcohol, then add the lobster stock, vegetable stock, and tomato sauce and toss once or twice. Cover the pan with a lid or another pan and let the shellfish steam until they open, about 3 minutes.

Discard the lemon wedges along with any shellfish that failed to open. Using a slotted spoon, transfer the mussels and clams to a large serving bowl. If the sauce in the pan seems too thick, add a bit more vegetable stock; if it seems too thin, return the pan to the heat and cook for another few minutes until it reaches the desired consistency. Pour the pan sauce over the mussels and clams and garnish with the parsley leaves and fennel pollen. Serve with the grilled bread.

SUNCHOKE SOUP WITH PICKLED FRESNO CHILES AND OREGANO

SERVES 8 AS A STARTER

On its own, this soup is much more delicate than anything you'd usually find on the Bestia menu. But I garnish it with pickled chiles, oregano, and fried capers, adding a lot of of intensity. Thinly slicing the sunchokes helps them cook quickly, and the soup's final texture is silky, rich, and hearty enough to be a comforting meal all by itself.

2¼ pounds sunchokes, scrubbed but not peeled

½ cup unsalted butter, plus 4 tablespoons

1 large red onion, halved and very thinly sliced

12 large fresh sage leaves

½ cup heavy cream

2 tablespoons plus 1 teaspoon kosher salt

Vegetable oil for frying

2 tablespoons capers, rinsed under warm water for 5 minutes (to tone down the saltiness)

Pickled Fresno Chiles (page 17) for garnish

Dried oregano for garnish

Extra-virgin olive oil for drizzling

With a bowl of ice water next to you, slice the sunchokes very thinly on a mandoline, transferring them to the ice water as you work to keep them from oxidizing.

In a saucepan over high heat, combine the ½ cup butter and the onion and cook, stirring occasionally, until the butter is melted. Turn the heat to low, cover, and continue to cook until the onion is soft, about 5 minutes. Drain the sunchokes and add them to the pan along with 2 quarts water. Increase the heat to high and bring to a boil, then lower the heat to a simmer and cook, uncovered, until the sunchokes are very tender, about 30 minutes.

Meanwhile, in a small saucepan over high heat, melt the 4 tablespoons butter with the sage leaves and cook until the butter begins to brown, about 3 minutes. Remove from the heat and set aside.

When the sunchokes are tender, remove from the heat and let cool slightly. Using a large ladle and working carefully to avoid splattering, transfer half of the contents of the pan to a blender, along with ¼ cup of the cream and half of the brown butter and sage leaves. Blend on high speed until completely smooth, then strain through a chinois or extra-fine-mesh strainer into a bowl. Repeat the process with the remaining sunchoke mixture, cream, and sage butter. Stir the two batches until thoroughly combined, then stir in the salt. (The soup can be covered and refrigerated at this point for up to 3 days.) Return to the saucepan and keep warm over low heat.

Line a plate with paper towels and set aside.

Pour vegetable oil into a small saucepan to a depth of 2 inches and preheat to 375°F. Using a slotted spoon or skimmer, add the capers to the hot oil and fry until crispy, about 1 minute. Using the spoon, transfer to the prepared plate to drain.

Ladle the soup into individual bowls. Top each with slices of pickled chile, a few fried capers, a pinch of dried oregano, and a drizzle of olive oil and serve hot.

SAFFRON CORN WITH DRIED SHRIMP

SERVES 4 AS A SIDE

Our daughter's name is Saffron, and our menus—both savory and sweet—have a lot of hidden saffron in them. This wasn't purposeful; just as kids change every other aspect of your life, Saffron has snuck her way into our cooking. But in this dish, the strong use of saffron is intentional. It somehow has a way of enhancing the corn's flavor to the point that it's almost aggressive; meanwhile, the dried shrimp adds sweetness and umami, the grill gives it a smoky flavor, and the buttermilk provides some acidity. All together, these flavors make the corn taste even more like corn.

---

3 large ears sweet corn, husks and silk removed

¼ cup buttermilk

¼ teaspoon packed saffron threads

½ clove garlic, grated on a Microplane or very finely minced

1 teaspoon freshly squeezed lemon juice

½ cup unsalted butter, at room temperature

¼ teaspoon shallot powder or onion powder

⅛ teaspoon Maldon or other flaky sea salt

2 tablespoons chopped dried shrimp (see Note)

2 tablespoons minced fresh chives

NOTE

Dried shrimp can be found in Asian markets and online.

Build a hot fire in a charcoal grill or preheat a gas grill to high. Place the corn on the grill grate directly over the heat and let sear until nicely grill-marked, about 30 seconds, before turning. Repeat until there are even grill marks on all sides. Transfer to a cutting board and let sit until cool enough to handle, then cut off the kernels with a knife.

In a small saucepan over low heat, combine the buttermilk and saffron and cook gently just until the buttermilk is warm. Remove from the heat and let the saffron infuse, 5 to 10 minutes.

In a small bowl, combine the garlic and lemon juice and let sit for 3 minutes.

In a food processor, combine the butter, saffron-infused buttermilk, garlic-lemon juice, and shallot powder and process until smooth. Set the saffron butter aside.

Preheat a large saucepan over high heat until smoking. Add 2 tablespoons of the saffron butter, followed by the grilled corn. Sauté for about 30 seconds, tossing once. Add another 2 to 3 tablespoons saffron butter and cook for 1 minute more, tossing once or twice. (Reserve any leftover butter for another use.) Add the salt and toss again, then remove the pan from the heat. Transfer the corn to a serving bowl, top with the dried shrimp and chives, and serve.

HOUSEMADE RICOTTA WITH BASIL, DRIED ZUCCHINI, LEMON ZEST, AND GRILLED BREAD

SERVES 4 AS A SIDE

This is a deconstructed fried zucchini blossom—the kind that's normally stuffed with ricotta and fried in a tempura batter. Here, I rearrange those traditional flavors, using our housemade ricotta as the rich, creamy centerpiece and finishing it with slivers of dehydrated zucchini for a delicate crispy texture. This is one place you definitely don't want to substitute store-bought ricotta . . . it's a whole different experience.

½ cup Creamy Ricotta (page 40)

¼ teaspoon freshly squeezed lemon juice

⅛ teaspoon freshly grated lemon zest

1 fresh basil leaf, torn into small pieces

Maldon or other flaky sea salt

10 slices dehydrated baby zucchini (see page 15)

1 dehydrated zucchini flower (see page 15)

½ teaspoon extra-virgin olive oil

Thick slices of grilled country bread, homemade (page 153) or crusty, rustic store-bought, for serving

Using a spoon, spread the ricotta across one side of a serving plate or in the bottom of a bowl. Sprinkle with the lemon juice and lemon zest. Garnish with the basil, a pinch of salt, the dehydrated zucchini slices, and the dehydrated zucchini flower. Drizzle with the olive oil. Serve with the grilled bread.

CHARRED SHISHITO PEPPERS WITH SQUID INK AIOLI

SERVES 4 AS A SIDE

Shishitos are amazing little peppers that are at their best in late summer or early fall. They're mostly sweet; as the saying goes, only one in ten is spicy. But I swear I once had a batch where every pepper was a hot one, and after a day of recipe testing, I was sweating and my stomach was burning so badly I had to get off the line. But the results, these blistered shishitos with our Squid Ink Aioli, are so addictive, you'll find yourself eating through the pain anyway. Have a beer close by.

---

2 tablespoons grapeseed oil

20 shishito peppers

1 clove garlic, lightly smashed

Maldon or other flaky sea salt

Freshly grated orange zest for garnish

Freshly squeezed lemon juice for garnish

Squid Ink Aioli (page 47) for dipping

Line a plate with paper towels.

In a saucepan over medium heat, warm the grapeseed oil until shimmering. Add the peppers and garlic clove and sauté until the skin on the peppers just starts to blister on one side, 1 to 2 minutes. Flip the peppers with tongs and repeat to blister the other side.

Transfer the peppers to the prepared plate to drain. Season with salt while still warm.

Transfer the peppers to a serving plate and garnish with a sprinkling of orange zest and a few drops of lemon juice. Serve with the aioli on the side.

GRILLED ENDIVE WITH BLACK BUTTER, APPLE BALSAMIC VINEGAR, PEAR, AND FRESH THYME

SERVES 4 AS A SIDE

In this recipe, crunchy heads of bitter endive or Coraline wilt, char, and absorb a ton of smoky flavor from the grill, then we dress a pile of them with the same apple balsamic and brown butter sauce that we use to finish our bone-in rib eye. The texture is incredible, with slices of ripe pear—make sure you find one that's super-ripe and very soft—almost melting into the endive, and the end result is so meaty, it can almost hold its own as an entrée.

---

3 tablespoons Black Butter (page 48)

1 tablespoon apple balsamic vinegar, aged balsamic vinegar, or saba

6 heads Belgian endive or Coraline chicory (see headnote, page 97), quartered lengthwise (do not remove the cores; they'll help the endive pieces hold together on the grill)

1½ tablespoons extra-virgin olive oil

Kosher salt and freshly ground black pepper

1 very ripe pear, cored and sliced ¼ inch thick

½ teaspoon fresh thyme leaves

Maldon or other flaky sea salt

In a small saucepan over medium heat, melt the butter. Add the vinegar and stir to combine. Remove from the heat and set aside.

Drizzle the endives with the olive oil, season with kosher salt and pepper, and toss well.

Build a hot fire in a charcoal grill or preheat a gas grill to very high. Brush the grill grate with olive oil. Arrange the endives on the hottest spot of the grill and sear, tossing occasionally with tongs, until the leaves are charred around the edges but remain somewhat firm, about 3 minutes. If the flame gets too high, or the endives start to burn, move them to a cooler spot of the grill.

Pile the charred endives on a large serving plate. Arrange the sliced pear on top and spoon the butter mixture over the dish. Finish with the thyme leaves and Maldon salt and serve.

BLISTERED SNAP PEAS WITH MINT

SERVES 4 AS A SIDE

This is about as simple as it gets at Bestia. Toss some sweet spring peas in a hot pan, pile on the fresh herbs, and eat. I like to serve it alongside grilled lamb chops or as a warm springtime salad. There's a healthy amount of mint in the recipe. Resist the urge to hold back—the dish needs it.

---

2 tablespoons extra-virgin olive oil

2 cloves garlic, smashed

1 sprig thyme

3 cups snap peas, trimmed and strings removed

¼ cup packed fresh mint leaves

1 teaspoon Maldon or other flaky sea salt

Freshly grated zest of ¼ lemon

Preheat a cast-iron frying pan or sauté pan over very high heat. Add the olive oil and, when shimmering, add the garlic and thyme. Sauté until the garlic is fragrant and begins to brown, about 1 minute.

Add the snap peas to the pan and cook, tossing occasionally, until the skins are blistered and browned in spots but the pods remain crisp, about 3 minutes.

Meanwhile, line a plate with paper towels.

Add the mint to the pan, toss, and cook until wilted, then transfer the whole mix to the prepared plate.

Discard the garlic cloves and thyme sprig. Pile the peas and mint in a bowl and toss with the salt. Garnish with the lemon zest and serve.

ROASTED CAULIFLOWER WITH PAPRIKA AIOLI AND SOFT HERBS

SERVES 4 AS A SIDE

I love cooking with cauliflower because it can handle anything: anchovies, chiles, olives—pretty much any strong, forceful flavors. Cauliflower is on every single menu in Israel, always roasted or fried, and whenever we put it on our menu, it's the most popular vegetable we serve. Nothing else comes close. Which is funny, because on its own it doesn't really taste like anything . . . but when the florets are seared and roasted until slightly charred, then swiped through our bright Paprika Aioli, that pale, bland vegetable turns into something amazing.

---

2 to 3 tablespoons grapeseed oil

2 cloves garlic, smashed

1 head cauliflower, cut into 2-inch florets

¼ cup dry white wine

Sea salt

½ teaspoon freshly grated lime zest

Leaves from 1 sprig flat-leaf parsley

Leaves from 1 sprig dill

10 fresh mint leaves

Paprika Aioli (page 47) for serving

Preheat the broiler and position the rack on the top shelf. Line a baking sheet with paper towels.

Preheat a large cast-iron frying pan over high heat. Add 2 tablespoons of the grapeseed oil and the garlic cloves, letting the garlic infuse the oil for about 1 minute. Add the cauliflower florets, toss to coat, and sear for 2 minutes. Toss again, then transfer the pan to the broiler until the cauliflower is a nice golden brown with some charred edges, 3 to 4 minutes. Remove the pan from the oven, add the wine, and return to the stovetop over medium heat until the wine has evaporated, about 1 minute.

Transfer the cauliflower to the prepared baking sheet to drain, then season with sea salt. Pile the cauliflower on a serving plate and garnish with the lime zest and fresh herbs. Serve with the aioli.

BREAD & PIZZA

COUNTRY BREAD

MAKES 2 LOAVES

Before Bestia, every restaurant I ever worked in bought their bread. It seems crazy now, in the midst of today's bread renaissance, but even ten years ago, that's just the way we did things. I had a year and a half gap between my last job and opening Bestia, and during that time, I decided to try my hand at baking bread. It's one of those skills that requires complete and total focus, and ideally, you're not trying to do anything else at the same time. I read a ton of books to understand all of the science behind bread making, and I began experimenting with different ways to bake at home. Because I had access to only my weak little home oven, I developed a method that involved baking the bread on a pizza stone, with a Dutch oven inverted over the top like a dome. That created an environment similar to a pizza oven—with increased heat and moisture—and it worked consistently well.

The key is a *biga*, or sourdough starter, which acts as the leavening agent as well as flavor enhancer. I made my own, which I've now been feeding for more than seven years, and it provides a pleasant acidic tang to everything from this bread to our pizza doughs (see pages 156 to 160) to homemade pici pasta dough (see page 217) and pita bread.

½ cup plus ⅓ cup (200 grams) Biga Sourdough Starter (page 155)

3¼ cups (750 grams) water, heated to 90°F

6¾ cups (850 grams) high-protein white flour (we like King Arthur's bread flour), plus more as needed

½ cup plus ⅓ cup (100 grams) whole-wheat flour

½ cup (50 grams) buckwheat flour

2 tablespoons (20 grams) kosher salt

SPECIAL EQUIPMENT

Scraper
Pizza stone
Dutch oven
Pizza peel

In a large bowl, combine the biga and water. (The biga should float, which indicates it is alive and active.) Stir to mix well.

In a second large bowl, whisk together the white flour, whole-wheat flour, and buckwheat flour, then add to the bowl with the water and biga and stir by hand, scraping down the sides of the bowl with a scraper as needed, until all of the flour is fully incorporated and a soft dough forms, about 5 minutes. Cover the bowl with plastic wrap and let the dough rest at room-temperature for 30 minutes.

Add the salt to the dough and stir by hand for 5 minutes until very thoroughly incorporated, making sure that no flour clumps or pockets of salt remain. Cover with plastic wrap and allow the dough to rise, or bulk-ferment, for 4 hours.

During the bulk-fermentation, you need to grasp a small portion of dough on the left side of the mass and pull it over and across to the right. Repeat the process

continued

on the other side, then pivot your hands to another spot on the mass and pull again from both sides. Re-cover and repeat every 30 minutes. Do this eight times total, grasping a different spot on the mass each time until all of the dough has been pulled. The dough should become less sticky after each pulling. By the end of the 4 hours, if the dough still feels sticky to the touch and has not fully doubled in size, allow to ferment for an additional 30 minutes.

Turn out the dough onto a lightly floured work surface and divide it in half. Shape the first piece of dough into a ball by cupping your hands around the side of the mass farthest from you, letting the outside of your hands rest on the work surface. Drag the mass toward you while letting the dough tuck over onto itself. Turn the dough mass 90 degrees and drag and tuck again. Repeat the process three or four times, adding more white flour to the work surface as needed to prevent sticking and rotating the dough ball each time, until it holds a round shape. Repeat with the second piece of dough. Cover the dough balls with a clean kitchen towel and let rest for 30 minutes.

Next, working one dough ball at a time, flip the dough onto the work surface and gently pat into a round disk. Pull each side at the top of the round into the center and pinch together. Repeat this process again in the middle of the round and again at the bottom of the round. Rotate the dough 90 degrees and repeat the pinching process two more times, once at the top and once at the bottom.

Flip the dough over and pull it towards you using the tucking and dragging motion used previously. Rotate the dough 90 degrees and pull it towards you again. Rotate the dough 90 degrees again and pull it towards you one final time. Repeat this process with the other dough ball.

Wrap each ball, seam-side down, in a clean kitchen towel dusted with flour, then place each in an 8-inch-wide container or bowl, cover with a lid or plastic wrap, and refrigerate until they are plump and develop flavor, 8 to 12 hours. The longer you let the dough sit, the more sour it becomes.

When ready to bake, position a pizza stone on the center rack of the oven. Invert a large Dutch oven on top of the stone and preheat the oven to 500°F for at least 30 minutes or preferably up to 1 hour. Meanwhile, remove a loaf from the refrigerator and let sit at room temperature for 20 minutes. Wearing thick oven mitts, remove the Dutch oven from the oven and place on the stovetop or other heatproof surface. Unwrap the towel and lift the loaf out of the container. Transfer the dough, seam-side down, onto a pizza peel. Using a bread knife, score the bread once between the center and right side, from the top to the bottom of the loaf. Slide the loaf from the peel onto the pizza stone. Cover it with the Dutch oven—this creates a mini pizza oven inside your oven. Bake at 500°F for 20 minutes, then uncover and bake at 450°F for 20 minutes longer, until the outside of the bread is deep golden brown and lightly bubbled. Transfer to a wire rack and let cool. Repeat with the second loaf.

Let the bread cool completely before slicing. Wrap in plastic wrap and store at room temperature for up to 2 days or freeze for up to 2 weeks.

MAKES 2 LOAVES

BIGA SOURDOUGH STARTER

PART 1

¾ cup (85 grams) high-protein white flour (we like King Arthur's bread flour)

2 tablespoons (15 grams) buckwheat flour

½ cup (100 grams) filtered water

PART 2

½ cup plus ⅓ cup (100 grams) high-protein white flour, plus more as needed

½ cup (100 grams) filtered water, plus more as needed

¼ cup (100 grams) fermented mixture from Part 1 (above), plus more as needed

For Part 1, in a 1-quart airtight container, combine both flours. Then, using your hands or spatula, mix in the filtered water until thoroughly combined. Cover the mixture and let sit at room temperature (at or above 70°F) until small fermentation bubbles form around the edges, up to 3 days. At this point the biga should look and smell a little "off" and have a tart taste. If any hard or oxidized bits have formed on the surface, pick them off, then stir.

For Part 2, in a clean airtight container, combine the flour, filtered water, and biga. Mix thoroughly, then cover and let sit at room temperature, feeding every 8 to 12 hours, depending on the temperature of the room. (The biga will ferment faster and need to be fed more frequently if stored in a room that is above 70°F.) You will know if it needs to be fed if there is an increase in volume by 30 to 50 percent.

From this point forward, for the next 3 days, you will be feeding the biga by discarding 200 grams of the biga and adding 100 grams of white flour and 100 grams of filtered water to it, mixing it as directed in part 1. This process is done to give the biga strength and a better flavor and aroma.

After 3 days of constant feeding, the biga should be ready to use. To check if the biga is ready to use, drop a small piece of the biga into a bowl of water—if it floats, it's ready to use.

Keep in the refrigerator in an airtight container. Do the 3-day feeding process when ready to use.

The biga can also be frozen. To use, thaw, then repeat the 3-day feeding process.

PIZZA DOUGH, TWO WAYS

EACH RECIPE MAKES ENOUGH FOR SIX 10-INCH PIZZAS

It was important for us to have pizza on the menu. Bestia is a place where people often come to mark a celebration, but pizza brings the restaurant down to earth enough for neighborhood people to come in and have a few slices and a beer on any kind of night.

Nevertheless, when we first opened, I was having trouble with my pizza dough, and I couldn't figure out why. I was doing everything by the book, but still, the dough was off. In fact, the one negative pointed out by then *LA Weekly* critic Besha Rodell in her otherwise rave review was about the texture of the pizza, and I was pissed because I knew she was right. Genevieve suggested it might be the water, so I finally had it tested, and it turns out that the chlorine levels were killing my sourdough starter, making the dough dense. We revived the starter with bottled filtered water, and then installed a reverse-osmosis system for the entire water supply to the restaurant. With something this simple, even the smallest detail can affect the end product, and the multiple dough recipes I've developed for this book take that into account. I recommend using filtered water in all of my recipes to ensure great results.

Dough is a living thing, and like all living things, its behavior is affected by its environment. At Bestia, we invested in a wood-fired pizza oven that can reach over 1,000°F, and while some might have access to this kind of high-temperature oven, not everyone does. So I've developed two different dough recipes, each capable of making a pizza that's as close as possible to the Bestia original, regardless of your equipment.

The first recipe is exactly what we make at the restaurant and uses *biga*, or sourdough starter, as its leavening agent. Because it relies entirely on a living, breathing organism, this dough is volatile and only truly works well in an oven capable of reaching temperatures of at least 800°F, so if you have a pizza oven, you have this option. I also developed a second, more forgiving version that uses both yeast and *biga* and bakes well in a conventional oven, producing a pizza that is still very similar to what we serve at the restaurant in flavor and texture. I add a little bread flour and a touch of yeast to give it more stability and lift.

continued

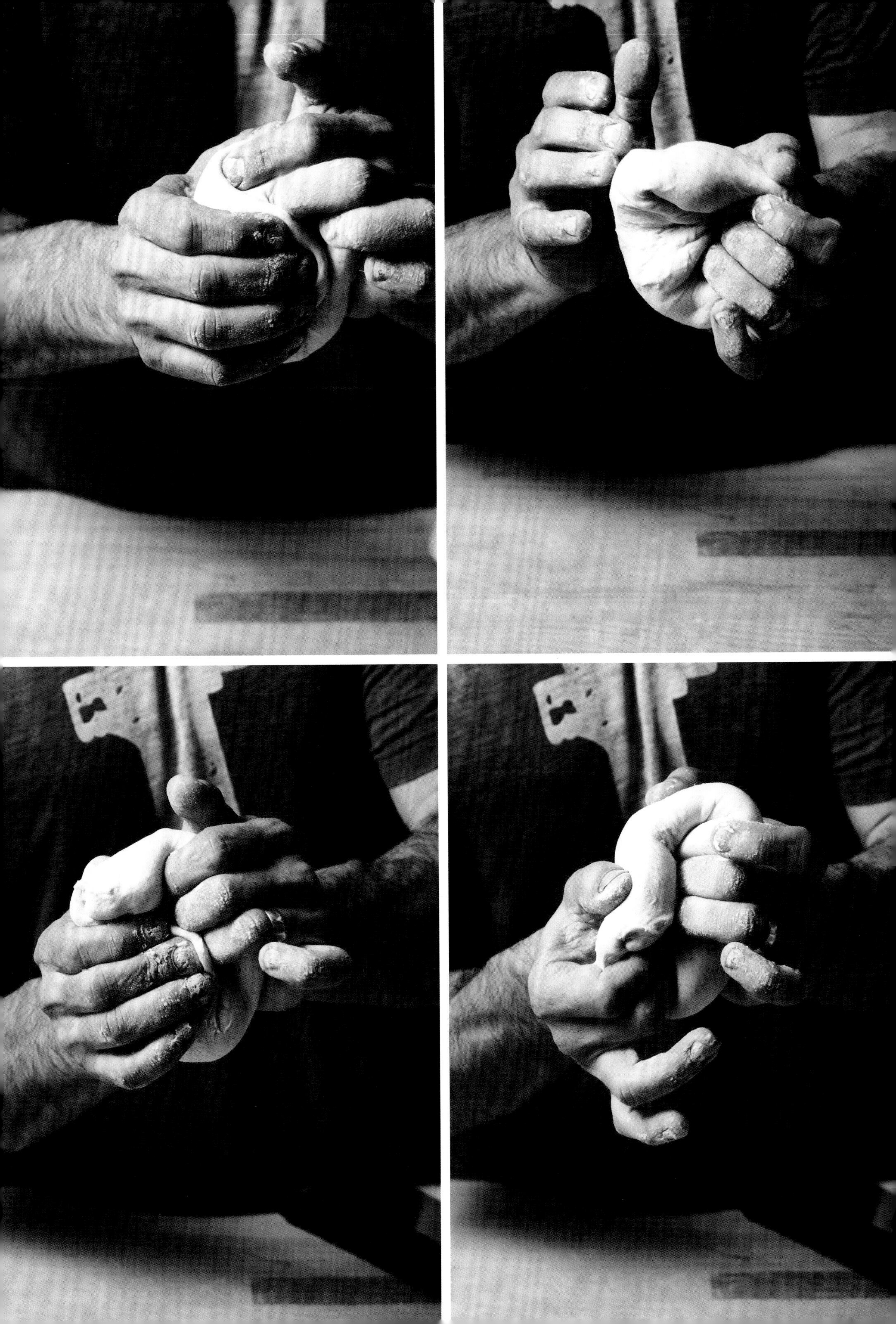

BIGA-BASED DOUGH FOR PIZZA OVENS

¾ cup (150 grams) Biga Sourdough Starter (page 155)

2⅔ cups (630 grams) filtered water, warmed to 80°F

7 cups plus 2 tablespoons (900 grams) 00 flour, preferably Antimo Caputo, plus more for dusting

½ cup plus ⅓ cup (100 grams) whole-wheat flour

2 tablespoons plus ½ teaspoon (23 grams) kosher salt

In the bowl of a stand mixer fitted with the dough hook attachment, combine the biga and warm water. (Note: the biga should float, which indicates it is alive and active.) Add both flours and beat on low speed for 10 minutes. Turn off the mixer, cover the bowl with plastic wrap, and let rest at room temperature for 30 minutes.

Mix again on low speed for about 7 minutes, then add the salt and continue to mix until well incorporated, about 3 minutes more. Transfer the dough to a lightly floured work surface and knead it into a ball. Return the dough to the bowl, cover with plastic wrap, and let rest at room temperature for 1 hour.

Turn out the dough onto a lightly floured work surface again and knead into a ball, then return it to the bowl, cover with plastic wrap, and let it rest for 1 hour more. By the end of this step, the dough has bulk-fermented for a total of 2 hours and should have increased in volume by one-third. If not, keep resting it until it does.

Turn out the dough again onto a lightly floured work surface. Shape into a large ball, then divide it into six 10-ounce portions (a digital scale takes the guesswork out of this step). Form each portion into a ball by stretching the outer layer of the dough with your hands, creating tension, and then pinching together at the bottom to close the seam and make a smooth ball. Repeat the process with the remaining dough portions, setting them aside on a floured surface as you work, then cover the dough balls with a clean kitchen towel and let rest for 15 minutes.

After 15 minutes, take a ball of dough and place it seam-side down in front of you on your work surface. Using both hands, drag the dough toward you while tucking it over onto itself, then turn a few degrees and drag and tuck again. Repeat ten times, until you have a very tense ball of dough that holds its shape. Transfer to a baking sheet. Repeat with the remaining five dough balls.

Cover and refrigerate for 24 to 48 hours before using.

continued

BIGA-AND-YEAST-BASED DOUGH FOR HOME OVENS

⅓ teaspoon active dry yeast

¼ cup (50 grams) filtered water, warmed to 110°F

4 cups plus 2 tablespoons (525 grams) 00 flour, preferably Antimo Caputo, plus more for dusting

3 cups (375 grams) high-gluten bread flour, preferably King Arthur Bread Flour

½ cup plus ⅓ cup (100 grams) whole-wheat flour

¾ cup (150 grams) Biga Sourdough Starter (page 155)

2⅔ cups (630 grams) water, warmed to 81°F

2 tablespoons plus ½ teaspoon (23 grams) kosher salt

In the bowl of a stand mixer fitted with the dough hook attachment, combine the yeast and the ¼ cup (50 grams) 110°F water and let sit until the yeast activates and floats to the surface, 5 to 10 minutes. Add all the flours, the biga, and 2⅔ cups (630 grams) 81°F water and mix on low speed for 3 minutes. Turn off the mixer, cover the bowl with plastic wrap, and let rest at room temperature for 30 minutes.

Add the salt to the bowl and mix again on low speed, about 7 minutes, then cover with plastic wrap and let rest for 1 hour.

Turn out the dough onto a lightly floured work surface and knead into a ball, then return it to the bowl, cover with plastic wrap, and let rest for 45 minutes.

Turn out the dough again onto a lightly floured work surface. Shape into a large ball, then divide it into six 10-ounce portions (a digital scale takes the guesswork out of this step). Form each portion into a ball by stretching the outer layer of the dough with your hands, creating tension, and then pinching together at the bottom to close the seam and make a smooth ball. Repeat the process with the remaining dough portions, setting them aside on a floured surface as you work, then cover the dough balls with a clean kitchen towel and let rest for 15 minutes.

After 15 minutes, take a ball of dough and place it seam-side down in front of you on your work surface. Using both hands, drag the dough toward you while tucking it over onto itself, then turn a few degrees and drag and tuck again. Repeat ten times, until you have a very tense ball of dough that holds its shape. Transfer to a baking sheet. Repeat with the remaining five dough balls.

Cover and refrigerate for 24 to 48 hours before using.

SHAPING THE PIZZA

Dust the top of the dough with a healthy amount of 00 flour, then with a spatula, gently lift a dough ball off the baking sheet as carefully as possible so as not to disrupt its shape. Place it upside down on your work surface and similarly dust the bottom with flour. Flip it back over and then press down on the center of the dough with your fingertips to form a flat disk, pressing the air into the outer rim to form a crust and being careful to keep the dough round.

Drape the dough over your fists and walk your fists around the edges of the dough while rotating it 360 degrees, letting gravity stretch it into roughly a 12-inch round. Lay it upside down on your work surface and lightly flour the bottom, then flip face-side up, assemble, and bake.

BAKING THE PIZZA

TO MAKE IN A PIZZA OVEN: Preheat your pizza oven or wood-burning oven to at least 850°F and keep it at that temperature for 45 minutes to 1 hour. Using a pizza peel, transfer the pizza to the oven and cook for 90 seconds to 2 minutes, until you see dark "leoparding" spots along the crust edges. If you see that the pizza is cooking more on one side than the other, use the pizza peel to rotate the pizza 90 degrees. Using the peel, transfer the finished pizza to a cutting board and let sit for 1 minute before cutting.

TO MAKE IN A HOME OVEN: Position a pizza stone on the center rack of the oven and preheat the oven to its highest temperature (500°F or more, if possible) for 45 minutes to 1 hour. About 5 minutes before you are ready to put your pizza in the oven, using thick oven mitts, transfer the pizza stone to the next highest rack of the oven and turn on the broiler for 5 minutes. Using a pizza peel, transfer the pizza to the pizza stone and broil for about 3 minutes, until you see dark "leoparding" spots along the crust edges. (If you have an oven light, turn it on so you can watch the cooking process.) If you see that the pizza is cooking more on one side than the other, use the pizza peel to rotate the pizza 90 degrees. Using the peel, transfer the finished pizza to a cutting board and let sit for 1 minute before cutting.

PIZZA SAUCE

MAKES ABOUT 3 CUPS; ENOUGH FOR SIX 10-INCH PIZZAS

Traditionally in Italy, you don't simmer the tomato sauce before putting it onto a pizza. The sauce gets cooked in the oven while the pizza bakes, but still maintains that bright, fresh tomato taste.

One trick for keeping the pizzas from getting too wet is to cube the mozzarella cheese ahead of time and let it sit on paper towels for about an hour to release some of its moisture. (I do the same thing with the burrata on the Burrata Pizza on page 169, but without cubing the cheese first.)

---

1 (28-ounce) can San Marzano whole peeled tomatoes, strained, juices reserved (see Note)

2 teaspoons kosher salt

1 clove garlic, Microplaned or very finely minced

½ teaspoon dried oregano

SPECIAL EQUIPMENT

Ricer

Pass the tomatoes through a ricer into a large bowl, or crush in the bowl by hand until they are the consistency of a chunky purée. If needed, add enough of the reserved tomato juice to reach a total of 2 cups.

Add the salt, garlic, and oregano to the bowl and stir to combine.

Store in an airtight container in the refrigerator for up to 3 days.

NOTE

You can use extra juices from the tomatoes for things like Lobster Stock (page 36), or even to make your own tomato paste: pour the juice onto a rimmed baking sheet and bake at your oven's lowest temperature, stirring occasionally, until thick and sweet, about 12 hours (depending on how much juice you start with). Transfer it to a jar, cover with a thin layer of olive oil, seal tightly, and refrigerate for up to 2 weeks.

MARGHERITA PIZZA

SERVES 1

Margherita pizza (pictured opposite) is the simplest pie on our menu, but it was actually the most difficult to develop. It is so simple that any imperfection will be noticed. The ratio of sauce to cheese to basil is as important as the ratio of garlic to oregano to salt in the sauce. It all has to be dialed in.

½ cup Pizza Sauce (page 163)

1 (10-inch) dough round from Pizza Dough, Two Ways, your choice (pages 156 to 160)

2 ounces fresh mozzarella cheese, cut into ½-inch cubes

5 or 6 fresh basil leaves

1 tablespoon freshly grated grana padano cheese

Maldon or other flaky sea salt

1 teaspoon extra-virgin olive oil

Using the back of a large spoon, spread the sauce evenly all over the dough round, leaving a ½-inch border. Evenly top the pizza with the mozzarella, basil, and grana padano. Finish with a pinch of salt, then drizzle with the olive oil and transfer to a pizza peel. See Baking the Pizza (page 161) to bake.

'NDUJA PIZZA

SERVES 1

This pie (pictured on page 167) is a kitchen favorite. In the early days, when we first opened Bestia and all of us were working fourteen- to eighteen-hour days, this is what we would eat on the line during service.

½ cup Pizza Sauce (page 163)

1 (10-inch) dough round from Pizza Dough, Two Ways, your choice (pages 156 to 160)

2 ounces fresh mozzarella cheese, cut into ½-inch cubes

¼ cup bite-size dollops of 'nduja, homemade (page 81 or 84) or store-bought

½ cup packed chopped cavolo nero (black kale)

1 green onion, tender green parts only, thinly sliced on the bias

1 tablespoon freshly grated grana padano cheese

Maldon or other flaky sea salt

1 teaspoon extra-virgin olive oil

Fennel pollen (see Note, page 18) for finishing (optional)

Using the back of a large spoon, spread the sauce evenly all over the dough round, leaving a ½-inch border. Evenly top the pizza with the mozzarella, 'nduja, cavolo nero, green onion, and grana padano. Finish with a pinch of salt, then drizzle with the olive oil and transfer to a pizza peel. See Baking the Pizza (page 161) to bake. After baking, finish with a pinch of fennel pollen (if using).

GORGONZOLA PIZZA

SERVES 1

This is the wine team's favorite pie on the menu because it pairs so well with white wines. The tangy flavor of the Gorgonzola cheese plays nicely with Riesling. That is why we have Riesling on the wine list, specifically to be enjoyed with this pizza.

---

1 (10-inch) dough round from Pizza Dough, Two Ways, your choice (pages 156 to 160)

2 ounces fresh mozzarella cheese, cut into ½-inch cubes

1½ ounces Gorgonzola cheese, preferably Gorgonzola Dolce, broken into 1-inch pieces

1 cup packed roughly chopped curly kale

1 tablespoon freshly grated grana padano cheese

Maldon or other flaky sea salt

1 teaspoon extra-virgin olive oil

Evenly top the dough round with the mozzarella, Gorgonzola, kale, and grana padano. Finish with a pinch of salt, then drizzle with the olive oil and transfer to a pizza peel. See Baking the Pizza (page 161) to bake.

BURRATA PIZZA

SERVES 1

The sweetness of the burrata, the acidity of the tomato sauce, the brininess of the olives, and the spice from the chiles all play off of one another for a completely balanced dish (pictured opposite).

½ cup Pizza Sauce (page 163)

1 (10-inch) dough round from Pizza Dough, Two Ways, your choice (pages 156 to 160)

2 ounces burrata, cut into 4 pieces

6 Castelvetrano olives, pitted, smashed, and cut in half

1 tablespoon freshly grated grana padano cheese

Maldon or other flaky sea salt

1 teaspoon extra-virgin olive oil

10 slices Pickled Fresno Chiles (page 17) or jarred Calabrian chiles packed in oil

Pinch of dried oregano

Using the back of a large spoon, spread the sauce evenly all over the dough round, leaving a ½-inch border. Evenly top the pizza with the burrata, olives, and grana padano. Finish with a sprinkle of salt, then drizzle with the olive oil and transfer to a pizza peel. See Baking the Pizza (page 161) to bake. After baking, finish with the chiles and oregano.

SALSA VERDE PIZZA

SERVES 1

I first made this pizza one night after service when I was hungry and we had leftover salsa verde. I liked the combination so much that I immediately put it on the menu. This is a pizza for people who like anchovies; but the salsa verde tones down some of the salty, fishy flavor.

½ cup Pizza Sauce (page 163)

1 (10-inch) dough round from Pizza Dough, Two Ways, your choice (pages 156 to 160)

2 ounces fresh mozzarella cheese, cut into ½-inch cubes

1 tablespoon freshly grated grana padano cheese

Maldon or other flaky sea salt

1 teaspoon extra-virgin olive oil

2½ tablespoons Salsa Verde (page 44)

1½ teaspoons Smoked Dried Anchovies (page 50), or 6 oil-packed anchovy fillets, or both (optional)

Using the back of a large spoon, spread the sauce evenly all over the dough round, leaving a ½-inch border. Evenly top the pizza with the mozzarella and grana padano. Finish with a pinch of salt, then drizzle with the olive oil and transfer to a pizza peel. See Baking the Pizza (page 161) to bake.

After baking, scatter dollops of the salsa verde over the pizza, then spread out with the back of the spoon to cover the surface evenly. Scatter the dried anchovies all over and serve. (Alternatively, arrange the oil-packed anchovy fillets in a circle, like the spokes of a wheel, pointing toward the center, or chop the oil-packed anchovies, combine them with the dried anchovies and sprinkle them over the top.)

PASTA

Fresh pasta was my very first foray into serious home cooking. When I was twenty-one, my sister bought me a pasta sheeter as a present, and as I began experimenting with it, I realized how empowering cooking can be. It was so rewarding to take this flavorless pile of flour, water, and eggs and transform it into something beautiful. You think it is going to be the most difficult thing ever, but once you learn how to manage it, how to be patient, and how to be both confident and gentle in your technique, you see how simple the process really is. Today, handmade pasta is considered a luxury, but at its heart it really is peasant food.

Of all the dishes at Bestia, the pastas are probably the most traditional. There's a familiarity to pasta that's key to its comfort; if the recipes aren't rooted in some semblance of a standard preparation, they become more off-putting than savory. That's not to say I'm afraid to make them my own—but even with those diversions from tradition, I often have Italians coming in to the restaurant and proudly comparing my pastas to the pastas of their *nonna*. And I'm okay with that.

You are welcome to use store-bought pasta in any of the recipes, though I should emphasize that the fresh pasta itself is an integral part of each preparation; and without it, the final dish won't be the same. Making pasta from scratch may sound daunting, but in reality it's a simple process that calls for only the most basic ingredients. If you do choose to use a store-bought product, opt for the highest quality you can find in a size and shape that's as similar as possible to the handmade version, then cook according to the package instructions.

PASTA INGREDIENTS

Italian food is all about simple recipes with few ingredients, but the quality of those ingredients needs to be high. This is definitely true of homemade fresh pasta.

Flour

I use two types of flour for my pasta: 00 flour, which is an Italian ultra-fine milled, low-gluten white flour (we like the Antimo Caputo brand); and semolina flour, a yellowish, higher-gluten flour made from durum wheat.

Eggs

Select fresh, large grade A eggs with bright yellow yolks—preferably local and free-range.

PASTA-MAKING TOOLS

Cavatelli Maker

This hand-cranked machine quickly and easily forms the ridged, curled cavatelli (see page 197) that are a denser version of gnocchi. I found a vintage version on eBay that works well with our soft dough, but if yours doesn't, knead in additional flour for added firmness.

Chitarra Pasta Maker

Chitarra translates to "guitar," thus the stringed tool used to cut the noodles is called the same name. Rolling and pressing the dough through the wire strings forms a perfect squared edge, which is what separates chitarra (see page 184) from similarly shaped knife-cut noodles.

Scraper

A scraper (see page 9) is handy for folding in flour.

Pasta Cutter

While in most cases a good knife will do, these roller cutters make it easy to cut along pasta sheets quickly and accurately for wider cuts like lasagne noodles and for ravioli. And for some pastas, like quadretti (see page 196), a serrated cutter is extra nice because it shapes the decorative edges.

Pasta Sheeter

This old-fashioned, simple machine clamps onto your countertop to use in place of a rolling pin to roll your dough relatively easily to even thinness. The dual steel rollers have a clickable 0 to 5 dial that sets the space between them at graduated thicknesses as you work. KitchenAid makes several reliable versions that attach to a stand mixer, but many inexpensive and dependable hand-crank pasta sheeters are available in the marketplace.

Piping Bags

Also called pastry bags, these triangular bags are made of canvas or sturdy disposable paper with interchangeable tips. Squeezing by hand gives you a controlled means for extruding elements for everything from pastas to desserts.

Spray Bottle of Water

Pasta can dry out easily, so I keep a spray bottle on hand to mist pasta as I work. It's also useful for dampening the edges of folded pasta like tortellini (see page 191) to help them stick.

NOTE

Some recipes call for ½ egg, 1½ eggs, or the like. One large egg beats up to about 4 tablespoons, so to add ½ egg to a recipe, beat 1 whole large egg until well blended and measure out 2 tablespoons.

KNEADING

Kneading, the repeated and lengthy process of pulling and stretching, is what forms the gluten necessary to give the noodles structure, helping them hold up to cooking as well as developing their tenderness. Each of the dough recipes here requires at minimum a full 15 minutes of hand kneading. It's a lot, but it's necessary. I've tried kneading for 5 or 10 minutes and the texture of the finished pasta just isn't right. I like to push down the dough and flatten it with the heel of my hand, then tuck it back and over itself and turn it 90 degrees.

How to Form and Knead Pasta Dough

On a smooth surface, pile the flour into a low mound. Make a well in the center and add all of your wet ingredients and salt.

Using a fork, gently stir the wet ingredients into the flour bit by bit, making wider and wider circles, until about half of the flour is incorporated and it just begins to form a small, shaggy dough ball. Using your hands or a scraper, fold the remaining flour over the dough and begin to knead until the mixture is just incorporated and forms a large, firm ball.

Continue to knead the dough, folding it toward you, pressing firmly with the heels of your hands, then turning it 90 degrees and folding again, for at least 15 minutes or up to 25 minutes, until the dough forms a dry, smooth ball that just bounces back when dimpled. Loosely drape the ball with plastic wrap and let rest for 1 hour at room temperature. Use immediately, or wrap tightly in plastic wrap and refrigerate for 24 to 48 hours. The chilling process is necessary to make the dough easier to shape and sheet.

STROZZAPRETI WITH TOMATO AND RICOTTA

SERVES 2

Genevieve and I took a two-week trip to Italy right before we opened Bestia. We started in Rome and went down the Amalfi Coast, eating at what people had told us were some of the area's greatest restaurants. We ended up mostly underwhelmed and couldn't understand where this magical Italian food everyone always talks about was.

The second half of our trip was a week spent in Umbria, starting in the medieval town of Bavagna. As we were walking around that first night looking at menus in the windows, we noticed one that seemed somehow different from all the others. Both the restaurant and the menu were so simple and unassuming, but there was an air of refinement about the place. We sat down, the chef asked if we wanted a tasting menu, and we said yes. The second course was a beautiful, simple ricotta-stuffed ravioli in a candy-sweet summer tomato sauce. Genevieve took one bite and started crying—like, actual full tears. We were both absolutely astonished not only by how delicious but also by how amazingly simple it was. Exactly the kind of rustic food you think about when you imagine Italian cooking at its best. This is my take on that dish and a souvenir of that incredible meal. At the restaurant, we serve this dish with housemade *casarecce*, but here we use *strozzapreti* instead, a free-form twisted noodle with a rustic, nonuniform look.

Kosher salt

1 tablespoon unsalted butter

¾ cup Tomato Sauce (page 43)

¼ cup vegetable stock, homemade (page 35) **or good-quality, low-sodium store-bought**

½ recipe Strozzapreti (page 180)

¼ cup freshly grated grana padano cheese, plus more for serving

⅓ cup Creamy Ricotta (page 40) **or store-bought whole-milk ricotta cheese**

2 teaspoons Basil Oil (page 180) **or high-quality olive oil**

In a large pot, bring 2 quarts water to a boil and add 2 tablespoons plus 2 teaspoons salt.

Meanwhile, in a sauté pan over medium heat, combine the butter, tomato sauce, vegetable stock, and salt to taste and bring to a simmer.

Add the pasta to the boiling water and boil for about 8 minutes, until tender but still with a bit of chew.

Using a slotted spoon, transfer the pasta to the sauté pan. Stir to coat and cook until the sauce begins to thicken, about 2 minutes. Remove from the heat, add the grana padano, and toss to mix. Transfer to a serving plate and pile the ricotta on top of the pasta. Finish with the basil oil and more grana padano and serve.

continued

BASIL OIL

MAKES 1 CUP

1 tablespoon kosher salt
4 ounces basil
1 cup olive oil

In a saucepan, bring 4 cups water to a boil. Add the salt and basil, cook for 30 seconds, then drain and immerse in ice water to stop the cooking. Drain, squeeze out all of the liquid, and transfer to a blender. Add the oil and purée. Strain the oil through a coffee filter, then store in an airtight container in the refrigerator for up to 5 days or in the freezer for up to 1 month.

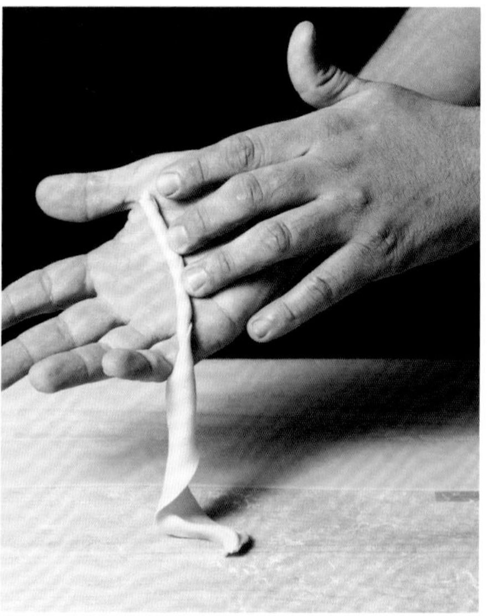

STROZZAPRETI

SERVES 4

1½ cups (240 grams) semolina flour
¼ cup (30 grams) 00 flour, preferably Antimo Caputo, plus more for dusting
1 large egg
¼ cup (70 grams) ricotta cheese whey (see page 40) or whole milk
1 teaspoon olive oil
1 teaspoon kosher salt

SPECIAL EQUIPMENT
Pasta Sheeter

Make the dough; see How to Form and Knead Pasta Dough on page 177.

Turn out the dough onto a work surface lightly dusted with 00 flour and divide in half. Form each piece into an oval about the width of your pasta sheeter. Lightly dust one piece of dough with 00 flour and pass it through the sheeter on the thickest setting once or twice, dusting with flour in between if it begins to stick.

Fold in the long sides to form a square the width of your pasta sheeter, then lower the thickness setting by one notch and pass the dough through the sheeter again. Repeat the process, decreasing the thickness by one notch each time, until you have a long rectangle of dough about ⅛ inch thick. Repeat with the second piece of dough.

Dust a baking sheet with 00 flour and set nearby. Using the tip of a knife, cut the pasta sheets into strips about 1 inch wide. Take one strip and, starting at the top, twirl between the heels of your hands so the dough twists in on itself, then pinch off a noodle about 3 inches long. Continue twirling and pinching off noodles every 3 to 4 inches down the remaining length of the strip. Repeat the process with all of the dough strips, transferring the pasta to the prepared baking sheet as you work. Dust the finished noodles with 00 flour, cover tightly with plastic wrap, and refrigerate for up to 24 hours or freeze for up to 1 week. Frozen pasta can be cooked the same way as fresh pasta.

SQUID INK CHITARRA WITH CUTTLEFISH

SERVES 2

Chitarra is Italian for "guitar," and as with so many shapes, the pasta is aptly named, in this case for the stringed tool used to form the noodles. The squid ink in this chitarra brings out the oceanic flavor of the cuttlefish. We toss in pesto and lemon zest to give it some complexity.

Kosher salt

5 ounces cuttlefish or squid

1 tablespoon grapeseed oil

1 tablespoon extra-virgin olive oil

2 cloves garlic, sliced paper-thin

1 tablespoon chopped fresh flat-leaf parsley, plus 1½ teaspoons

1 teaspoon red pepper flakes

¼ cup dry white wine

1 cup vegetable stock, homemade (page 35) or good-quality, low-sodium store-bought

½ recipe Squid Ink Chitarra (page 184)

1 tablespoon Pesto (page 44)

1 teaspoon Parsley Bread Crumbs (page 55)

Freshly grated lemon zest for garnish

In a large pot, bring 2 quarts water to a boil and add 2 tablespoons plus 2 teaspoons salt.

Pull off and discard the head and innards from each cuttlefish body, then cut off the tentacles, rinse them, and set aside. Butterfly the bodies so they lie flat, rinse well, and lightly score the inside with a crosshatch pattern. Generously season the scored side with salt.

Preheat a large sauté pan over high heat. Add the grapeseed oil and, when smoking, the cuttlefish, scored-side down, and tentacles and sear for about 1 minute, then flip the cuttlefish and remove from the heat. Using tongs, slowly curl the cuttlefish body in on itself, then transfer to a cutting board along with the tentacles.

With the sauté pan still off the heat, add the olive oil, garlic, 1 tablespoon parsley, and red pepper flakes and sauté for about 1 minute. Return the pan to very low heat and sauté for about 1 minute longer, until the garlic just begins to turn golden around the edges. Increase the heat to medium, add the wine, and swirl and cook for about 1 minute, until the wine evaporates. Add ½ cup of the stock and bring to a simmer.

Add the chitarra to the boiling water, tossing with the tongs to make sure the noodles don't stick together, and boil for 1 minute. Drain and transfer to the sauté pan. Add the remaining ½ cup stock and bring to a simmer, then sauté the pasta and sauce together until the sauce is creamy and has thickened slightly, 2 to 3 minutes.

Meanwhile, chiffonade the rolled cuttlefish into strips roughly the same width as the chitarra. Add two-thirds of the cuttlefish strips to the sauté pan and toss, then add the pesto and 1 teaspoon parsley and toss again. Taste and add more salt, if necessary. Transfer the pasta to a platter, pile the remaining cuttlefish strips and tentacles on top of the pasta, and garnish with the bread crumbs, lemon zest, and remaining ½ teaspoon parsley and serve.

continued

SQUID INK CHITARRA

SERVES 4

1½ cups (180 grams) 00 flour, preferably Antimo Caputo, plus more for dusting

6 tablespoons beaten egg (about 1½ large whole eggs; see Note, page 176), plus 3 large egg yolks

1 teaspoon extra-virgin olive oil

Pinch of kosher salt

1½ teaspoons squid ink (see Note, page 47)

SPECIAL EQUIPMENT

Pasta Sheeter
Chitarra

Make the dough; see How to Form and Knead Pasta Dough on page 177.

Turn out the dough onto a lightly floured work surface and divide in half. Form each piece into an oval about the width of your pasta sheeter. Lightly dust one piece of dough with flour and pass it through the sheeter on the thickest setting once or twice, dusting with flour in between if it begins to stick. Fold in the long sides to form a square the width of your pasta sheeter, then lower the thickness setting by one notch and pass the dough through the pasta sheeter again. Repeat the process, decreasing the thickness by one notch each time, until you have a very long rectangle of dough about ⅛ inch thick. Repeat with the second piece of dough.

Dust a baking sheet with flour and set nearby. Using the tip of a sharp knife, cut the pasta sheets into pieces about 1 inch shorter than the length of your chitarra machine (usually about 9 inches). Lay a piece of dough on top of the chitarra strings and, using a rolling pin, roll back and forth over the dough while pressing down so the strings cut the dough into strips. If any noodles stick, use your fingers to finish pressing the dough through the chitarra strings. Dust the finished noodles with flour. Use immediately, or cover tightly with plastic wrap and refrigerate for up to 48 hours. Do not freeze.

STINGING NETTLE PAPPARDELLE WITH MUSHROOMS AND FRIED EGGS

SERVES 2

We have this dish on the menu only three months of the year, when nettles are in season. The nettles impart a mineral greenness and forest-like taste that reminds me of mushrooms; it seemed perfect to combine them. But that gave the dish an overwhelming mossy flavor, so I added the eggs and that brought it back into balance, mellowing those stronger notes and creating a rich sauce at the same time.

Kosher salt

1 tablespoon plus 1½ teaspoons grapeseed oil

2 sprigs thyme

2 cloves garlic, smashed

8 ounces mixed mushrooms such as shiitake, oyster, and shimeji, trimmed

Freshly ground black pepper

2 tablespoons unsalted butter, plus 1½ teaspoons

2 tablespoons finely minced shallot

1 cup Mushroom Stock (page 36), Vegetable Stock (page 35), or good-quality, low-sodium store-bought versions

½ recipe Stinging Nettle Pappardelle (page 188)

1 tablespoon plus 1½ teaspoons crème fraîche

¼ cup freshly grated grana padano cheese

2 large eggs

Maldon or other flaky sea salt

Fennel pollen (see Note, page 18) for finishing (optional)

Fresh stinging nettle leaves, fried and seasoned as in Herb Confetti (page 222), for garnish (optional; see Note on page 189 for how to safely work with stinging nettles)

Fill a large pot with 2 quarts water and bring to a boil, then add 2 tablespoons plus 2 teaspoons kosher salt.

Meanwhile, in a sauté pan over medium heat, warm the grapeseed oil. Add 1 sprig of the thyme and the garlic and cook until the garlic is fragrant, about 1 minute. Discard the garlic and thyme, then turn the heat to low and add the mushrooms. Season with kosher salt and pepper and sauté until the mushrooms begin to brown, about 3 minutes. Remove from the heat.

In a large sauté pan over medium heat, melt the 2 tablespoons butter. Add the shallot and cook, stirring, until translucent, about 5 minutes. Add the remaining thyme sprig, stock, and cooked mushrooms and bring to a simmer.

At this point, add the pappardelle to the boiling water and cook for 1 to 2 minutes, then drain and transfer to the pan with the mushrooms and sauce and toss to coat. Return the sauce to a boil, then stir in the crème fraîche and toss to mix. Simmer, stirring, until the sauce is thickened and the pasta is tender but still with a bit of chew, 1 to 2 minutes longer. Remove from the heat, add the cheese, and toss to mix well. Cover to keep warm.

Preheat a nonstick sauté pan over medium heat and melt the remaining 1½ teaspoons butter. Crack in the eggs, season lightly with kosher salt and pepper, then turn the heat to low. Cook until the egg whites are no longer translucent, about 3 minutes.

Divide the pappardelle between two serving plates. Slide an egg on top of each portion, then finish each serving with a pinch of Maldon salt and the fennel pollen and fried nettle leaves (if using).

continued

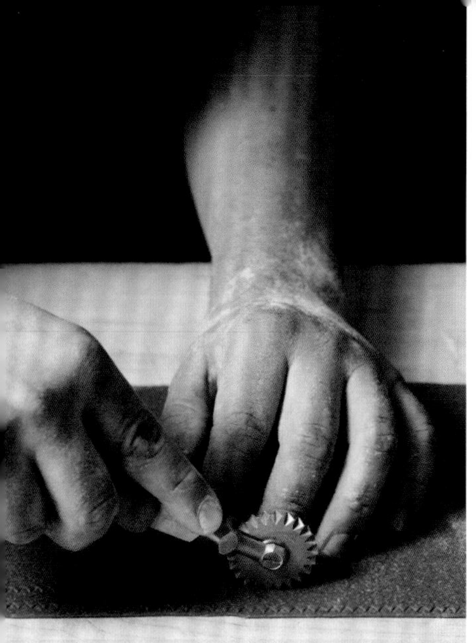

SERVES 4

1 pound stinging nettles, tough stems removed (see Note), and puréed

1 large whole egg, plus 1 large egg yolk

1 cup (120 grams) 00 flour, preferably Antimo Caputo, plus more for dusting

½ cup (85 grams) plus 1 tablespoon semolina flour

1 teaspoon extra-virgin olive oil

1 teaspoon kosher salt

SPECIAL EQUIPMENT

Pasta sheeter
Pasta cutter

STINGING NETTLE PAPPARDELLE

Bring a large pot of water to a boil and fill a large bowl with ice water. Blanch the nettle leaves in the boiling water until wilted, 1½ to 2 minutes, then drain and plunge into the ice water bath to stop the cooking process. Squeeze the nettles to remove as much water as possible (at this point, they are no longer stinging), then transfer the leaves to a blender. Blend until smooth. Measure 1¼ cups (225 grams) purée for the dough. (This will make slightly more nettle purée than you need for your pasta; store the remaining purée in the freezer to use for your next batch of pappardelle.)

Make the dough with the stinging nettle purée; see How to Form and Knead Pasta Dough on page 177.

Turn out the dough onto a work surface lightly dusted with 00 flour and divide in half. Form each piece into an oval about the width of your pasta sheeter. Lightly dust one piece of dough with 00 flour and pass it through the sheeter on the thickest setting once or twice, dusting with flour in between if it begins to stick. Fold in the long sides to form a square the width of your pasta sheeter, then lower the thickness setting by one notch and pass the dough through the sheeter again. Repeat the process, decreasing the thickness by one notch each time, until you have a long rectangle of dough that is almost paper-thin and slightly transparent—you should be able to see the outline of your hand through it. Repeat with the second piece of dough.

Lay out a pasta sheet lengthwise in front of you on a work surface lightly dusted with 00 flour and cut crosswise into 8-inch lengths.

Dust each piece on both sides with flour. Take each sheet of dough and, using a pasta cutter or knife, cut along the cut side into ¾-inch-wide strips. Carefully unwrap the noodles and toss gently to separate. Transfer to a large baking sheet and dust with more flour. Repeat with the second dough piece. Cover and refrigerate for 24 to 48 hours. Do not freeze.

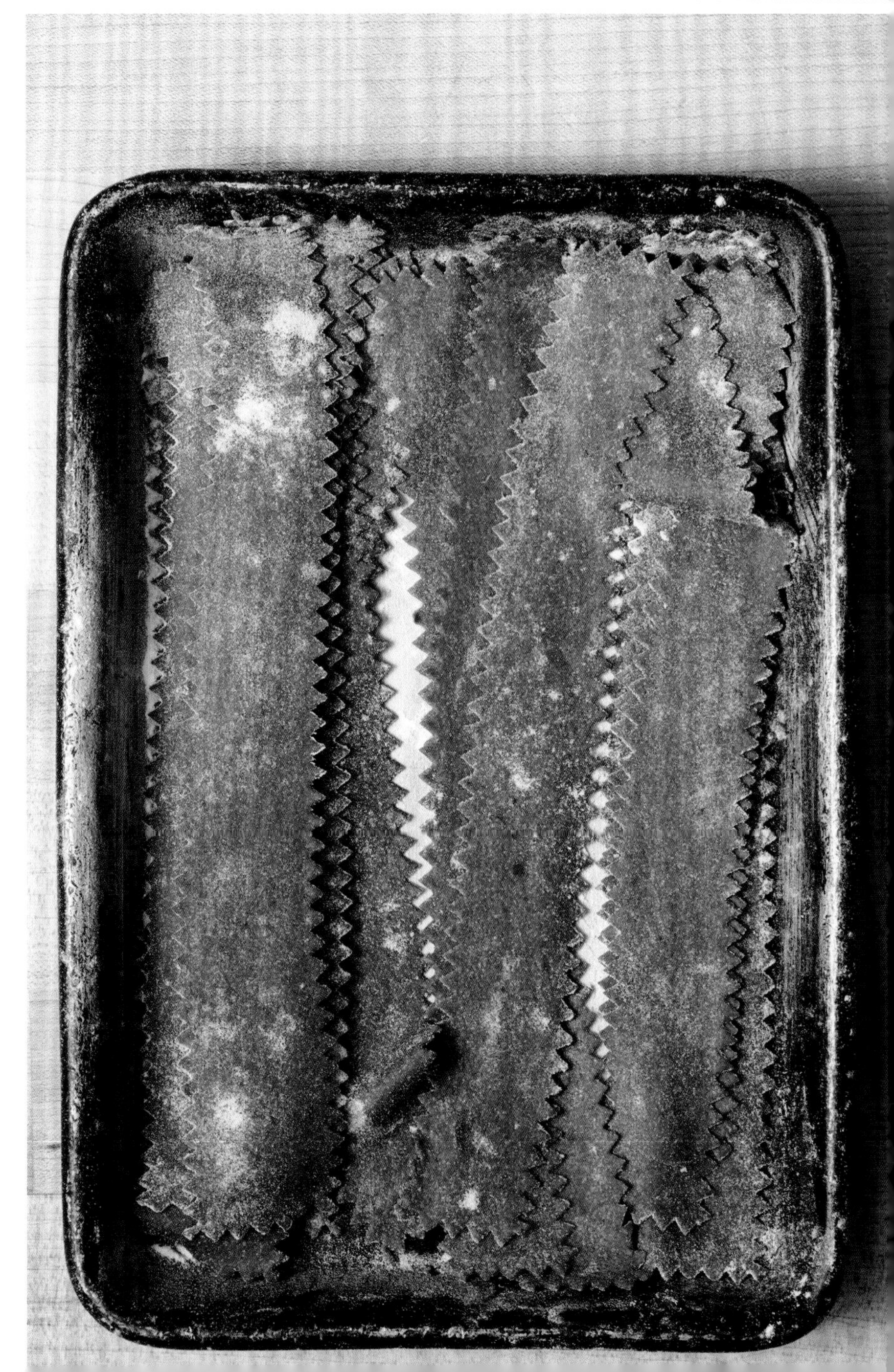

NOTE

Be sure to wear gloves whenever you're handling raw nettles. When there is a new employee at the restaurant, I don't tell them anything and wait until they start to feel the itching sensation. That's when we laugh and say, "That's why you need to wear gloves."

TORTELLINI DI MORTADELLA

SERVES 4

This pasta is a play on *cotechino*, a northern Italian sausage that's paired with lentils to celebrate the new year. This sauce has lentils as well as a bit of spinach and thyme to lighten up the filling, a savory mix of ricotta and mortadella.

FILLING

- 5 ounces mortadella, homemade (page 85) or store-bought, diced
- 3½ ounces (about ½ cup) whole-milk ricotta cheese
- 1½ teaspoons unsalted butter
- 5 fresh sage leaves

PASTA DOUGH

- 25 threads saffron (optional)
- 1½ cups (180 grams) 00 flour, preferably Antimo Caputo, plus more for dusting
- 1 large whole egg, plus 5 egg yolks
- 2 teaspoons extra-virgin olive oil
- 1 teaspoon kosher salt

- Kosher salt
- 6 tablespoons unsalted butter
- 2 tablespoons dry white wine
- 1 cup Basic Lentils (page 39)
- Freshly ground black pepper
- 2 cups packed baby spinach leaves
- 2 cups vegetable stock, homemade (page 35) or good-quality, low-sodium store-bought
- 6 tablespoons freshly grated Parmesan cheese
- 2 teaspoons minced mortadella, homemade (page 85) or store-bought
- ½ teaspoon fresh thyme leaves

SPECIAL EQUIPMENT

- Pasta sheeter
- Piping bag

To make the filling, in a food processor, combine the mortadella and ricotta and process to a smooth paste, scraping down the sides of the bowl periodically with a spatula as needed.

In a small saucepan over low heat, combine the butter and sage and slowly cook, swirling the pot occasionally, until the butter is a dark even brown, about 5 minutes. Add the butter and sage to the mixture in the food processor and process again until very smooth. Scrape the mixture into a bowl, cover, and refrigerate for 45 minutes to 1 hour to firm up.

To make the pasta, if using the saffron, place the threads in a small, heatproof bowl. Pour in 2 teaspoons hot water and stir. Let sit for 10 minutes, then stir again.

Make the dough with the saffron water; see How to Form and Knead Pasta Dough on page 177.

Turn out the dough onto a lightly floured work surface and divide in half. Form each piece into an oval about the width of your pasta sheeter. Lightly dust one piece of dough with flour and pass it through the sheeter on the thickest setting once or twice, dusting with flour in between if it begins to stick. Fold in the short sides to form a square that's roughly the same width as your pasta sheeter and pass it through once more. Lower the thickness setting by one notch and pass the dough through the sheeter again. Repeat the process, decreasing the thickness by one notch each time, until you have a very long rectangle of dough about 1⁄16 inch thick.

Lay out the pasta sheet in front of you on a lightly floured surface. Using a knife, cut the dough crosswise into 1½-inch-wide strips, and then cut the strips into 1½-inch squares. Repeat the process with the remaining dough piece.

Once the filling has chilled, transfer it to a piping bag with a small plain tip. Pipe a small ball of filling, about ½ teaspoon, into the center of each pasta square. (If the filling seems too thick to pipe easily, let it rest at room temperature for a minute or so to soften.)

continued

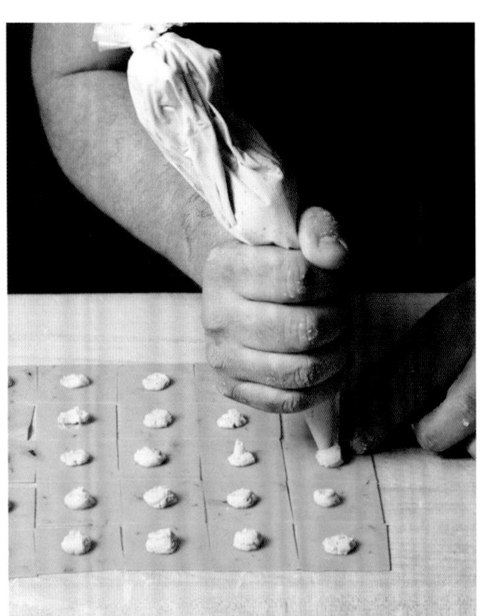

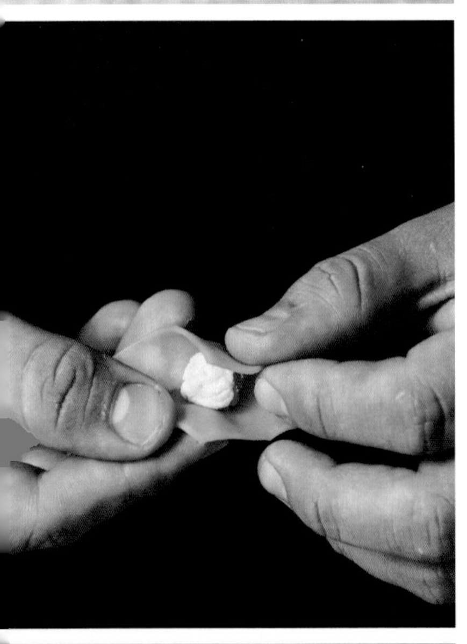

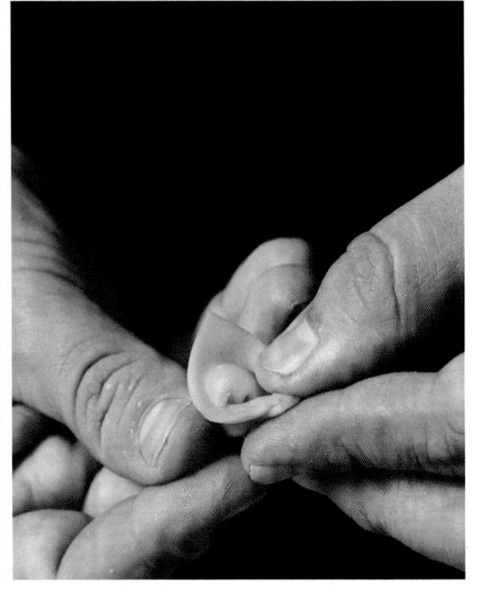

TORTELLINI, continued

With a small bowl of water next to you, wet a pastry brush or your finger and lightly moisten all four sides of the pasta square. Fold the top corner over to meet the bottom to form a downward-facing triangle and press the edges to seal. Then fold the other two corners up toward each other, overlapping the points, and pinch closed. (See photos, left.)

Repeat until all of the dough has been formed into tortellini. Boil immediately, or dust lightly with flour, place in an airtight container, and refrigerate for up to 24 hours or freeze for up to 4 days.

Fill a large pot with 2 quarts water and bring to a boil, then add 2 tablespoons plus 2 teaspoons salt.

Meanwhile, in a large saucepan over medium heat, melt the butter. Add the wine and cook until the liquid evaporates, about 2 minutes. Add the lentils and toss, then season with a pinch each of salt and pepper. Add the spinach and toss to wilt, then add the vegetable stock and bring to a simmer.

Add the tortellini to the boiling water and cook, stirring once or twice, until tender but still with some bite, about 2 minutes. Using a slotted spoon, transfer the tortellini to the saucepan. Turn the heat to high and gently sauté for about 2 minutes. Add the Parmesan and toss to mix, then scoop onto individual plates. Garnish with the mortadella and thyme and serve.

CARROT QUADRETTI WITH RABBIT RAGU AND FRESH PEAS

SERVES 4

We source the majority of our produce from two of the city's largest farmers' markets: Santa Monica and Hollywood. One farm at both markets, Jimenez, raises amazing rabbits. One day we bought a couple rabbits and decided to make a ragu, but I didn't know what noodle to serve with it. I'm always focused on keeping our pasta flavors from getting repetitive, so I thought I could use carrot juice in the dough to be funny—rabbit, get it? When I put it on the menu, some people thought the combination was cruel; but those people probably aren't going to be eating rabbit anyway. Everyone else loved it. It may be based on a joke, but the pairing is seriously good.

In Italy, *quadretti* are tiny square pastas that are mainly for little kids to eat, but I didn't know that when I created my version. I just knew I wanted a flat, square shape that would work well with the dots of carrot purée in the rabbit ragu dish. A longer, twirling pasta would mess up the plate as you eat.

RABBIT RAGU

1 rabbit (about 3 pounds), prepared and cut into serving parts by your butcher (see Note)

Kosher salt and freshly ground black pepper

2 tablespoons unsalted butter

2 tablespoons extra-virgin olive oil

1 cup dry white wine

1 shallot, cut in half

3 sprigs thyme

2 sprigs sage

2 fresh bay leaves or 1 dried

5 juniper berries, smashed

2 whole star anise

5 black peppercorns

1 cup Vegetable Soffritto (page 38)

4 cups vegetable stock, homemade (page 35) or good-quality, low-sodium store-bought, plus more if needed

¼ cup good-quality, low-sodium beef stock

2 carrots, peeled and very thinly sliced (we use a mandoline); save the tops, if present

1 to 2 cups whole milk

Kosher salt

2 tablespoons unsalted butter

¾ cup fresh peas

1 recipe Carrot Quadretti (page 196),

Freshly ground black pepper

⅓ cup freshly grated Parmesan cheese

Fresh tarragon leaves and carrot tops (optional) for garnish

SPECIAL EQUIPMENT

Cheesecloth
Kitchen string

To make the rabbit ragu, preheat the oven to 350°F.

Season the rabbit pieces with 1 tablespoon plus 1 teaspoon salt and ¼ teaspoon pepper. Preheat a sauté pan over high heat until smoking. Melt 1 tablespoon of the butter in 1 tablespoon of the olive oil. Add half of the rabbit pieces and sear until nicely browned on all sides, 3 to 5 minutes. Using tongs, transfer the rabbit to a large bowl. Wipe the pan clean and repeat the process with the remaining butter, olive oil, and rabbit.

continued

Meanwhile, place a small saucepan over high heat. Add the wine and boil until it has reduced to 2 tablespoons, 8 to 10 minutes.

Cut a 10-inch square of cheesecloth and place the shallot, thyme, sage, bay leaves, juniper berries, star anise, and peppercorns in the middle. Wrap them tightly in the cheesecloth, then wrap kitchen string around the bundle several times to form a tight sachet. Tie to close.

Preheat a Dutch oven over medium heat. Add the soffritto, herb sachet, browned rabbit pieces and any juices accumulated in the bowl, the wine reduction, vegetable stock, and beef stock. Cover, transfer to the oven, and braise until the meat is completely fork-tender and falling off the bone, about 2 hours.

Using tongs, transfer the rabbit to a large bowl and set aside until cool enough to handle, about 30 minutes. Carefully remove the rabbit meat from the bones and shred with your fingers or two forks, then return the shredded meat to the braising liquid. (You should have about 3 cups ragu. Store in an airtight container in the refrigerator for up to 3 days. Or freeze for up to 2 weeks, then thaw in the refrigerator before using.)

Place the carrots in a small saucepan and add enough of the milk just to cover. Place the saucepan over medium-high heat and bring to a boil, then turn the heat to low, cover, and simmer until the carrots are soft, about 20 minutes. Strain the carrots, reserving the milk, and transfer the carrots to a blender. Blend to a creamy purée. If there's not enough liquid for the blender to work, add a small amount of the reserved milk. You want the purée to be thick. Add a pinch of salt, blend to combine, and set aside.

In a large pot, bring 2 quarts water to a boil and add 2 tablespoons plus 2 teaspoons salt.

Meanwhile, in a large sauté pan over medium heat, melt the butter. Add the rabbit ragu and peas and heat until simmering.

Add the quadretti to the boiling water and cook for 1 to 1½ minutes, until the first squares start to float, then scoop out with a slotted spoon and add to the pan with the rabbit ragu and toss. Increase the heat to high and bring the ragu back to a boil, then sauté the pasta and ragu together until the sauce begins to thicken, about 1 minute. Remove from the heat. (If the sauce seems too thick, thin it with a small amount of vegetable stock.) Taste and adjust the seasoning with salt and pepper. Toss in the Parmesan.

Transfer the pasta to a serving plate and top with 10 to 12 teaspoon-size dollops of carrot purée. Garnish with the tarragon leaves and the carrot tops, if you have them, and serve.

NOTE

If you're breaking down the rabbit yourself, first remove the giblets. Remove the arms and legs from the loin. Remove the silver skin with a knife, then remove the boneless belly flaps just past the rib cage. Using a knife or kitchen shears, remove the loin from the rib cage and use a cleaver to divide the loin into three pieces.

continued

CARROT QUADRETTI

SERVES 4

5 tablespoons (75 grams) fresh carrot juice

Pinch of saffron threads

1 cup plus 3 tablespoons (144 grams) 00 flour, preferably Antimo Caputo, plus more for dusting

½ cup (80 grams) plus 1 tablespoon semolina flour

1 large egg yolk

¼ cup (65 grams) whole-milk ricotta cheese

1 teaspoon kosher salt

SPECIAL EQUIPMENT

Pasta sheeter
Serrated pasta cutter

Pour the carrot juice into a small saucepan and warm over medium-low heat until it reaches a light simmer, about 30 seconds. Remove from the heat, add the saffron, and let it infuse until the carrot juice cools down.

Make the dough with the carrot juice; see How to Form and Knead Pasta Dough on page 177.

Turn out the dough onto a work surface lightly dusted with 00 flour and divide in half. Form each piece into an oval about the width of your pasta sheeter. Lightly dust one piece of dough with 00 flour and pass it through the sheeter on the thickest setting once or twice, dusting with flour in between if it begins to stick. Fold in the short sides to form a square the width of your pasta sheeter, then lower the thickness setting by one notch and pass the dough through the sheeter again. Repeat the process, decreasing the thickness by one notch each time, until you have a very long rectangle of dough about ⅛ inch thick—slightly thicker than some of the other pastas. Repeat the process with the second dough piece.

Using the serrated pasta cutter, cut the pasta into ¾-inch squares. Dust with 00 flour, cover, and transfer to the freezer for 1 hour or up to 3 days before cooking.

CAVATELLI ALLA NORCINA

SERVES 4

Norcina sauce includes two of the most wonderful things you find in Umbria: pork and truffles. But there's no single definitive recipe for the sausage-based sauce—everyone has his or her own version. Once, Genevieve and I visited the town of Norcia and tried a cold recipe with ricotta folded in among the pasta. The temperature was a little weird, but I liked the addition of the ricotta and thought of that when pairing my own Norcina sauce with a light, ricotta-based cavatelli. This is not going to be an inexpensive dish if you're buying fresh winter truffles—but it is impressive, addictive, and easily one of the most popular dishes at the restaurant. We go through so much cavatelli each day, I have to get a new cavatelli maker every two months.

Speaking of which, my cavatelli recipe makes an especially soft and sticky dough that can be too delicate to use with some countertop cavatelli makers. I use an old Viantonio Cavatelli No. 50 machine that I found on eBay, and it works well, but if yours struggles with the soft dough, knead in some additional flour until it's firm enough to go through the machine easily.

CAVATELLI DOUGH

1½ cups (200 grams) 00 flour, preferably Antimo Caputo, plus more for dusting

2 tablespoons beaten egg (about ½ large egg; see Note, page 176)

2 teaspoons whole milk

½ cup packed (120 grams) whole-milk ricotta cheese

1 teaspoon kosher salt

Kosher salt

1½ ounces black truffle, preferably fresh winter (see Note)

¼ cup extra-virgin olive oil

1 teaspoon packed anchovy paste, homemade (page 50) or store-bought

¼ teaspoon fresh thyme leaves

1 clove garlic, smashed

1½ teaspoons grapeseed oil

8 ounces Norcina sausage, homemade (page 78) or store-bought

1 cup mushroom stock, homemade (page 36) or good-quality, low-sodium store-bought

1 cup vegetable stock, homemade (page 35) or good-quality, low-sodium store-bought, plus more as needed

3 tablespoons unsalted butter

⅓ cup freshly grated Parmesan cheese

SPECIAL EQUIPMENT

Pasta sheeter
Cavatelli maker

Make the dough; see How to Form and Knead Pasta Dough on page 177.

Lightly flour the outside of the cold dough round, flatten gently, and pass it through the pasta sheeter once on the thickest setting. Remove, fold in the short sides to form a square that's roughly the same width as your sheeter, and pass it through once more. Decrease the thickness setting one notch and roll the pasta through again. Repeat the process, decreasing the thickness by one notch each

continued

time, until you have a very long rectangle of dough about ⅛ inch thick. Lay out the dough on a lightly floured surface. Using a knife, cut the dough into long strips about 1 inch wide.

Secure the cavatelli maker to the counter. Dust the dough strips and the rollers with flour and feed the strips one at a time through the wood spindles while turning the crank. The machine will spit out the formed cavatelli. Dust the finished cavatelli with more flour. Cover and refrigerate for up to 24 hours or freeze for up to 1 week.

When ready to cook, bring 2 quarts water to a boil in a saucepan and add 2 tablespoons plus 2 teaspoons salt. Line a plate with paper towels.

While the water is heating, cut a 1-ounce piece of the truffle into small dice, then add it to a small saucepan along with the olive oil, anchovy paste, thyme, and garlic. Place the pan over medium heat and cook until the oil just begins to bubble around the edges, about 1½ minutes seconds. Remove from the heat and set aside to let the oil infuse.

Preheat a large saucepan over high heat. Add the grapeseed oil and the sausage, breaking up the meat with a wooden spoon. Brown the sausage just until cooked through, about 3 minutes, then transfer it to the prepared plate to drain. Wipe the saucepan clean and return it to the stove over low heat. Add the mushroom stock, vegetable stock, and butter and bring to a simmer.

Drain the diced truffle, reserving the oil, and add the truffle to the saucepan. Stir and return the mixture to a simmer.

Meanwhile, add the cavatelli to the boiling water and boil until tender but still slightly chewy, about 5 minutes. (If frozen, cook an additional 3 minutes.) Using a slotted spoon, transfer the cavatelli to the saucepan along with the cooked sausage. Increase the heat to high and sauté the pasta and sauce together, stirring occasionally, until the sauce begins to thicken and become creamy, 3 to 5 minutes. Remove from the heat. Add the Parmesan and reserved truffle oil to the pan and toss. (If the pasta seems dry, add more vegetable stock.)

Transfer the pasta to a serving plate or bowls, shave the remaining ½ ounce truffle over the top, and serve.

NOTE

Fresh winter truffles can be purchased online.

SPINACH GNOCCHETTI WITH ROASTED MARROWBONES

SERVES 2

This has been on our menu nonstop for the last six years. And it'll stay on the menu for another six years because I know that if I ever take it off, I may get stabbed in the dark alley behind the restaurant. It's that popular. We serve the marrowbones over a plate of fresh spinach gnocchetti, and the marrow is scooped and tossed into the pasta to create a rich, decadent sauce.

---

2 tablespoons grapeseed oil, plus 1 teaspoon

2 cloves garlic, smashed

1 cup packed spinach leaves

¼ cup plus 2 tablespoons whole milk

1 large egg yolk

Kosher salt

¾ cup (90 grams) 00 flour, preferably Antimo Caputo

4 tablespoons freshly grated Parmesan cheese

1 center-cut beef marrowbone (about 5 inches long), split in half
4 cups lengthwise by your butcher

Freshly ground black pepper

Maldon or other flaky sea salt

⅓ cup vegetable stock, homemade (page 35) or good-quality, low-sodium store-bought, plus more as needed

1 tablespoon unsalted butter, at room temperature, cut into small cubes

Fennel fronds for garnish

Pinch of Parsley Bread Crumbs (page 55)

Aged balsamic vinegar for drizzling

SPECIAL EQUIPMENT

Spaetzle maker

In a large sauté pan over high heat, warm 1 tablespoon of the grapeseed oil and 1 garlic clove and cook until the garlic begins to brown around the edges, about 1 minute. Add the spinach and toss until completely wilted, then remove from the heat and set aside to let cool slightly. Discard the garlic clove and transfer the spinach mixture to a blender along with the milk and egg yolk. Blend to a smooth purée.

Bring 2 quarts water to a boil in a large saucepan, then add 2 tablespoon plus 2 teaspoons kosher salt. Fill a large bowl with cold water and about 5 ice cubes and place nearby. Line a plate with paper towels.

Meanwhile, in a large bowl, whisk together the flour and 2 tablespoons of the Parmesan. Make a well in the center with your fingers and pour in the spinach purée. Add 1 teaspoon kosher salt and stir until a smooth, thick batter forms.

Add half of the batter to the spaetzle maker and, moving the hamper back and forth with your hands, press through the holes over the boiling water. Cook for 1 to 2 minutes, until the water returns to a boil, then, using a slotted spoon, gently transfer the gnocchetti to the ice water bath for 1 minute to stop the cooking. Repeat with the remaining batter. Drain well in a colander set in the sink, then transfer to the prepared plate to drain completely. Refrigerate the pasta, uncovered, for 30 minutes so it dries out before cooking. It will spatter oil if there is still water content. This also helps the pasta crisp up when cooking it.

Preheat the oven to 500°F. Bring the split marrowbone to room temperature.

Season the marrowbone with a pinch of pepper. Place, cut-side up, in a roasting pan, slide onto the top rack of the oven, and roast for 5 minutes. Turn the oven to broil

continued

and finish cooking for another 2 minutes, until the marrow has formed a golden crust. (If you have a blowtorch, you can use it instead of broiling.) Remove the marrowbone from the oven and season with a pinch of Maldon salt. Keep warm. (You can roast the marrowbone up to 1 hour ahead and rewarm in the oven before serving.)

Transfer the gnocchetti to a bowl, add the 1 teaspoon grapeseed oil, and toss to coat.

Preheat a large nonstick frying pan over medium-high heat. Add the remaining 1 tablespoon grapeseed oil and the remaining garlic clove and sauté until the garlic turns golden brown, about 1 minute. Add the gnocchetti and let cook on one side undisturbed until they begin to brown, about 2 minutes. Stir to flip the gnocchetti, then turn the heat to medium-low and brown lightly on the other side, about 2 minutes longer. Increase the heat to high for 1 minute more. The final texture should be chewy and slightly crispy.

Remove the pan from the heat and add the vegetable stock to deglaze, scraping the bottom with a spatula to incorporate all of the browned bits then add the butter and remaining 2 tablespoons Parmesan and mix until creamy. (If the sauce seems too dry, add a bit more vegetable stock.)

Spoon the pasta into a serving bowl and rest the split roasted marrowbone on top at an angle. Garnish with fennel fronds, finish with the bread crumbs or another pinch of Maldon salt, drizzle with balsamic vinegar, and serve.

SPAGHETTI RUSTICHELLA WITH SEA URCHIN

SERVES 2

This dish is an ocean bomb, in the best way possible. There are three different elements of the sea here: lobster stock, sea urchin, and bottarga. Sea urchin is one of the few local seafood items we can get super-fresh regularly.

Before buying sea urchin, make sure the lobes seem firm and their color is vibrant. Once it's a bit passed, sea urchin has sort of a wilted look to it. Smell it and, if possible, taste it. It should smell of the deep ocean and slightly sweet. A clean, sweet, saline taste is important to the dish.

Kosher salt

1 tablespoon extra-virgin olive oil, plus 1 teaspoon

1 tablespoon finely chopped shallot

½ teaspoon minced garlic

¼ teaspoon finely chopped hot, fruity chile such as Calabrian

1 teaspoon chopped fresh flat-leaf parsley, plus more for garnish

2 tablespoons dry white wine

⅓ cup vegetable stock, homemade (page 35) or good-quality, low-sodium store-bought

¼ cup Lobster Stock (page 36)

2 grinds of black pepper

¾ ounce fresh sea urchin, plus 2 whole lobes for garnish

3 ounces dried spaghetti

Squid Ink Bottarga (page 53) for garnish

Maldon or other flaky sea salt

Freshly squeezed lemon juice for finishing

In a large saucepan, bring 2 quarts water to a boil and add 2 tablespoons plus 2 teaspoons kosher salt.

Meanwhile, in a large sauté pan over medium heat, warm the 1 tablespoon olive oil. Add the shallot, garlic, chile, parsley, and ½ teaspoon salt and sauté until fragrant and the garlic just begins to turn golden, about 3 minutes. Add the wine to deglaze the pan, scraping the bottom with a spatula to incorporate all of the browned bits. When the wine has evaporated, add both stocks and remove from the heat. Add the pepper and stir to combine. Set aside.

In a small bowl, mash the ¾-ounce sea urchin with a rubber spatula until it becomes a chunky paste. Set aside.

Add the spaghetti to the boiling water and cook for 2 minutes less than whatever the package recommends. Drain, then add to the sauté pan, place over high heat, and cook, tossing occasionally, until the sauce is mostly absorbed, about 2 minutes. Remove the pan from the heat. Add the mashed sea urchin and the 1 teaspoon olive oil and toss until creamy.

Transfer the pasta to individual shallow bowls or pasta plates and garnish with parsley and a few grates of bottarga. Top each portion with 1 whole lobe of sea urchin, finish with a pinch of Maldon salt, a few drops of lemon juice, and serve.

AGNOLOTTI ALLA VACCINARA WITH CACAO PASTA, BRAISED OXTAIL, GRANA PADANO, PINE NUTS, AND CURRANTS

SERVES 4

Coda alla vaccinara is an Italian stew that traditionally has a sweet-and-sour profile, and some preparations incorporate chocolate into the oxtail braise. Our version uses a heavy amount of cocoa powder in the pasta dough instead of the braise, which gives the pasta a deep, slightly bitter, savory note and beautiful color.

OXTAIL FILLING

1½ pounds oxtail, cut into 3 or 4 pieces

Kosher salt and freshly ground black pepper

5 tablespoons grapeseed oil, plus 1½ teaspoons

1 tablespoon unsalted butter

½ cup dry red wine

5 cloves garlic, plus 1 tablespoon minced

2 fresh bay leaves or 1 dried

½ sprig rosemary, plus 1 teaspoon finely chopped fresh rosemary

1 sprig sage

1 sprig thyme

5 black peppercorns

4 juniper berries, smashed

1 small yellow onion, diced

1 carrot, peeled and diced

1 celery stalk, trimmed and diced

4 cups vegetable stock, homemade (page 35) or good-quality, low-sodium store-bought

½ cup good-quality, low-sodium beef stock

2 tablespoons minced shallots

1 teaspoon finely chopped fresh marjoram

1 cup packed chopped Swiss chard

½ cup whole-milk ricotta cheese

3 tablespoons packed freshly grated grana padano cheese

CACAO PASTA DOUGH

1⅓ cups (170 grams) 00 flour, preferably Antimo Caputo, plus more for dusting

⅓ cup (30 grams) 50 to 70 percent cocoa powder

2 large whole eggs, plus 2 large egg yolks

3 teaspoons extra-virgin olive oil

1 teaspoon kosher salt

Kosher salt

4 tablespoons currants

1 cup dry white wine

2 tablespoons unsalted butter

¼ cup vegetable stock, homemade (page 35) or good-quality, low-sodium store-bought

3 tablespoons good-quality, low-sodium beef stock

1½ teaspoons toasted pine nuts

1 to 2 tablespoons freshly grated grana padano cheese

SPECIAL EQUIPMENT

Cheesecloth
Kitchen string
Piping bag
Pasta sheeter
Spray bottle of water
Serrated pasta cutter

Preheat the oven to 350°F.

To make the filling, season the oxtail with salt and pepper. In a large sauté pan over high heat, combine 3 tablespoons of the grapeseed oil and the butter. When hot, add the oxtail pieces and sear until golden brown on all sides, 5 to 10 minutes. Remove from the heat and set aside.

Meanwhile, place a small saucepan over high heat. Add the wine and boil until it has reduced to 1 tablespoon, about 10 minutes.

Cut a 10-inch square of cheesecloth and place the garlic cloves, bay leaves, rosemary sprig, sage, thyme, peppercorns, and juniper berries in the middle. Wrap them tightly in the cheesecloth, then wrap kitchen string around the bundle several times to form a tight sachet. Tie to close.

Preheat a Dutch oven over medium heat. Add 2 tablespoons grapeseed oil, then add the onion, carrot, and celery and cook for about 15 minutes, until well caramelized.

continued

Add the herb sachet and browned oxtail along with any liquids that accumulated in the pan and the vegetable and beef stocks. Cover and transfer to the oven. Braise until the meat is completely fork-tender and falling off the bone, about 4 hours. Using tongs, transfer the oxtail to a large bowl and set aside until cool enough to handle. Strain the vegetables, reserving the liquid in an airtight container. Remove the oxtail meat from the bones and shred with your fingers or two forks. Finely chop with a knife to form a paste. Transfer the vegetables to a food processor and pulse until very finely chopped. (Alternatively, transfer to a cutting board and chop by hand.) Transfer the meat and vegetables to a second airtight container and refrigerate along with the reserved liquid for at least 2 hours or up to 24 hours. A hard layer of fat will rise to the surface of the reserved braising liquid; scrape off with a spoon and discard.

In a saucepan over medium-low heat, warm the 1½ teaspoons grapeseed oil. Add the shallots, minced garlic, marjoram, and chopped rosemary and cook, stirring occasionally, until the aromatics are fragrant and beginning to soften, 3 to 5 minutes. Add the Swiss chard, oxtail meat, chopped vegetables, and the reserved braising liquid. Continue to cook over medium-low heat, stirring occasionally, until the liquid is completely reduced, being careful not to allow the bottom of the pot to scorch. Remove from the heat, then transfer to a large bowl and refrigerate until cool. Once cool, adjust the seasoning of the salt and pepper if necessary and stir in the ricotta and grana padano. (Store in an airtight container in the refrigerator for up to 3 days. Alternatively, freeze the reduced meat mixture on its own for up to 1 month, then thaw in the refrigerator before incorporating the cheese to make the filling.)

Make the dough; see How to Form and Knead Pasta Dough on page 177.

When ready to fill the agnolotti, transfer the filling to a piping bag with a small plain tip.

Turn out the pasta dough onto a lightly floured work surface and divide in half. Form each piece into an oval about the width of your pasta sheeter. Lightly flour one piece of dough and pass it through the sheeter on the thickest setting once or twice, dusting with flour in between if it begins to stick. Fold in the long sides to form a square the width of your pasta sheeter, then lower the thickness setting by one notch and pass the dough through the sheeter again. Repeat the process, decreasing the thickness by one notch each time, until you have a long rectangle of dough that is almost paper-thin and slightly transparent—you should be able to see the outline of your hand through it. Repeat with the second piece of dough. Cut your sheets into 3-inch strips. You should get 2 to 3 strips from the full sheet.

Lightly flour your work surface, then lay a pasta sheet on it with a long side facing you. Pipe 1-teaspoon portions of the filling about 1 inch apart along the sheet, just below the middle. Using a spray bottle, lightly spray the pasta with water to keep it from drying out. Fold the bottom half of the pasta up and over the filling to meet the top. Then, with your thumb and forefinger pointed downward, pinch the dough together between the lumps of filling, forming a long upward crease. Spray with water again.

Using the serrated pasta cutter, trim the long edges about ¼ inch above and below the filling and discard the scraps. Then cut between the agnolotti, rolling firmly away from you with the pasta cutter while gently bracing the filling between your thumb and forefinger, allowing just the sides of each agnolotto to roll over on itself. Repeat the rolling, filling, and shaping process with the second pasta sheet. Dust the finished agnolotti with flour, cover with plastic wrap, and transfer to the freezer for at least 2 hours or up to 3 days so the agnolotti will firm up and hold their shape and won't burst open when cooking.

In a large saucepan, bring 2 quarts water to a boil and add 2 teaspoons salt.

In a small saucepan over medium heat, combine the currants and white wine and bring to a boil. Remove from the heat and let cool to room temperature; drain, then measure out 1 tablespoon of the currants and set aside. (Transfer the remaining currants to an airtight container and store in the refrigerator for another use.) In a large sauté pan over high heat, melt the butter. Once melted, turn the heat to the lowest setting and let cook, undisturbed, until the solids have settled to the bottom of the pan and begin to brown.

Drop the frozen agnolotti into the boiling water and boil until they float to the surface, about 2 minutes. Drain.

Add the 1 tablespoon currants, the vegetable stock, and the beef stock to the pan with the butter and whisk to combine. Add the cooked pasta and toss, sautéing until the sauce is thick and creamy. Remove from the heat, add the pine nuts and grana padano, toss to mix well, and serve.

TAGLIATELLE AL SUGO DI MAIALE WITH PORK RAGU, SPECK, CABBAGE, AND CARAWAY SEEDS

SERVES 4

Tagliatelle is a long, fat, ribbony noodle that's ideal for capturing meaty sauces. Traditionally it goes with Bolognese, but it works great with all kinds of ragu. With caraway seeds, speck, and cabbage, this pork ragu is inspired by that part of Italy near the Austrian border. The long strips of cabbage lighten the dish, cutting the heavy starchiness—while also adding a touch of sweetness.

The ragu can be made and frozen up to 1 month ahead and makes enough for a couple of extra meals—a reward for all that slow cooking.

PORK RAGU

5 cloves garlic

3 sprigs thyme

1 small sprig rosemary

1 sprig marjoram

1 sprig sage

2 fresh bay leaves or 1 dried

2¼ pounds bone-in pork shoulder, boned (bones reserved) and cut into ½-inch cubes

1 tablespoon plus 1 teaspoon kosher salt

½ teaspoon freshly ground black pepper

3 tablespoons grapeseed oil

3 tablespoons unsalted butter

1 cup dry white wine

1 tablespoon plus 1 teaspoon extra-virgin olive oil

1 cup Vegetable Soffritto (page 38)

½-ounce piece speck or speck skin (optional, for added flavor)

6 cups vegetable stock, homemade (page 35) or good-quality store-bought

1 tablespoon finely chopped dried porcini mushrooms

1 tablespoon unsalted butter

1 ounce speck, cut into thin strips

¼ head green cabbage, thinly sliced

½ cup heavy cream

Kosher salt

1 recipe Tagliatelle (page 213)

Freshly ground pepper

1 teaspoon caraway seeds

½ cup freshly grated Parmesan cheese

SPECIAL EQUIPMENT

Cheesecloth
Kitchen string

To make the ragu, cut a 10-inch square of cheesecloth and place the garlic, thyme, rosemary, marjoram, sage, and bay leaves in the middle. Wrap them tightly in the cheesecloth, then wrap the kitchen string around the bundle several times to form a tight sachet. Tie to close.

Line a plate with paper towels.

In a large bowl, season the pork with the salt and pepper and toss well. Preheat a saucepan over high heat until smoking. Add 1 tablespoon each of the grapeseed oil and butter. When the butter has melted, add one-third of the pork and sear, turning as needed, until nicely browned on all sides, 3 to 5 minutes. Using a slotted spoon, transfer the pork to the prepared plate to drain. Wipe the pan clean and repeat the process twice with the remaining grapeseed oil, butter, and pork.

Meanwhile, preheat the oven to 375°F. Arrange the reserved pork bones on a baking sheet and roast for 45 minutes.

Pour the wine into a small saucepan over high heat. Bring to a boil and reduce to 1 tablespoon, about 10 minutes. In a large pot over medium heat, combine the olive

continued

oil, soffritto, sachet of aromatics, and the ½-ounce piece of speck, (if using). Add the reduced wine, 5 cups of the stock, and the roasted pork bones (this will add more flavor to the ragu without making an actual pork stock for this dish) and bring to a boil, stirring occasionally. Lower the heat to a simmer.

After browning the last batch of pork, deglaze the pan with the remaining 1 cup stock, scraping the bottom with a spatula to incorporate all of the browned bits. Pour the deglazing liquid into the pot along with all of the browned pork meat. Return to a boil, then turn the heat to low and simmer, uncovered, for 1½ hours, periodically skimming off the fat that accumulates on the surface with a spoon. Stir in the dried porcini, remove from the heat, and let the ragu rest for about 15 minutes so the porcini can infuse. Remove and discard the pork bones. You should have about 6 cups ragu. (The ragu may seem thin, but it will thicken when you cook it with pasta for the final dish. Set aside 2 cups for this recipe and store the rest in an airtight container in the refrigerator for up to 3 days, or freeze for up to 1 month, then thaw in the refrigerator before using.)

In a large sauté pan over medium heat, melt the butter. Add the speck strips and cook until crispy and all of the fat has rendered, about 2 minutes. Add the cabbage and cook until it is just wilted but still has some texture, about 1 minute. Stir in the cream and sauté until the sauce begins to thicken, then add the 2 cups pork ragu and return to a simmer.

Meanwhile, in a large saucepan, bring 2 quarts water to a boil and add 2 tablespoons plus 2 teaspoons kosher salt. Add the tagliatelle and boil for about 40 seconds. Then, using tongs, transfer the noodles to the sauté pan with the ragu. Increase the heat to high, bring the ragu back to a boil, and sauté the pasta and ragu together until the sauce begins to thicken, about 2 minutes. Remove from the heat. If the sauce seems too thick, add a small amount of water to thin it out and sauté for another minute. Taste and adjust the seasoning with salt and pepper if needed, then add the caraway seeds and Parmesan and toss and serve.

TAGLIATELLE

SERVES 4

1½ cups (200 grams) 00 flour, preferably Antimo Caputo, plus more for dusting

1 large whole egg, plus 5 large egg yolks

1½ teaspoons extra-virgin olive oil

1 teaspoon kosher salt

SPECIAL EQUIPMENT

Pasta sheeter

Make the dough; see How to Form and Knead Pasta Dough on page 177.

Turn out the dough onto a lightly floured work surface and divide in half. Form each piece into an oval about the width of your pasta sheeter. Lightly dust one piece of dough with flour and pass it through the sheeter on the thickest setting once or twice, dusting with flour in between if it begins to stick. Fold in the long sides to form a square the width of your pasta sheeter, then lower the thickness setting by one notch and pass the dough through the sheeter again. Repeat the process, decreasing the thickness by one notch each time, until you've reached the thinnest setting. If the dough begins to stick at any point, lightly dust the sheet of dough with flour before passing it through again. You should end up with a long rectangle of dough that is almost paper-thin and slightly transparent—you should be able to see the outline of your hand through it. Repeat with the second piece of dough.

On a clean, dry work surface, spread out a pasta sheet and cut it into equal 10-inch segments, about the length of a chef's knife. Then, one piece at a time, dust the sheet with flour and roll it into a long roll about 2 inches in diameter. Using a chef's knife, slice the roll into ½-inch-wide strips. Separate the strips into noodles with your fingers, dust them with flour, and lay them flat until dry, 10 to 15 minutes. Line a baking sheet with parchment. Gently bundle each segment's worth of noodles together and drop in loose piles on the baking sheet. Repeat with the second pasta sheet. Use immediately, or refrigerate in an airtight container for up to 48 hours.

PICI WITH LAMB RAGU

SERVES 4

I hate throwing anything away, and that includes our sourdough starter. Even after baking all of our bread and making all of our pizza each day, we always have a little bit of extra starter left over. I was saving it in the refrigerator, but it began to accumulate, so I started experimenting with putting it into pasta dough as a nontraditional way of making pici, which is traditionally an extruded pasta. The slight leavening effect of the starter gives the noodles a chewy texture and tanginess, that's enhanced by the addition of yogurt whey (see Note, page 217).

I love the look of the handmade pici—some are a little thicker, some are thinner. They're rustic and perfectly imperfect. The pasta's acidic sourdough quality is the perfect accompaniment for the rich, slightly gamy lamb ragu—which is incredible with nearly any handmade pasta. It's also delicious served on top of polenta (see page 39).

LAMB RAGU

2 cloves garlic, smashed

2 sprigs thyme

2 sprigs sage

1 sprig marjoram

2 fresh bay leaves or 1 dried

1 fresh fig leaf, or 1 cinnamon stick

5 juniper berries, smashed

10 black peppercorns

2½ pounds bone-in lamb shoulder, boned (bones reserved) and cut into ½-inch cubes

Kosher salt and freshly ground black pepper

3 tablespoons grapeseed oil

3 tablespoons unsalted butter

1 cup dry red wine

1 tablespoon plus 1 teaspoon extra-virgin olive oil

1 cup Vegetable Soffritto (page 38)

Heaping 1 tablespoon tomato paste

6 cups vegetable stock, homemade (page 35) or good-quality, low-sodium store-bought

12 saffron threads

Kosher salt

1 recipe Pici (page 217)

1 tablespoon Black Butter (page 48), unsalted butter, or olive oil

2 tablespoons roughly chopped fresh flat-leaf parsley

⅓ cup freshly grated Parmesan cheese

1 teaspoon toasted bread crumbs

Freshly grated Capra Sarda or Parmesan cheese for garnish

SPECIAL EQUIPMENT

Cheesecloth

Kitchen string

To make the ragu, cut a 10-inch square of cheesecloth and place the garlic, thyme, sage, marjoram, bay leaves, fig leaf, juniper berries, and peppercorns in the middle. Wrap them tightly in the cheesecloth, then wrap the kitchen string around the bundle several times to form a tight sachet. Tie to close.

Line a plate with paper towels.

In a large bowl, season the lamb with the salt and pepper and toss to coat. Preheat a saucepan over high heat until smoking. Add 1 tablespoon each of the grapeseed oil and butter. When the butter has melted, add one-third of the lamb and sear, turning as needed, until nicely browned on all sides, 3 to

continued

5 minutes. Using a slotted spoon, transfer the lamb to the prepared plate. Wipe the pan clean and repeat the process twice with the remaining lamb, grapeseed oil, and butter.

Meanwhile, preheat the oven to 375°F. Arrange the reserved lamb bones on a baking sheet and roast for 45 minutes.

Pour the wine into a small saucepan over high heat. Bring to a boil and reduce to 1 tablespoon, about 10 minutes. In a large pot over low heat, combine the olive oil, soffritto, sachet of aromatics, and tomato paste and cook, stirring occasionally, until the tomato paste has started to bubble and caramelize, about 5 minutes. Add the reduced red wine, 5 cups of the stock, and the roasted bones and bring to a boil, stirring occasionally. Lower the heat to a simmer.

After browning the last batch of lamb, deglaze the pan with the remaining 1 cup stock, scraping the bottom with a spatula to incorporate all of the browned bits. Pour the deglazing liquid into the pot along with all of the browned lamb. Return to a boil, then turn the heat to low and simmer, uncovered, for 1½ hours, periodically skimming off the fat that accumulates on the surface with a spoon.

Remove the ragu from the heat. Stir in the saffron and let the ragu rest for about 15 minutes to let the flavors infuse. Remove and discard the lamb bones. You should have about 7 cups ragu. (The ragu may seem thin, but it will thicken when you cook it with pasta for the final dish. Set side 3 cups for this recipe and store the rest in an airtight container in the refrigerator for up to 3 days, or freeze for up to 1 month, then thaw in the refrigerator before using.)

In a large saucepan, bring 2 quarts water to a boil and add 2 tablespoons plus 2 teaspoons salt. Add the pici and cook for about 6 minutes, until soft and chewy. Drain and set aside.

Meanwhile, in a saucepan over medium heat, warm the 3 cups ragu until simmering. Add the pici and toss with tongs, then stir in the black butter. Continue to simmer until the ragu has thickened and coats the noodles. Add 1 tablespoon of the the parsley and toss, then remove the pan from the heat. Add the Parmesan and toss once more.

Transfer the pasta to individual plates or a large platter and finish with the bread crumbs, the remaining 1 tablespoon parsley, and a few gratings of the Capra Sarda and serve.

PICI

¾ cup plus 1 tablespoon (100 grams) 00 flour, preferably Antimo Caputo plus more for dusting

½ cup (85 grams) plus 1 tablespoon semolina flour

1 large egg yolk

2 tablespoons (25 grams) Biga Sourdough Starter (page 155), or 2 tablespoons 00 flour mixed with 2 tablespoons water

¼ cup (50 grams) whey from plain whole-milk Greek yogurt (see Note)

3 tablespoons (45 grams) water

½ teaspoon kosher salt

SPECIAL EQUIPMENT

Pasta sheeter

NOTE

The whey from Greek yogurt adds extra tang to this pasta dough. For ¼ cup whey, place a fine-mesh strainer lined with cheesecloth over a bowl and scoop in 2 cups yogurt. Let drain in the refrigerator for about 1 hour.

Make the dough; see How to Form and Knead Pasta Dough on page 177.

Remove the chilled dough from the refrigerator and unwrap. Turn out the dough onto a work surface lightly dusted with 00 flour and divide in half. Form each piece into an oval about the width of your pasta sheeter. Lightly dust one piece of dough with 00 flour and pass it through the sheeter on the thickest setting once or twice, dusting with flour in between if it begins to stick. Fold in the long sides to form a square the width of your pasta sheeter, then lower the thickness setting by one notch and pass the dough through the sheeter again. Repeat the process, decreasing the thickness by one notch each time, until you have a long rectangle of dough about ¼ inch thick. Lay out the dough in front of you on a lightly floured surface. Using a knife, cut into ¼-inch strips and roll each piece back and forth with the heels of your hands until the dough forms a skinny noodle about 8 inches long. Repeat the process until all of the dough has been formed into noodles. Use immediately, or place the noodles on a lightly floured plate, cover with plastic wrap, and refrigerate for up to 8 hours. Due to the sourdough starter, the noodles may rise and thicken a bit in the fridge. If they get too thick, quickly reroll each noodle by hand once more before cooking. Do not freeze.

MAIN DISHES

GRILLED STUFFED QUAIL WITH BLISTERED SHISHITO PEPPERS

SERVES 4

Stuffed with farro, shiitakes, and mascarpone, and piled on top of blistered shishitos, these tiny, beautifully flavored birds become a substantial, satisfying main course. You can ask your butcher to snip the wing tips or you can do it yourself with kitchen shears.

- 1 cup Cooked Farro (page 102)
- 4 Pickled Smoked Shiitake Mushrooms (page 20) or rehydrated dried shiitakes, julienned
- 1 teaspoon chopped fresh thyme
- 3 tablespoons mascarpone
- Kosher salt and freshly ground black pepper
- 4 semiboneless quail, wing tips removed
- 2 tablespoons extra-virgin olive oil, plus more for serving
- 2 cloves garlic
- 24 shishito peppers
- 2 sprigs thyme
- Juice of ½ lemon
- 3 tablespoons good-quality, low-sodium beef stock or chicken stock
- 32 capers, rinsed
- 16 fresh Thai basil leaves
- 16 fresh mint leaves
- Maldon or other flaky sea salt

Combine the farro, pickled shiitakes, thyme, and mascarpone in a bowl and mix well. Add ½ teaspoon salt and a pinch of pepper and stir to combine.

Place the quail, breast-side down, on a cutting board and lightly season inside the cavity with salt and pepper. Fill the cavity of each quail with about 2 tablespoons of the farro stuffing, press down to flatten, and refrigerate for at least 1 hour or up to overnight. Bring to room temperature before grilling.

Build a hot fire in a charcoal grill or preheat a gas grill to high. Place a cast-iron pan directly on the grill grate. Add 1 tablespoon of the olive oil and the garlic cloves to the pan and cook, letting the garlic infuse the oil for 2 to 3 minutes, then add the shishitos and sauté, tossing occasionally, until blistered on all sides, about 3 minutes. Season with salt and pepper and continue to sauté for another 30 seconds. Remove the pan from the heat and set aside.

Lightly season the outside of the quail with salt and pepper and drizzle with 2 teaspoons olive oil. Grill the quail, breast-side down, for 2 minutes, then rotate 90 degrees and grill for another 2 minutes. Flip the quail and place on a medium-heat area of the grill for an additional 4 minutes, rotating again after 2 minutes. The quail should be golden brown and the legs should start to have some give when you wiggle them. Transfer the quail to a platter, cover loosely with aluminum foil, and let rest.

Transfer the shishitos to a serving platter and return the cast-iron pan to the grill. Add the thyme and lemon juice to the hot pan and let cook for a few seconds, then stir in the stock and bring to a simmer. Add the remaining 1 teaspoon olive oil and whisk to emulsify, then lightly season with salt and pepper and cook until slightly thickened. Remove from the heat and discard the thyme.

Return the quail to the hot grill for a few seconds on each side to reheat. Then, arrange the quail on top of the shishitos and top with the pan sauce, capers, basil, and mint. Finish with a splash of olive oil and pinch of Maldon salt and serve.

GRILLED WHOLE BRANZINO WITH HERB CONFETTI

SERVES 2

The preparation of this fish is grilled, but because of the pea-tendril stuffing, it has the moistness of a steamed fish. The fried herbs and garlic add crunch, reminiscent of the fish's crispy skin, and the preserved lemon peel provides a great flavor that you just can't get from anything else. Ask your butcher to debone the fish in the following way: butterflied from the spine so the belly is attached. Make sure the fish is clean of bones but remains whole and intact.

HERB CONFETTI

- 5 cloves garlic, sliced very thinly (we use a mandoline)
- 4 cups grapeseed oil
- 1 whole Fresno chile, sliced very thinly
- 3 sprigs flat-leaf parsley
- 3 sprigs mint
- 8 large leaves fresh basil
- Kosher salt

- 1 whole branzino or other white fish (about 1½ pounds), filleted and butterflied from the spine
- Kosher salt and freshly ground black pepper
- 1 teaspoon rinsed and chopped Preserved Lemon (page 23)
- 1 cup packed pea tendril leaves or baby spinach leaves
- 1 teaspoon extra-virgin olive oil
- 1 lemon, halved

SPECIAL EQUIPMENT

Deep-frying thermometer

To make the herb confetti, in a small pot of boiling water, blanch the sliced garlic for 1 minute. Drain and pat dry completely.

Line a plate with paper towels.

In a saucepan, heat the grapeseed oil to 250°F. Fry the garlic in the oil until golden brown, about 5 minutes, then use a slotted spoon to transfer to the prepared plate to drain. Increase the heat until the oil reaches 275°F, then fry the chile slices until crispy and browned, 3 to 5 minutes. Add to the plate. Raise the temperature once more until the oil reaches 350°F, then fry the herbs until crisp, 30 to 40 seconds, and add to the plate. Season everything with salt and set aside.

Season the inside of the fish with salt, pepper, and the chopped preserved lemon. Stuff the fish with the pea tendril leaves and olive oil and press to close. Then, season the outside with salt and pepper.

Build a hot fire in a charcoal grill or preheat a gas grill to medium. If using a charcoal grill, move the coals a bit to one side. Make sure your grill is clean and brush the grates with oil.

Place the fish on the grill with the head near the warmer part and the tail pointed toward the cooler spot. Grill the fish on one side until the exposed flesh turns from translucent to white, 6 to 8 minutes. Don't touch it or try to move it too early or it may stick. Using a fish spatula, carefully flip the fish to the other side and continue cooking until it's fully cooked and the flesh is opaque, about 6 minutes longer. Meanwhile, place the lemon halves facedown on the grill until warmed through.

Transfer the fish to a large platter and top it with a heaping pile of the herb confetti. Squeeze the grilled lemon over all and serve.

PORCINI AND WILD FENNEL–RUBBED COPPA STEAK

SERVES 2 TO 4

A coppa steak comes from the pork shoulder and part of the neck. It's high in connective tissue, which can turn some people off, but when cooked correctly it has an awesome range of textures from fatty to chewy and has a deep, dark porcine taste. Unlike most cuts, coppa should be grilled to slightly over medium; otherwise, it can be tough. The yogurt-based marinade helps tenderize and infuse the meat with flavor. Serve the steak with an assertive salad like the Arugula, Radish, and Tarragon Salad on page 99.

- 1 tablespoon ground dried porcini mushrooms
- 1 teaspoon apple cider vinegar
- ½ cup plain whole-milk Greek yogurt
- 2 teaspoons yellow mustard seeds, toasted and ground
- 1 tablespoon roughly chopped wild fennel fronds (see Note, page 97) or regular fennel fronds
- 1 teaspoon ground red pepper flakes
- 1 clove garlic, Microplaned or very finely minced
- 2 (8-ounce) coppa steaks
- Kosher salt
- Extra-virgin olive oil for drizzling
- Maldon or other flaky sea salt
- 10 slices Pickled Smoked Shiitake Mushrooms (page 20)

In a small bowl, combine the ground mushrooms, vinegar, yogurt, mustard seeds, fennel, red pepper, and garlic and stir until thoroughly mixed. Rub the steaks liberally with the marinade on all sides, then cover and refrigerate for 24 hours.

Two hours prior to grilling, remove the steaks from the refrigerator and bring to room temperature. Build a hot fire in a charcoal grill or preheat a gas grill to high (see Grilling Basics, page 226). Holding your hand high above the steaks, generously shower the meat on all sides with kosher salt, then drizzle with olive oil and pat gently to set. Place the steaks directly onto the hottest part of the grill. Cook until the steaks easily lift off the grill without sticking. Turn them 45 degrees and give them another sear for 2 to 3 minutes. Then, flip the steaks and repeat the same process on the second side. Remove the steaks from the grill and let them rest for 3 to 5 minutes. You're looking for a temperature between medium and slightly over medium.

Just before serving, return the steaks to the grill over high heat for 1 minute to reheat, then transfer them to a cutting board. Using a sharp knife, slice the steaks against the grain on the bias. Arrange on individual plates, finish with Maldon salt and a drizzle of olive oil, top with the pickled shiitakes, and serve.

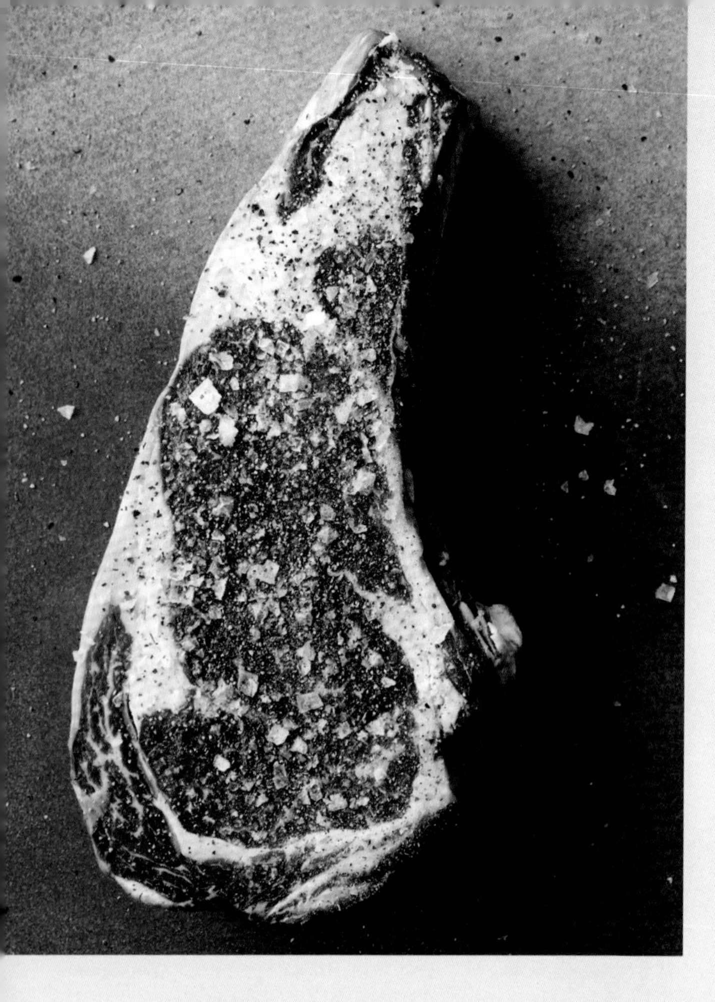

GRILLING BASICS

There's something primal about eating a piece food that's been cooked over a wood fire. Wood smoke provides layers of acidity, aroma, sweetness, and bitterness to anything you cook over it, which is why we have a wood-burning grill at Bestia. At home, though, I'm forced to be more pragmatic. I would love to have charcoal or wood if I could, but like most people, the only tool I have at home is a gas grill. Whatever your fuel, you can reliably grill most anything with the proper setup and technique.

Build Temperature Zones

You want to set up your grill with a gradation of heat. For a gas grill, set half of the burners at very high and the other half at medium-low. For charcoal, push most of the coals to one side, forming a slope. The different zones allow you to sear over high heat, then transfer your ingredients to a lower temperature for low-and-slow cooking. The cooler spots also serve as safe zones in case of flare-ups.

Use a Meat Thermometer

At this point in my experience, I can just look at a piece of meat, touch it quickly with the tip of my finger, and know if it's at the proper temperature. But that skill took years of professional cooking to acquire. If you're at all in doubt, don't guess. A basic meat thermometer will allow you to grill meat with consistency and precision, and build your confidence to learn the look and feel of meat at different temperatures.

Sear, Then Low and Slow

I always cook my meat the same way: sear over high heat to give it a flavorful crust, then move it to low heat. Cooking over high heat the entire time is quick, but it forces out all of the juices. Cooking large cuts of meat low and slow breaks down the muscle proteins, so what you end up with is tender and juicy.

Sear Again After Resting

Most people grill meat, take it off to rest, and then slice it. Doing so, you often end up eating something that's not as hot as it should be. I take my meat off the grill a little before one normally would, check its temperature after resting a few minutes, and then return it to high heat for another few seconds right before serving. This not only reheats and recrisps the exterior of the meat, but it gives you some leeway for overcooking. If after letting the meat rest it has not quite reached the temperature you want, you can leave the meat on a little longer to raise the temperature a few degrees.

SLOW-ROASTED LAMB NECK WITH SALSA VERDE AND ARUGULA, FENNEL, AND BLACK SESAME SALAD

SERVES 4

A few months before we opened the restaurant, we wanted to cook dinner for our Armenian neighbors, Soren and Norah, who lived above us and were always generously sending the most amazing food down. Cooking was always such a huge hassle because our kitchen was so tiny that you couldn't open the refrigerator or the oven without having to step aside to swing open the door. (Working together in that kitchen was a true testament to the solidity of our marriage.) Ori chose to make a lamb neck—it's a cheap and flavorful cut of meat, and at the time, we couldn't afford much else. He marinated it and then slow-roasted it for hours. The end result was falling-off-the-bone tender morsels of lamb meat, topped with a surprisingly bright salsa verde. Norah, who is quite the chef herself, was floored and insisted that we put it on our opening menu.

—Genevieve

---

1 or 2 lamb necks (about 2½ pounds total weight; see Note)
1 tablespoon kosher salt
2 tablespoons chopped fresh dill
1 teaspoon packed chopped fresh rosemary
1 teaspoon chopped fresh marjoram
2 teaspoons freshly grated lemon zest
2 cloves garlic, chopped
Pinch of freshly ground black pepper
3 tablespoons extra-virgin olive oil
¼ cup Salsa Verde (page 44)
½ teaspoon ground toasted fennel seeds

ARUGULA, FENNEL, AND BLACK SESAME SALAD

2 cups loosely packed arugula
¼ cup julienned Pickled Fennel (page 18)
¼ cup thinly sliced fresh fennel
Leaves of 2 sprigs dill
½ teaspoon toasted black sesame seeds
Pinch of fennel pollen (see Note, page 18)
Kosher salt and freshly ground black pepper
1 tablespoon Lemon-Chile Vinaigrette (see page 32)

½ lemon

Season the lamb neck on all sides with the salt. In a small bowl, mix the fresh herbs, lemon zest, garlic, black pepper, and 2 tablespoons of the olive oil. Rub the mixture all over the lamb neck, then cover and marinate in the refrigerator for at least 8 hours or up to overnight.

Bring the lamb neck to room temperature and preheat the oven to 325°F. Rub the lamb neck with the remaining 1 tablespoon olive oil, then place it on a rimmed baking sheet and tightly cover the entire pan with aluminum foil. Roast for 2½ hours on the top rack of your oven, or as far away from the heat

continued

source as possible; then flip the lamb, re-cover, and continue to roast for about 30 minutes more, until the meat is fork-tender and falling off of the bone.

Remove the baking sheet from the oven, uncover the lamb neck, and baste it with the juices that have accumulated. Discard the foil and wrap the lamb in plastic wrap. Let sit at room temperature for 1 hour to steam and soften the outer crust. (Alternatively, wrap the entire baking sheet in plastic wrap.) Before serving, unwrap the lamb neck and rewarm in a 450°F oven for 5 to 10 minutes.

In a small bowl, stir together the salsa verde and ground fennel.

Meanwhile, make the salad. In a bowl, combine the arugula, pickled fennel, fresh fennel, dill, sesame seeds, and fennel pollen and toss gently to mix. Season with salt and pepper, drizzle with the vinaigrette, and toss to coat.

Transfer the lamb neck to a serving platter. Squeeze the juice from the lemon half over the lamb and spread with a thick layer of the salsa verde mixture. Pile the salad alongside and serve.

NOTE

Most better butchers will sell you a lamb neck. Just ask for it slightly trimmed with a thin layer of fat remaining.

WHOLE ROASTED DUCK WITH CITRUS AND DILL

SERVES 4

This is my go-to recipe for every holiday feast. It's one of those recipes where you can just season it, put it in the oven, and then walk away. That's because we're cooking the meat for a longer time at a lower temperature until it falls apart. This way you get the flavor from the bones into the meat. The key is dry-aging the duck first in the refrigerator to help the fat render and the skin to crisp, and then cooking the meat breast-side down for added moisture.

---

1 whole duck (3½ to 4 pounds)

Kosher salt and freshly ground black pepper

3 cloves garlic

6 juniper berries, smashed

10 black peppercorns

6 sprigs dill, cut in half

3 sprigs thyme, cut in half

1 sprig sage

1 small sprig rosemary

2 fresh bay leaves or 1 dried

1 orange, cut into 8 wedges

1 tablespoon grapeseed oil

Fennel pollen (see Note, page 18) for garnish

Blistered Snap Peas with Mint (page 146) for serving

Basic Polenta (page 39) for serving

SPECIAL EQUIPMENT

Kitchen string

Using a sharp knife, remove the wing tips from the duck. Season the body cavity of the duck with 1 tablespoon salt and ¼ teaspoon black pepper. Place the garlic, juniper berries, and peppercorns in the cavity. Line the bottom of the cavity with half of the dill sprig pieces, half of the thyme sprig pieces, the sage, rosemary, and bay leaves. Top with the orange wedges, then pile the remaining herbs on top of the oranges.

Cut two 10-inch lengths of kitchen string. Use one piece to tie the ends of the legs together. Use the second piece of string to tie the wings closed behind the back. Place the duck, breast-side up, on a baking sheet lined with a clean kitchen towel and refrigerate uncovered for 24 to 72 hours.

Preheat the oven to 325°F.

Rub the outside of the duck with the grapeseed oil. Season the duck exterior with 1 tablespoon plus 1 teaspoon salt, applying a bit more salt to the breast, then season with ¼ teaspoon pepper. Transfer the duck, breast-side down, to a roasting pan and roast for 3½ hours. Wearing oven mitts and working carefully, rotate the bird at the following intervals: 45 minutes breast-side down; 45 minutes left-side down; 45 minutes right-side down; 25 minutes left-side down; and 25 minutes right-side down.

Remove the bird from the oven, rotate it onto its back, and let rest, breast-side up, for 15 to 30 minutes.

To carve, pull the legs back from the body; they should easily separate. Using a sharp chef's knife, cut half of the breast meat off the body and transfer to a cutting board. Repeat to remove the other half. Carve the breast into thick slices against the grain on the bias. Arrange the slices on a serving platter and finish with a pinch of fennel pollen. Serve with the peas and polenta.

GRILLED PORK PORTERHOUSE

SERVES 4 TO 6

We keep the belly on our pork porterhouse, which adds a third cut of meat to the traditional two-cut porterhouse. This recipe calls for a vinegar-based marinade instead of a brine, which breaks down the proteins and softens the meat. The added sugars char on the grill to give the meat a deep, caramelized flavor and helps crisp up the fat.

Serve with Pineapple Mostarda (page 26) and a simple salad of crisp greens, like Arugula and Opal Basil Salad (page 99).

---

8 tablespoons ground fennel seeds

3 tablespoons paprika

1 tablespoon fresh marjoram leaves

1 tablespoon fresh thyme leaves

1 clove garlic, Microplaned or very finely minced

2 teaspoons kosher salt

1 teaspoon freshly ground black pepper

¼ cup extra-virgin olive oil, plus more for drizzling

¼ cup sherry vinegar

2 pork porterhouse steaks, with belly or without (see recipe introduction), each about 1½ pounds and 1½ inches thick

Maldon or other flaky sea salt

SPECIAL EQUIPMENT

Instant-read thermometer

In a small bowl combine the ground fennel, paprika, marjoram, thyme, garlic, kosher salt, pepper, olive oil, and vinegar. Add ¼ cup water and stir until a thick paste forms. If the consistency is too dry, add a splash more of each liquid. Slather the pork with a very thick coating of the vinegar rub, then cover with plastic wrap and refrigerate for 24 to 48 hours.

Two hours prior to grilling, remove the steaks from the refrigerator and let them to come to room temperature.

Build a fire in a charcoal grill for both a hot area and a medium-low area, or preheat a gas grill with half of the burners on high heat and half on medium-low heat. (See Build Temperature Zones, page 226.) Brush the grates with oil. Holding your hand high above the steaks, generously shower the meat on all sides with kosher salt, then drizzle with olive oil.

Place the steaks, bone-side down, over high heat and cook undisturbed for about 3 minutes; then begin to sear the steaks on all sides over high heat, flipping and moving frequently to avoid flare-ups, until evenly charred and crusted.

Move the steaks to medium-low heat and cook undisturbed until the thickest part of the meat reaches 118°F.

Transfer to a cutting board to rest, uncovered, until the temperature reaches 125°F. Using a sharp knife, separate each steak into its three parts: the belly, the loin, and the fillet.

Return each belly to the grill over high heat. Add the loins and fillets and quickly sear again just until the meat is hot and the surface is crisp, 2 to 3 minutes. Slice the loins against the grain on the bias into slices ¼ to ½ inch thick. Repeat the process with the fillets and, last, the bellies, which take the longest to cook. All of the meat should be cooked to medium at this point.

Transfer the meat to a platter and finish with a drizzle of olive oil and a pinch of Maldon salt and serve.

GRILLED FENNEL-CRUSTED PORK CHOP

SERVES 4

This is the most impressive cut of meat that we serve at the restaurant. It's massive it really looks like a weapon. Like the rib-eye, the size here allows you to leave it on the grill for a longer period of time without overcooking it, which allows it to develop savory, smoky flavors you couldn't achieve with a smaller chop. You can ask your butcher to prepare this cut—a pork chop with the loin and belly attached to the rib—or you can use the same recipe for regular thick-cut bone-in pork chops.

BRINE

2 tablespoons fennel seeds
¾ cup kosher salt
⅓ cup sugar
1 whole head garlic, halved crosswise
Whole peel (not just zest) and juice of 1 orange
3 fresh bay leaves or 1 dried
10 juniper berries, smashed
2 sprigs rosemary
3 sprigs thyme
20 black peppercorns

2 tomahawk pork chops, each about 2 pounds and ¾ thick, or 4 bone-in pork chops, each about 1 pound and 1 inch thick
Kosher salt and freshly ground black pepper
Ground fennel seeds for rubbing
Maldon or other flaky sea salt
Extra-virgin olive oil for drizzling

SPECIAL EQUIPMENT

Instant-read thermometer

To make the brine, in a small sauté pan over medium heat, toast the fennel seeds until just fragrant, about 2 minutes. In a large saucepan over high heat, bring 2 quarts water to a boil. Add the kosher salt and sugar and return to a boil, stirring to dissolve the salt and sugar. Add the toasted fennel seeds, garlic, orange peel and juice, bay leaves, juniper berries, rosemary, thyme, and peppercorns, then remove from the heat and let cool to room temperature.

Place the pork chops in a large container and add the brine to cover. Transfer to the refrigerator for 4 hours, but no longer or they will be too salty. Rinse the pork chops in cold water, then pat dry and transfer to a plate or cutting board for 2 hours, until room temperature. (You can transfer them to a plate lined with a clean kitchen towel after rinsing and refrigerate until 2 hours *before* you're ready to grill.)

Build a fire in a charcoal grill for both a hot area and a medium-low area, or preheat a gas grill with half of the burners on high heat and half on medium-low heat. (See Build Temperature Zones, page 226.) Brush the grates with oil. Holding your hand high above the pork chops, generously season one side with kosher salt and pepper, then rub with a thick layer of ground fennel seeds. Flip the chops and repeat on the other side, then less heavily season the fat cap and sides.

Place the chops over high heat and sear, rotating frequently, until the chops have an even crust on all sides. Lean them up against the side of the grill to help them stand on end if necessary. Watch for flare-ups and move them away from the hot spots if the flame gets too high. Move the chops to medium-low heat and cook until the thickest part reaches 120°F.

Transfer the chops to a cutting board and let rest until the thickest part reaches 132°F to 135°F, about 5 minutes. Using a sharp knife, remove the loin from the rest of each chop, leaving the belly and bone attached. Return each belly to high heat to crisp; then 2 to 3 minutes later, add the loins as well. Grill for 1 minute more, then transfer to a cutting board. Slice each loin against the grain on the bias, then cut each belly off of the rib and slice it on the bias as well. Season with Maldon salt, then liberally drizzle with olive oil and serve.

GRILLED RIB-EYE WITH APPLE BALSAMIC–BLACK BUTTER SAUCE

SERVES 3 OR 4

I taste a piece of every single steak that leaves the kitchen, which means that I pretty much eat an entire steak every night. It's not great for my cholesterol, but it's necessary to make sure that each steak we serve is absolutely perfect. I don't like neat, linear grill marks on my steaks. Instead, I want the entire surface of the steak to be one big grill mark. That blackened crust is where the flavor is.

---

1 rib-eye steak, about 2 pounds and 2 inches thick, aged preferred (ask your butcher for the top 3 ribs near the shoulder)

3 tablespoons Black Butter (page 48)

1 tablespoon apple balsamic vinegar, aged balsamic vinegar, or saba

Kosher salt and freshly ground black pepper

Fresh thyme leaves for garnish

Maldon or other flaky sea salt

SPECIAL EQUIPMENT

Instant-read thermometer

Bring the steak to room temperature, about 2 hours.

Meanwhile, in a small saucepan over medium heat, melt the black butter, then add the apple balsamic and stir to combine. Remove from the heat and set aside.

Holding your hand high above the steak, generously shower one side with kosher salt and pepper, then flip and repeat the process on the other side. Hold the steak on end and blot up the leftover seasoning, then lightly coat the short sides.

Build a fire in a charcoal grill for both a hot area and a medium-low area, or preheat a gas grill with half of the burners on high heat and half on medium-low. (See Build Temperature Zones, page 226). Brush the grates with oil.

Place the steak directly over high heat and sear, rotating frequently, until evenly grill-marked on all sides, about 8 minutes. Balance the steak bone-side down, leaning up against the side of the grill if necessary, and grill for 3 to 4 minutes. Transfer the steak to low heat and grill until the thickest part of the steak reaches 110°F.

Transfer to a cutting board and let rest for 5 to 10 minutes, until the temperature is 117°F and the juices run clear. Return the steak to the grill over medium-low heat for 1 to 2 minutes to warm it up, then transfer it to high heat for 1 minute more, flipping frequently, until the thermometer reads 125°F for medium-rare. Remove from the heat and let rest for another 2 to 3 minutes before slicing. Using a sharp knife, cut the meat from the bone, then slice against the grain on the bias.

Transfer the meat to a serving plate, garnish with thyme leaves and a pinch of Maldon salt, then spoon the balsamic-butter sauce over the top and serve.

IN BERKELEY CALIFORNIA

SLOW-ROASTED SUCKLING PIG

SERVES 8 TO 10

I'm proud to call myself a hunter. The experience of killing an animal in the wild is central to my philosophy of being a chef. It's why I insist on cooking whole animals whenever possible, and why no piece ever goes to waste. About two months before we opened Bestia, I went boar hunting with some friends under a full moon.

We went out around midnight and by two o'clock in the morning we still hadn't seen any pigs, so everyone decided we should just head on home. We piled in the car and began driving, when suddenly a giant herd of eighty or ninety boar appeared out of nowhere. They surrounded the car, running alongside us. We sped up to get out of the way, but two of them passed right in front of the car and—boom!—we hit them. When we got out to see what we had killed, we saw that it was two babies. Baby boar are very difficult to hunt—they're so tiny and almost impossible to see—so we knew this was something special. We couldn't just let them go to waste.

My friend and I each took one home and decided to do right by them and prepare a feast. I brined mine for a day or two, butterflied it, and roasted it with a ton of herbs and aromatics. I was invited over to another friend's house for the dinner along with a bunch of other chefs and hunters. Everyone sat down at the table and began cutting off chunks of moist pig and shatteringly crisp skin. Suddenly, we all stopped eating and stared at one another in silence, then everyone started to laugh. The flavor was like nothing I'd ever tasted before. Next thing you know, we're all dancing and hugging around the table—a bunch of adult chefs, hunters, and friends. There was an overwhelming feeling of excitement and festivity around this miracle that we'd been gifted. It was a sensation that I still have trouble describing, and I'm not sure that I'll ever recapture.

I said to everyone that night that when I open the new place, I'm going to put a suckling pig on the menu to honor this once-in-a-lifetime meal. And I did—for the first two nights of Bestia, suckling pig ran as a special. I still put it on the menu every once in a while, but for the most part, this is something I reserve for a special occasion. I recommend you do the same.

continued

SLOW-ROASTED SUCKLING PIG, continued

BRINE

2 tablespoons fennel seeds

3¾ cups kosher salt

1⅔ cups sugar

2 whole heads garlic, halved crosswise

Whole peel (not just zest) and juice of 2 oranges

10 fresh bay leaves or 3 dried

20 juniper berries, smashed

4 sprigs rosemary

6 sprigs thyme

30 black peppercorns

1 (18-pound) suckling pig

Extra-virgin olive oil for rubbing, plus 1 cup

Kosher salt and freshly ground black pepper

2 to 3 tablespoons ground fennel seeds

2 whole heads garlic, halved crosswise

10 bay leaves, crumbled

5 sprigs rosemary

2 handfuls thyme sprigs

2 handfuls fennel fronds

About 2 quarts vegetable stock, homemade (page 35) or good-quality, low-sodium store-bought

Juice of 1 orange

1 sprig tarragon

1 lemon wedge (optional)

4 cups canola oil

10 large leaves cavolo nero (black kale)

8 cups Basic Polenta (page 39)

Strawberry Mostarda (page 27) or Pineapple Mostarda (page 26) for serving

SPECIAL EQUIPMENT

Kitchen string
Instant-read thermometer
Deep-frying thermometer

To make the brine, in a small sauté pan over medium heat, toast the fennel seeds until just fragrant, about 2 minutes. In a large stockpot over high heat, combine 10 quarts water, the salt, and sugar and bring to a boil, stirring to dissolve the salt and sugar. Once boiling, add the toasted fennel seeds, the garlic, orange peel and juice, bay leaves, juniper berries, rosemary, thyme, and peppercorns, then remove from the heat and let cool to room temperature.

Place the pig in a large container or brining bag and add the brine to cover. Transfer to the refrigerator for 24 hours.

Rinse the pig under cold water, then return to the refrigerator uncovered for another 24 hours to air-dry.

Bring the pig to room temperature, about 2 hours.

Preheat the oven to 375°F.

Rub the pig with a thin layer of olive oil and lightly season with salt (remember, the pig has been brined, so you don't need to use as much salt), pepper, and ground fennel seeds. Arrange the garlic halves, bay leaves, 3 of the rosemary sprigs, and 1 handful each of the thyme sprigs and fennel fronds on a large rimmed baking sheet. Splay out the legs of the pig and press down to flatten, then lay, skin-side up, on top of the aromatics on the baking sheet. Stir together the vegetable stock and orange juice, then pour into the baking sheet until the level reaches just below the skin.

Meanwhile, make a basting brush out of the remaining 2 sprigs rosemary and handful each of thyme sprigs and fennel fronds, tying the ends together with kitchen string. Dip the herb basting brush into the 1 cup olive oil.

Roast the pig at 375°F for 30 minutes, then lower the temperature to 275°F and cook for 2½ to 4 hours, depending on the pig's size, basting every 45 minutes with the herb brush and olive oil. After 1 hour, check the ears to see if they are getting too dark; if so, cover them with aluminum foil. The pig is done when the thigh meat reaches an internal temperature of 185°F and when you press on the thigh of the pig, there is no tension and the bone feels loose.

Remove from the oven, tent with aluminum foil, and let rest for 25 to 30 minutes.

Meanwhile, use a turkey baster to remove the juices from the baking sheet and pour them into a small saucepan. Cook over medium heat until the liquid has reduced by half; remove from the heat and add the tarragon sprig. Taste, and if it needs more acidity, squeeze in the juice from the lemon wedge.

While the pig is resting, pour the canola oil into a large, heavy saucepan and place over medium heat until the oil reaches 375°F on a deep-frying thermometer. Add the cavolo nero and fry for 2½ minutes, until crisp, then, using a skimmer or a slotted spoon, transfer to paper towels to drain. Season with salt.

Carve the suckling pig into eight to ten pieces. Spoon 1 cup polenta onto each serving plate. Top with one piece of suckling pig and spoon the sauce around the plate (but not on the meat; you want to keep the skin crispy). Lay some fried kale chips on top of the pig and spoon a tablespoon or two of the mostarda alongside and serve.

DESSERTS

At Bestia, we feel that finishing with dessert is imperative to a complete experience. An ideal night would begin with appetizing bites that tempt the palate, move to a main course that satisfies your hunger and cravings, and then finish with a touch of sweetness to complete the dining arc—sending a signal to your brain that the meal has come to an end.

But that doesn't mean that all desserts need to register as sweet and decadent. A great dessert can be light, refreshing, and even slightly savory. Our pastry program strives to have something on the menu for everyone while remaining true to our core philosophy: if the first thing that you taste is sugar, we failed. Every dessert, no matter how simple, should be composed in such a way that it showcases the beautiful tannins of a walnut, the tartness of citrus, or the coolness of cream—not the prevalence of sugar.

You won't find a lot of unusual flavor combinations on our dessert menu. I'm not trying to reinvent the wheel, I'm trying to make the wheel as perfect as possible. Every dessert we make takes into account texture, flavor, and mouthfeel so that the act of eating it is as pleasurable as possible. Your fork needs to push through the crust with the same force it goes through whatever is inside it. Rice pudding needs to be thick, with the pastry cream enveloping the rice so the flavors and textures stay as intended during the whole chewing process, not causing a separation between cream and rice. Every detail is important, no matter how small, and we test and retest until we make sure that each element is the best it can be.

That said, both my husband and I try to keep all of the work behind the scenes, and off the plate. So while our sweet and savory dishes may be complex to execute, we try to keep the technique as hidden as possible from the diner and aim to present flavors in their pure, simple, and elegant form.

—Genevieve

DESSERT-KITCHEN INGREDIENTS

While proper, well-cared-for tools and beautiful ingredients are keys to success in every arena of the kitchen, for desserts, I think using top-quality ingredients is even more important than your gear. With some ingredients, like butter, chocolate, and vanilla, it's easy to tell if they're high quality; but there are variables with other ingredients that are harder to notice. For example, make sure your baking powder and baking soda are fresh—use baking soda within 3 months of opening and baking powder within 6 months. It's not just about the expiration date on the box or can; with baking soda particularly, it can lose its activation power when exposed to humidity.

It may sound like a broken record, but it's a timeless hit: fresh, fresh, fresh is of the essence, from pantry to produce. Choose good-quality pantry items from responsible producers. With fruit, remember, "organic" doesn't necessarily mean "good." Even fruit from the farmers' market can be mealy and flavorless. I've found peaches at the grocery store that are better than ones found at a roadside stand. Smell and, if possible, taste the fruit to make sure. At the store, I'll bite into a peach, and if it's good, I'll buy what I need and cut around the bite mark. (If it's not what I'm looking for, I'll still buy the bitten fruit, of course, and give it to my daughter, whose currently three-year-old tastes are a little less discerning than mine.) It's better to buy one bad peach than eight bad peaches.

Following are a few more of my baking and dessert basics.

Eggs

High-quality eggs are more essential than most people think. Yolks from average grocery-store eggs typically have no flavor and lack viscosity, whereas a pasture-raised yolk is sweet, deep golden, and has a thick, sticky texture. This affects everything in cooking, but especially ice cream bases and crème anglaise, where good yolks make all of the difference.

Nearly all of the recipes in this chapter, as throughout the book, call for large grade A eggs. In some cases, the egg quantity includes "½ egg." For half an egg, beat 1 whole egg until well blended and measure out 2 tablespoons (or just double the recipe and make two desserts!).

Flour

Bad flour is like sawdust. Good flour should smell malty and fresh, not dusty. If you are lucky enough to have access to heritage wheats, use them. They carry an extra dimension of flavor, a taste that we've sadly lost over the last hundred years of industrial farming and modification. But even plain white flour has a beautiful malted fragrance if it's freshly milled. If you are buying at the grocery store, I recommend King Arthur or anything with a hippie-looking label.

Salt

All of the salt in these recipes is kosher salt unless otherwise noted. You may notice that my recipes call for more salt than you are used to seeing. This is not an error, and no, your desserts will not be salty tasting (with the exception of a few that I note are supposed to be a little salty). Salt and sugar are the yin and yang of flavor enhancements. They're opposites, but reliant on each other to coax out the flavors of each dish. Desserts require a certain amount of salt to round out the sugars. With the right amount of salt, you can actually use less sugar, because salt enhances everything, even sweetness.

The order in which I add salt to a recipe matters, too. If I want something to be evenly salted—like a pastry dough, which should have a well-rounded, buttery savoriness—I'll add salt in the beginning so that it fully dissolves and is evenly dispersed. But in some cases letting the salt dissolve throughout doesn't work as well and can muddle flavors. In that case I will add salt at the end, so it dissolves only partially and you end up with bright little sparkles of salt within each bite.

Sugar

Muscovado is real brown sugar, and I prefer to use it instead of conventional brown sugar in everything but my coconut tart, where I want that sort of nostalgic American butterscotch flavor. Muscovado provides an almost savory intensity and delicious dark, rich caramel flavor that you can't achieve with conventional brown sugar. You can find it at most specialty markets like Whole Foods, gourmet shops, and online retailers.

DESSERT-MAKING TOOLS

Chinois

You'll see that most of my recipes, especially the ice creams, call for an extra-fine-mesh strainer, or what the French call a *chinois*. It gets out all the tiniest bits of fibrous or solid ingredients and creates an incredibly smooth end product.

Oven Thermometer

Eighty percent of women are wearing the wrong bra size, and an even higher percentage of home ovens are set at the wrong temperature. Long before I ever played around with the idea of being the pastry chef, I was baking at home and couldn't figure out why the bottoms of all my cookies and cakes were burning while the centers remained raw. I tried lowering my oven temperature by 10 to 15 degrees, but it didn't help. I thought it was just a really bad oven. But then one day I was at a kitchen supply store, bought an oven thermometer, and came home to discover that my oven was actually running 45 degrees higher than its set temperature. So when I was supposedly baking at 350°F, I was actually baking at almost 400°F. I lowered my oven to 300°F and suddenly my cookies were baking at 345°F—and they were perfect. You can spend lots of money getting your oven calibrated, or use a $10 oven thermometer and do the math.

Pastry Rings

These small metal rings help things to not lose shape while baking, and they're essential for some of the crostatas that use small, juicy fruit like berries. I use 3½-inch rings for the individual crostatas (see variation, page 256).

Silicone Mats

You can use parchment for almost all of our recipes (except macaroons), but I always tell people to get a few different sizes of silicone mats instead. They're sustainable, they're less work than cutting parchment, and they last for years and years, which saves money—and trees.

Tamis

Basically a large, flat, cake-pan-shaped fine-mesh sifter, a tamis is great for quickly sifting dry ingredients as well as removing the pulp from fruit purées. It's quicker than using a sifter—you can dump an entire pound of powdered sugar or flour onto a tamis, run your hand over it, and have it lump-free in about 20 seconds. (See also page 9.)

ON MEASURING AND THE KITCHEN SCALE

Many home cooks have this innate fear of weighing ingredients, but believe me, using a scale means way fewer dishes to wash with way better results. You can place a bowl on the scale and dump directly from the package of flour or carton of milk instead of dirtying all of your measuring cups or wondering if your lightly spooned flour was too light or not light enough.

If you are still unsure about using a scale, know this: I think I could possibly be the only person ever to graduate from the University of Southern California in this millennium without ever knowing how to send an e-mail or use a computer. But I use a scale and only a scale. Unless I'm eyeballing it—but don't do that! My team hates me for it, and it's a surefire way to ruin a lot of expensive ingredients. If you choose not to listen to me, I've listed every recipe in cups and tablespoons in the pastry-based recipes that follow. But I'm hoping you'll be inspired to forgo that old style of measuring.

When making desserts at Bestia, we weigh ingredients as much as possible for accuracy. Measuring cups are not 100 percent accurate. Even the difference of one or two teaspoons sugar can affect getting the correct caramelization on a cake. For panna cotta, if your liquid is off even slightly, it will affect the resulting texture. If you aren't going to weigh ingredients, please be sure to take the time to measure them correctly. With flour, for example, gently spoon it into the measuring cup until it reaches the top. One cup of flour can weigh anywhere from 4 to 6 ounces depending on how you handle it—that's a 33 percent difference! So if you aren't going to weigh, for god's sake, please spoon, don't scoop.

FLEXIBILITY

I know that sometimes it's daunting to substitute ingredients in a cookbook, but a lot of the fruit desserts here are designed to have fruit substituted depending on seasonality and preference. If you love blackberries or mangoes, there's nothing wrong with using our crostata dough and frangipane and making a blackberry or mango crostata. If you don't see what you want, don't be afraid to make these recipes your own. And if you use very high-quality fruit, they most likely will turn out delicious.

KITCHEN CONFIDENCE

You need to have confidence in the kitchen. If I didn't have any confidence I wouldn't be here. Always remember, I probably don't have much more experience than the average person reading this book, so be thoughtful and confident in your choices. No one's going to die if it doesn't turn out perfect. The sun will still come up tomorrow.

GENEVIEVE'S PASTRY DREAM TEAM

There's something very special about starting a journey with a group of people and then continuing to grow together. The chefs in this photo represent a team that has been the heart and soul of Bestia's pastry program. Every single person here has played an essential role in making sure that the pastries we put out at Bestia are as delicious and consistent as possible, night after night. If I'm going to take credit for anything, it's that I handpicked a group of very special people, all of whom have a fire within them to put out nothing but the very best. They won't let themselves do otherwise. That level of caring and talent is not cultivated by me. It's because of who they are.

MATILDE Can make you laugh with just a look

DANIELA My responsible alter-ego

GENEVIEVE

LEMON–POPPY SEED OLIVE OIL CAKE

MAKES ONE 9-INCH CAKE

This is the moistest, most flavorful cake we make. In fact, it's so moist, it's almost like pudding, and it'll stay that way for a couple of days. With a dollop of our Crème Fraiche Whipped Cream (page 266) and a scoop of our Blueberry Mascarpone Ice Cream (page 303), it's the perfect way to finish off a simple dinner—and then eat the rest of the cake for breakfast.

¼ cup plus 2 tablespoons (85 grams) freshly squeezed orange juice

2 tablespoons (29 grams) freshly squeezed lemon juice

½ teaspoon kosher salt

1 cup plus 2 tablespoons (142 grams) all-purpose flour

¼ teaspoon baking powder

¼ teaspoon baking soda

3 tablespoons (23 grams) poppy seeds

6 tablespoons beaten egg (about 1½ large eggs; see page 245)

1 cup (200 grams) sugar

Freshly grated zest of 3 lemons (about ¼ cup loosely packed)

¾ cup (155 grams) extra-virgin olive oil

2 tablespoons (29 grams) Grand Marnier

½ cup plus 2 tablespoons (150 grams) buttermilk

Preheat the oven to 350°F.

In a small saucepan, combine the orange juice and lemon juice and cook over medium-low heat until thick, syrupy, and reduced by one-fourth, about 10 minutes. Remove from the heat and add the salt, stirring to dissolve. Set aside.

In a small bowl, whisk together the flour, baking powder, baking soda, and poppy seeds. Set aside.

In the bowl of a stand mixer fitted with the whisk attachment, beat the eggs on medium speed until slightly foamy. Add the sugar and lemon zest and beat until well mixed, about 1 minute, scraping down the sides of the bowl with a rubber spatula to make sure all of the sugar gets incorporated. Add the olive oil, Grand Marnier, and reduced citrus juices and mix until emulsified, 30 seconds to 1 minute.

Turn off the mixer and add one-third of the flour mixture. Mix on low speed until just barely incorporated, scraping down the sides with a spatula. Add half of the buttermilk and beat on low speed until combined, followed by another one-third of the flour mixture. Repeat the process, scraping down the sides of the bowl periodically, until all of the wet and dry ingredients are just combined. Be careful not to overmix. Remove the bowl from the mixer and gently fold the batter with the spatula, scraping the bottom of the bowl.

Cut a 9-inch round of parchment paper. Butter the bottom and sides of a 9-inch springform cake pan, line it with the parchment paper, and then butter the parchment. Pour the batter into the pan and bake until a toothpick inserted in the center comes out with moist crumbs and the edges are golden, about 25 minutes.

Transfer the pan to a wire rack and let cool slightly. Remove the pan sides and slide an offset spatula between the parchment and the pan bottom. Gently lift up one side of the cake, slide your hand between the parchment and the cake, and then peel off the parchment. Place on a serving plate. Store any leftovers in an airtight container at room temperature for up to 3 days.

CROSTATAS

I knew very few things when we opened Bestia. What I did know was that I was a pastry chef with no actual skills. So as I was designing the opening dessert menu, I tried to come up with dishes that I could pull off without having to make them look perfect. A free-form fruit crostata is completely Italian, absolutely delicious, and rustic enough that you can get away with any rough-hewn edges. Today it's one of our staples. We switch the seasonal fruit throughout the year, and you should, too. Use whatever peak-season produce you like; the only thing that matters is the quality—if it's out of season, mealy, or flavorless, this crostata will be terrible. This is one of those dishes where, because it's so simple, every single element has to be perfect.

Before Bestia opened, I'd been having some trouble with my crostata dough. If I didn't incorporate the butter thoroughly enough, the pea-sized bits would melt and create holes in the dough that leaked filling. If I did incorporate it enough, it was never as flaky or as tender as I hoped. One day, I was staging at Chez Panisse and I watched as they smashed every butter square into disks with their hand after tossing it in the flour. My whole world opened up. They explained it was a Jacques Pépin technique—that something this brilliant came from him shouldn't surprise anyone. Use this recipe for our crostatas, fill it with jam for a pocket pie, or roll it out to top a potpie.

An almond-flavored cream, frangipane adds a beautiful scent and complexity to every fruit, but especially stone fruits. Its main scent is bitter almond, which comes from the pits of stone fruits, most typically the apricot. We add a layer of frangipane to most of our crostatas for both heft and flavor.

CROSTATA DOUGH

MAKES ONE 11-INCH CROSTATA OR EIGHT 3½-INCH INDIVIDUAL CROSTATAS

2¼ cups (270 grams) all-purpose flour
4 teaspoons (17 grams) sugar
¾ teaspoon kosher salt
¾ cup (170 grams) cold unsalted butter, cubed
¼ to ½ cup (55 to 110 grams) ice water

In the bowl of a stand mixer fitted with the whisk attachment, combine the flour, sugar, and salt and whisk to blend. Remove the bowl from the mixer. Let the butter cubes become pliable but not too soft, then add them to the flour mixture and toss to coat. Using your hands, pick up each butter cube and smash it between your palms into a thin, flat disk about ⅛ inch thick and then drop

NOTE

After you've wrapped your dough in plastic wrap and formed it into a disk, gently but firmly pound all of the edges on the work surface. Do this once more just before rolling; this will keep the edges of your dough from feathering.

it back into the bowl. Repeat the process until all of the butter cubes have been flattened. Then, using your fingers, gently crumble each of the butter disks into nickel-size chunks and drop back into the flour mixture until you have a very coarse meal.

Return the bowl to the stand mixer and fit the mixer with the paddle attachment. With the mixer on the lowest speed, drizzle in ¼ cup (55 grams) of the ice water and beat until just incorporated. Stop the mixer, remove the paddle, and finish mixing gently by hand. If the dough feels too dry, add up to ¼ cup (55 grams) ice water, 1 tablespoon at a time. The finished dough should feel moist, and if you squeeze a small handful, it should hold together securely.

Knead the dough gently by hand or with a spatula in the bowl until it forms a shaggy ball. Turn the dough out onto a lightly floured work surface, then roll into a ball, wrap in plastic wrap, and flatten into a disk about 1 inch thick. If making individual crostatas, divide into eight equal balls, wrap in plastic wrap, and flatten into disks, about ½ inch thick. You will still see butter streaks, but break up any large lumps. Refrigerate for 2 hours or up to 3 days before rolling out. (Or freeze for up to 2 weeks.)

To make your own sweet or savory crostata, add the filling of your choice and bake at 375°F until the crust is golden brown, generally 30 to 40 minutes. The exact bake time will vary depending on the filling.

FRANGIPANE

MAKES ABOUT 1¾ CUPS

1 cup (230 grams) almond paste
½ cup (113 grams) unsalted butter
1 large egg
⅛ teaspoon almond extract
2 tablespoons (25 grams) sugar
1 tablespoon all-purpose flour

Combine the almond paste and butter in the bowl of a stand mixer fitted with the paddle attachment. Beat on medium speed until the mixture is light and fluffy, about 5 minutes. Add the egg and almond extract and beat on low speed until incorporated, then add the sugar and flour and beat until smooth, about 1 minute.

Transfer to an airtight container and refrigerate for up to 2 weeks.

NOTE

Use any extra frangipane to spread between slices of French toast, or make a traditional French pastry, *bostock*, by spreading frangipane on top of brioche, sprinkling with sliced almonds, and then baking at 375°F for 20 minutes. Sprinkle with powdered sugar before serving.

RHUBARB-RASPBERRY CROSTATA

MAKES ONE 11-INCH CROSTATA OR EIGHT 3½-INCH CROSTATAS

Rhubarb and strawberries both have the same sort of lemony tartness—their flavors meld as one when baked together. Raspberries, on the other hand, have the sweetness to balance out the rhubarb, but with a brighter, more wine-like vinegar quality. Also, raspberries have more concentrated flavor than strawberries. Even when used thinly as a glaze, the raspberry flavor shines very brightly while allowing the rhubarb flavor to remain distinct.

---

1 recipe Crostata Dough (page 252), at room temperature

1 cup Frangipane (page 253)

10 stalks fresh rhubarb

4 tablespoons unsalted butter, at room temperature

¼ cup sugar

¼ cup raspberry jam, preferably seedless

2 teaspoons raspberry liqueur

Crème Fraîche Whipped Cream (page 266) for serving

SPECIAL EQUIPMENT

Scraper
Eight 3½-inch metal pastry rings (optional; see variation, page 256)

Line a rimmed baking sheet with parchment paper.

On a lightly floured work surface, roll out the dough into a very thin 14-inch round. Using a scraper, transfer the dough round to the prepared baking sheet, cover with plastic wrap, and refrigerate for 30 minutes.

Take the chilled crostata dough out of the refrigerator and spread with an even layer of the frangipane, leaving about 2 inches around the edges uncovered. Using a vegetable peeler, remove the stringy outer layer of the rhubarb and scrape the stalks to about the thickness of your frangipane layer. If the rhubarb still seems thick, cut lengthwise into ¼-inch-wide strips. Arrange the rhubarb side by side on top of the frangipane, trimming off any bits that overhang the uncovered dough.

Fold the uncovered edges of the dough over the rhubarb, crimping every few inches to form a pleated round crust that tucks in the fruit but leaves the center exposed.

Using a pastry brush, spread the butter in a generous layer over the crust edges, then sprinkle the sugar over the entire surface of the crostata and refrigerate until firm, about 20 minutes.

Preheat the oven to 375°F. Bake the crostata until the crust is golden brown and crisp, 40 to 45 minutes. Transfer to a wire rack and let cool for 10 minutes (see Note, page 256).

In a small saucepan, stir together the raspberry jam, raspberry liqueur, and 1 tablespoon water and cook over low heat until warm, stirring to dissolve. If your jam has seeds, strain the glaze through a chinois or extra-fine-mesh strainer into a small bowl, making sure you yield a full ¼ cup.

Brush a thick layer of the raspberry glaze over the exposed fruit on the crostata. Serve warm with the whipped cream.

continued

VARIATION

To make individual crostatas, divide the crostata dough into eight equal pieces. On a lightly floured work surface, roll out each piece of dough into a very thin 5-inch round, then transfer to parchment paper–lined rimmed baking sheets and refrigerate for 10 minutes. Spread a heaping 1 tablespoon of frangipane across the middle of each round, leaving about 1½ inches of the edges uncovered. Fill, fold in the crust, brush with butter, and sprinkle with sugar as directed for the large crostata. Refrigerate until firm, about 20 minutes. Preheat the oven to 400°F. Butter the insides of eight 3½-inch pastry rings and place a ring around each chilled crostata. Bake until the crusts are completely golden, about 25 minutes. Check to make sure they're golden underneath as well by lifting one with an offset spatula. Remove from the oven and use the spatula to carefully remove the rings. Let cool for 10 minutes before glazing.

NOTE

The unglazed crostata can be baked up to 6 hours before serving. Reheat in a 275°F oven for 10 minutes until warm and glaze just before serving.

APPLE AND CURRANT CROSTATA WITH WARM CRÈME ANGLAISE

MAKES ONE 11-INCH CROSTATA OR EIGHT 3½-INCH CROSTATAS

When I was nineteen, I moved to Austria for a year to study the French horn at the Vienna Academy of Music. Much like becoming a pastry chef, it was a spontaneous decision. Basically, I just showed up on the doorstep of the school like an orphan.

During my time in Austria, I eventually made a trip to Salzburg, the birthplace of Mozart. One day when lunchtime rolled around, I was starving, so I stopped at a café, and then quickly realized I didn't have enough money for anything except the apple strudel. It was served warm in a pool of vanilla crème anglaise, and maybe it was because I was hungry and poor or maybe it was because it was the middle of winter and I was thousands of miles from home, but the first bite of that apple strudel was one of the most sublime moments of my life. No version will likely ever top it, but I think this crostata—with its delicate crust, thinly sliced apples, and warm crème anglaise—captures a lot of what made that Salzburg lunch strudel so memorable.

---

1 recipe Crostata Dough (page 252), at room temperature

¼ cup brandy

¼ cup dried currants

1 recipe Frangipane (page 253)

5 large Pink Lady or any peak-season apple, cored and thinly sliced

4 tablespoons unsalted butter, at room temperature

¼ cup sugar

1 recipe Crème Anglaise (page 261) for serving

SPECIAL EQUIPMENT

Scraper
Eight 3½-inch metal pastry rings (optional; see Variation)

VARIATION

To make individual crostatas, see directions on page 256.

Line a rimmed baking sheet with parchment paper.

On a lightly floured work surface, roll out the dough into a very thin 14-inch round. Using a scraper, transfer the dough round to the prepared baking sheet, cover with plastic wrap, and refrigerate for 30 minutes.

Meanwhile, in a small saucepan over medium heat, combine the brandy and currants and bring to a boil. Remove from the heat and set aside to cool and infuse for at least 1 hour or until ready to use; then strain the currants, reserving the brandy, and set aside.

Take the chilled crostata dough out of the refrigerator and spread with an even layer of the frangipane, leaving about 2 inches around the edges uncovered. Starting from the outside, arrange the apple slices in a spiral pattern on top of the frangipane.

Fold the uncovered edges of the dough over the apples, crimping every few inches to form a pleated round crust that tucks in the fruit but leaves the center exposed. Using a pastry brush, spread the butter in a generous layer over the crust edges, then sprinkle the sugar over the entire surface of the crostata and refrigerate until firm, about 20 minutes.

continued

Preheat the oven to 375°F. Bake the crostata until pale golden and starting to set, 25 to 30 minutes. Quickly remove the crostata from the oven, scatter with the currants, and drizzle 4 teaspoons of the reserved currant-soaking brandy over the top. (If making individual crostatas, drizzle ½ teaspoon on each.) Place back in the oven immediately and bake until the crust is golden brown and crisp, 10 to 15 minutes longer. Transfer to a wire rack and let cool for 10 minutes or up to 6 hours (see Note page 256).

Prepare a double boiler or make one by filling a saucepan with 2 inches of water and bringing it to a simmer over low heat. Nestle a heatproof bowl in the saucepan over the boiling water, making sure the bottom of the bowl isn't touching the water. Add the crème anglaise to the top pan of the double boiler or bowl and heat until warm, stirring gently and scraping the bottom of the pan or bowl with a rubber spatula.

To serve, cut the crostata into eight slices. Spoon about 3 tablespoons of the warm crème anglaise onto each dessert plate and nestle a warm slice (or individual crostada) on top. Or pass the warm crème anglaise at the table for guests to drizzle onto their plates.

MAKES ABOUT 2 CUPS

⅓ cup sugar

1½ cups heavy cream

½ cup whole milk

½ vanilla bean, seeds scraped, pod reserved

5 whole coffee beans

Pinch of kosher salt

¼ teaspoon freshly grated Meyer lemon zest

5 large egg yolks

1½ teaspoons apple brandy

CRÈME ANGLAISE

Measure out 2 tablespoons of the sugar and set aside. In a saucepan over medium heat, combine the remaining sugar, cream, milk, vanilla seeds and pod, coffee beans, salt, and lemon zest and bring to a simmer.

Meanwhile, in a large, heatproof bowl, whisk together the egg yolks and 2 tablespoons sugar. Slowly pour the warm cream mixture into the yolks while whisking constantly until fully incorporated.

Pour the egg-cream mixture back into the saucepan and cook over very low heat, stirring constantly with a spatula, until the custard is very thick and coats the back of a spoon (also called *nappé*), about 10 minutes. Strain through a chinois or extra-fine-mesh strainer into a bowl and discard the solids. Stir in the apple brandy until well blended. Cover with plastic wrap, pressing it against the surface of the custard so it doesn't form a skin. Use immediately, or refrigerate for up to 3 days.

NOTE

Crème anglaise is a classic egg yolk–based custard that forms the base of many things, including ice cream. Here we use it to create a warm, creamy sauce for apple crostata.

RICOTTA-PEAR TART

MAKES ONE 11-INCH TART

Pears reach their peak right at the start of autumn. If you close your eyes and picture fall, you probably imagine pumpkins and apples and such things. But personally, I feel like pears have always been the most emblematic fruit of the season. Didn't anyone else get the Harry & David catalogs in the mail, where the pears were wrapped in gold like crown jewels?

1⅓ cups (340 grams) whole-milk ricotta cheese

½ cup (115 grams) mascarpone

1 large egg

½ cup (100 grams) sugar, plus 2 tablespoons (25 grams)

⅛ teaspoon kosher salt

⅛ teaspoon freshly grated nutmeg

1 teaspoon freshly grated lemon zest

4 tablespoons Frangipane (page 253), at room temperature

1 Pâte Sucrée Tart Shell (page 264), blind-baked

4 large very ripe pears, preferably Taylor or Warren (about 1¾ pounds total weight)

Juice of ½ lemon

Preheat the oven to 375°F.

In a large bowl, combine the ricotta, mascarpone, egg, ½ cup (100 grams) sugar, salt, nutmeg, and lemon zest and whisk until smooth. Spread the frangipane in an even layer across the bottom of the baked tart shell, followed by a layer of the ricotta cream thick enough to reach halfway up the sides of the shell. (Don't feel the need to overfill. You might have a little left over, depending on the size of your tart shell and the height of the crust.)

Peel and core the pears and cut them into ¼-inch-thick wedges. Transfer to a large bowl. Sprinkle with the remaining 2 tablespoons sugar and add the lemon juice. Gently toss to coat thoroughly. Working from the outside in, arrange the pear slices in the tart, overlapping them on the ricotta in a spiral pattern until fully covered.

Gently cover the very edges of the crust with aluminum foil to prevent them from burning and bake until the ricotta has puffed and is fully cooked in the center (test by lifting one of the pears in the middle; the ricotta should look fully set and hold its shape) and the pears are fork-tender and browned along the edges, about 1 hour. Transfer to a wire rack and let cool slightly, then remove the pan sides, slice and serve.

This tart is best served the same day. At the restaurant, we serve it warm with our black pepper ice cream and hand-whipped cream. It's just as delicious served with a dollop of our Crème Fraîche Whipped Cream (page 266).

VARIATION

You can substitute very ripe Fuyu persimmons for the pears in this tart. Just marinate the slices in lemon juice and omit the nutmeg from the ricotta cream. We serve the persimmon version at the restaurant with our buttermilk ice cream and a spoonful of Fermented Blackberry Jam (page 28).

continued

MAKES ONE 11-INCH TART SHELL

PÂTE SUCRÉE TART SHELL

1¼ cups (150 grams) all-purpose flour

¼ cup (50 grams) sugar

⅛ teaspoon kosher salt

1 large egg yolk

2 tablespoons (30 grams) heavy cream

½ cup (113 grams) unsalted butter, cubed and frozen

SPECIAL EQUIPMENT

Scraper
11-inch removable-bottom tart pan

In a food processor, combine the flour, sugar, and salt and pulse to mix. In a small bowl, stir together the egg yolk and cream. Set aside.

With the food processor running, add the butter cubes a small handful at a time to the flour mixture until the butter is completely and evenly incorporated into a sandy mix. Stop the machine and scrape down the sides of the bowl with a spatula as needed, making sure there is no butter stuck in the corners. With the machine running again, drizzle in the egg-cream mixture and process again just until a dough ball forms.

Transfer the dough onto a nonstick silicone mat or a cold, clean countertop. Using what's called the *fraisage* method, grab a small handful of dough, about ¼ cup, and smear it across the mat with the heel of your hand to make sure all of the ingredients are thoroughly incorporated. Repeat with the remaining dough until the whole batch has been smeared. Using a scraper, gather all of the smeared dough into a ball, press into a disk, wrap in plastic wrap, and refrigerate for at least 2 hours or up to 2 days.

To blind-bake the shell: On a large nonstick silicone mat or wooden cutting board (something that will fit in your refrigerator), roll out the dough into a round about 12 inches in diameter and ⅛ inch thick. Cover with plastic wrap and refrigerate for 30 minutes.

Remove the dough from the refrigerator and bring to cool room temperature; it should be pliable but still cool to the touch. Butter an 11-inch, removable-bottom tart pan and place it on top of a rimmed baking sheet. Carefully transfer the rolled dough to the pan and gently press it into the corners, trimming off any overhang. (Save the dough scraps to fix any tears and cracks after baking.) Wrap the tart shell in plastic wrap and freeze for at least 30 minutes or up to 3 days. We've found that freezing helps the tart to hold its shape better during baking.

Preheat the oven to 325°F.

Remove the tart shell from the freezer, transfer to a baking sheet, and place in the oven. Lower the oven temperature to 300°F. Bake until light golden brown, 25 and 30 minutes. Transfer to a wire rack and let cool for 5 minutes. Inspect the crust for cracks, paying special attention to the corners, and fix any you find by gently filling with a bit of the reserved dough. Let the shell cool completely.

CHESTNUT ZEPPOLE

MAKES ABOUT 36 ZEPPOLE

Zeppole, small Italian donuts resembling American donut holes, are delicious, and our version is made with chestnut flour.

The measurements and ingredients are precise, so you shouldn't attempt to make these without the proper flours or without a scale. The ingredients are very volatile, and if your measurements are over or under in any way, the dough will be too loose or too tough to work with. But if made correctly, chestnut flour gives the zeppole a very special, nutty warmth all to its own.

⅓ cup (78 grams) filtered water

1 large egg, cold

½ teaspoon vanilla extract

½ cup (115 grams) whole milk

1 tablespoon (12 grams) sugar, plus ⅓ cup (70 grams)

2 teaspoons active dry yeast

2 cups (250 grams) high-protein (at least 13 percent) bread flour

¾ cup plus 3 tablespoons (85 grams) chestnut flour

1 teaspoon kosher salt

⅛ teaspoon ground mace

4 tablespoons (55 grams) unsalted butter, melted

Grapeseed or canola oil for greasing, plus more for frying

Spiced Sugar (page 266) for serving

Crème Fraiche Whipped Cream (page 266) for serving

SPECIAL EQUIPMENT

Deep-frying thermometer

In a small bowl, whisk together the water, egg, and vanilla and refrigerate until chilled, about 15 minutes.

In a small saucepan over low heat, warm the milk. Then, remove from the heat, add the 1 tablespoon sugar, and stir to dissolve. When the milk mixture has cooled to 110°F (it should feel like a warm bath to the touch), add the yeast. Set the bowl aside in the warmest part of your kitchen to proof until the mixture becomes frothy and puffed, about 15 minutes. (Another way to test that your yeast is good is to sniff and make sure the mixture smells sweet.)

In the bowl of a stand mixer fitted with the paddle attachment, beat together both flours, the salt, ⅓ cup (70 grams) sugar, and mace. Add the yeast mixture and chilled egg mixture and begin beating on low speed to combine. Then, with the mixer still running, drizzle in the melted butter and mix until incorporated. Turn off the mixer and scrape the paddle clean with a rubber spatula.

Replace the paddle with the dough hook and knead the mixture on medium speed for about 15 minutes, until it starts to form a very loose ball. Once the loose ball is formed, turn the speed to medium-low and continue to knead for about 10 minutes, until the dough starts to form a soft ball and pulls away from the sides of the bowl. Test for doneness with the "windowpane test": see if you can spread a small piece of dough thin enough between your fingers to see light through it without it tearing.

Grease a large bowl with grapeseed oil, add the dough ball, and turn it seam-side down. Cover with plastic wrap and refrigerate for 8 hours.

continued

Lightly oil a baking sheet and a work surface. Using a rolling pin, roll out the dough into a rectangle about ¼ inch thick and transfer to the prepared baking sheet. Refrigerate the dough for 30 minutes, then cut into small rounds using a 1¼-inch cookie cutter. (Alternatively, use a knife and cut the dough into 1¼-inch squares.) Cover with plastic wrap. (At this point you can refrigerate for up to 8 hours.) Let the dough proof at room temperature for 30 minutes, until slightly risen and light and airy feeling when lifted. Meanwhile, line a plate with paper towels.

Pour grapeseed oil into a saucepan to a depth of 1½ inches and warm over high heat to 350°F on a deep-frying thermometer. Using a slotted spoon, drop the dough rounds into the hot oil in batches of about six at a time; be sure not to crowd the pan. Fry until the undersides are browned, about 1 minute, then flip with the slotted spoon and fry until nicely golden brown on all sides, about 1 minute more. Using the slotted spoon, transfer to the prepared plate to drain. While they're still hot and slightly oily, toss the zeppole in spiced sugar to coat evenly. Serve warm with the whipped cream for dipping.

SPICED SUGAR

MAKES ABOUT ¾ CUP

½ cup granulated sugar
¼ cup firmly packed light brown sugar
¾ teaspoon ground allspice
½ teaspoon ground cinnamon
Pinch of kosher salt

In a bowl, whisk together all of the ingredients. Store in an airtight container at room temperature for up to 1 week.

CRÈME FRAÎCHE WHIPPED CREAM

MAKES ABOUT 2 CUPS

1 cup very cold heavy cream
2 tablespoons crème fraîche
1 tablespoon sugar

In a bowl, combine all of the ingredients. Beat until soft peaks form. Use immediately, or cover with plastic wrap and store in the refrigerator for up to 4 hours. If storing, before using, lightly whisk the mixture to bring back together any liquid and solids that may have separated.

BUTTERSCOTCH-COCONUT TART

MAKES ONE 11-INCH TART

My favorite Girl Scout cookie is a Samoa. Most people seem to love Thin Mints, but to me, Samoas are the best. So, I thought, what if I made a grown-up dessert. The top layer bakes into a chewy, crackly glaze, and just beneath that lies the gooey butterscotch filling—all of it held together by a crumbly, buttery cookie crust. "But doesn't a true Samoa have chocolate on it?" you might say. Well, yes—but it's that horrible waxy chocolate that doesn't taste like anything. On the other hand, if you use high-quality chocolate, it completely overpowers the coconut, so I decided to omit it altogether. Even with the chocolate missing, it still has the nostalgia of that perfect girlhood cookie.

1⅔ cups (115 grams) finely shredded unsweetened coconut

⅓ cup plus 1 tablespoon (85 grams) heavy cream

1 tablespoon (15 grams) dark rum

½ teaspoon vanilla extract

6 tablespoons (85 grams) cold unsalted butter

⅔ cup (135 grams) very tightly packed light brown sugar

⅓ cup (70 grams) granulated sugar

Rounded ¾ teaspoon kosher salt

3 large egg yolks (50 grams)

1 Pâte Sucrée Tart Shell (page 264), blind-baked

Fresh coconut sorbet and blackberries for serving (optional)

NOTE

The slow melting gives the sugar time to absorb and emulsify with the butter. If the butter melts too quickly, the butter and sugar will remain separate and will become an oily mess that's almost impossible to bring back together.

Preheat the oven temperature to 325°F.

Spread the shredded coconut in an even layer on a baking sheet. Bake, stirring once halfway through, until an even golden brown, about 8 minutes. Remove from the oven and let cool. Leave the oven on.

In a small bowl, stir together the cream, rum, and vanilla and set aside.

In a small saucepan over low heat, combine the butter, both sugars, and salt and whisk gently, making sure the butter incorporates evenly with the sugars as it slowly melts. Once all of the butter has been incorporated, increase the heat to medium-high and begin whisking constantly until the caramel mixture is pale, thick, and bubbly, 2 to 3 minutes. Remove from the heat, add the cream mixture, and whisk thoroughly for about 20 seconds. If the caramel seems grainy, return the pan to low heat for another 30 seconds, stirring continuously, to dissolve the remaining sugars. Remove from the heat and let the mixture cool for 2 to 3 minutes.

Add the egg yolks to the caramel and whisk until smooth, then gently fold in the toasted coconut with a spatula.

Spread the filling in the tart shell and bake until mostly set but the center has a slight jiggle to it, 20 to 25 minutes, rotating halfway through the cooking time. Transfer the tart to a wire rack and let cool completely. Look for any caramel bits that have stuck to the pan and use a small paring knife to separate. Then carefully remove the sides of the pan, cut into slices, and serve with sorbet and blackberries, if desired.

MAPLE-RICOTTA FRITTERS

MAKES ABOUT 30 FRITTERS

Growing up, my hermit parents barely took us anywhere. We never even went to Disneyland, even though we lived an hour away. But once a year, one of them would begrudgingly take us to the local fair, and these fritters were inspired by the funnel cakes I used to see, smell, and very occasionally get to taste at the Conejo Valley Days.

Maple sugar is becoming increasingly more common and can be found at grocery stores like Whole Foods, Sprouts, Trader Joe's, and other specialty food stores or online.

⅓ cup (42 grams) fine-ground cornmeal

½ cup (57 grams) very fine cake flour

2 teaspoons baking powder

½ teaspoon kosher salt

¾ cup plus 3 tablespoons (227 grams) whole-milk ricotta cheese

½ cup plus 1½ tablespoons (80 grams) maple sugar

2 tablespoons freshly grated lemon zest (from about 2 large lemons)

1 teaspoon vanilla extract

1 large egg, at room temperature

Grapeseed oil for frying

Powdered sugar for dusting

Maple Butter for serving (recipe follows)

SPECIAL EQUIPMENT

Deep-frying thermometer

In a small bowl, whisk together the cornmeal, cake flour, baking powder, and salt. Set aside.

In a large bowl, beat together the ricotta, maple sugar, lemon zest, and vanilla. Add the egg to the ricotta mixture and whisk until thoroughly combined. Gently fold the dry ingredients into the wet ingredients until just combined. Do not overmix. (If not frying right away, keep your wet and dry ingredients separate until just before cooking.)

Pour grapeseed oil into a large heavy saucepan to a depth of 2 inches and warm over high heat to 375°F on a deep-frying thermometer. Working in batches to avoid crowding the pan, carefully drop small scoops (about 2 teaspoons each) of batter into the hot oil. When the fritters are golden brown on one side—about 1½ minutes—using a slotted spoon, flip and continue cooking until golden brown on the other side, about 1 minute longer. Using the spoon or a skimmer, transfer to paper towels to drain. Repeat with the remaining batter.

Dust the fritters with powdered sugar and serve warm with the maple butter alongside for dipping.

MAPLE BUTTER

MAKES ABOUT 1 CUP

6 tablespoons unsalted butter, at room temperature

½ cup maple syrup

½ teaspoon kosher salt

Combine all of the ingredients in the bowl of a stand mixer fitted with the whisk attachment. Whisk on medium-high speed until well-blended and airy, 10 to 15 minutes. Serve at room temperature, or cover and refrigerate for up to 2 weeks. Bring to room temperature and rewhip briefly before serving.

APPLE CIDER DONUTS

MAKES ABOUT 24 DONUTS
AND 24 DONUT HOLES

Just so everyone knows, I've never lived on the East Coast. Every year I buy sweaters I will barely wear while picturing changing leaves, crisp fresh air, and days full of apple picking. Of course, I live in L.A., so that's not happening. Ever. But I still find myself feeling nostalgic for the idea of an East Coast fall that I've never actually experienced. That's where this recipe came from—wistful nostalgia. The batter is made more like a traditional cake batter, rather than a donut dough. Creaming of the butter and folding in egg whites creates a more aerated finish, while the whole wheat gives the outside a crispy, short texture. Last, the grated apple, when cooked, releases liquid into the cake donut and gives it a boost of moisture.

---

4 cups (960 grams) unfiltered apple cider

¼ cup (57 grams) sour apple liqueur

6 strips orange zest

14 whole cloves

3⅔ cups (450 grams) all-purpose flour

1 cup (113 grams) very fine cake flour

2 cups (227 grams) Sonora flour, einkorn flour, or whole-wheat pastry flour

4 teaspoons (18 grams) baking powder

2 teaspoons (10 grams) baking soda

2 teaspoons ground cinnamon

½ teaspoon mace

2¾ teaspoons kosher salt

½ cup (115 grams) buttermilk

1 teaspoon vanilla extract

¾ cup (170 grams) solid, cold Black Butter (page 48)

1 cup plus 5 tablespoons (260 grams) granulated sugar

4 large eggs, separated

2¾ cups (320 grams) peeled and grated tart apple such as Pink Lady or Granny Smith (5 to 6 apples)

SUGAR COATING

1 cup (200 grams) granulated sugar

½ cup (100 grams) packed light brown sugar

⅛ teaspoon kosher salt

Neutral oil such as grapeseed for frying

Crème Fraîche Whipped Cream (page 266) for dipping

SPECIAL EQUIPMENT

Deep-frying thermometer

In a saucepan over high heat, combine the cider, apple liqueur, orange zest, and cloves and bring to a boil. Cook until reduced by about three-fourths, about 10 minutes. Remove from the heat and set aside.

In a large bowl, whisk together all three flours, the baking powder, baking soda, cinnamon, mace, and salt. Set aside.

In a small bowl, stir together the buttermilk and vanilla and set aside.

In the bowl of a stand mixer fitted with the paddle attachment, cream the black butter with the sugar, beating on medium speed until light and fluffy, about 5 minutes. Turn the speed to low and add the egg yolks one by one, beating after each addition until incorporated. Scrape down the sides of the bowl with a rubber spatula, then add

continued

the apple cider reduction and beat on medium speed until thoroughly incorporated. Add the buttermilk mixture and beat until thoroughly mixed in. Add the grated apples and mix on low speed until incorporated. Turn off the mixer, dump in the flour mixture, and then continue to mix on very low speed until almost fully incorporated. Remove the bowl from the stand mixer and scrape the bottom of the bowl with a spatula to make sure all of the dry ingredients are mixed with the wet, then set aside.

In a large metal bowl, whisk the egg whites until they hold stiff peaks. Gently fold the beaten egg whites into the batter with a rubber spatula until just combined.

Line a baking sheet with a flour-dusted silicone baking mat. Transfer the dough to the silicone mat, sprinkle it with flour, then cover the dough with a large sheet of plastic wrap and begin to gently press it into a flat, even layer. Remove the plastic wrap, dust your hands with flour, and finish pressing the dough until it's about ¼ inch thick.

Cover the baking sheet with plastic wrap and freeze for 30 minutes or refrigerate for 1 hour, until the dough is firm enough to cut.

Meanwhile, line another baking sheet with parchment paper and lightly dust with flour. When the dough is firm, flip it onto the parchment-lined sheet. (This will keep the dough from sticking to your pan like glue, so you will be able to remove the circles.) Using a round cutter 2 to 2½ inches in diameter, cut out circles of the dough; then use a 1-inch round cutter to cut holes out of the center of each round, reserving the holes. Try to keep everything cold while working, and dust everything with all-purpose flour as you work to keep it from sticking. If the dough begins to stick too much, return it to the refrigerator until it firms up. (At this point, you can cover the dough and refrigerate for up to 6 hours.)

To make the sugar coating, when you're ready to fry: Whisk together all of the ingredients in a shallow bowl, making sure to break up any lumps, and set aside.

Pour oil in a heavy-bottomed pot or Dutch oven to a depth of 3 inches and warm over high heat to 350°F on a deep-frying thermometer. Using a slotted spoon, carefully add the donuts and holes to the oil, a few at a time. When the bottoms are deep golden brown, after about 1 minute, use the slotted spoon to flip; cook until they are a nice golden brown all over, 45 seconds to 1 minute longer. Using the slotted spoon, transfer to paper towels to drain, then immediately coat lightly in the sugar mixture and transfer to a baking sheet. Repeat until you've finished frying the remaining donuts and holes.

Serve warm with the whipped cream for dipping.

CHOCOLATE BUDINO TART

MAKES EIGHT 4-INCH TARTS

A lot of the early desserts at Bestia wound up on the menu for one of two reasons: I either already knew how to make them, or they seemed somewhat Italian. My chocolate budino tart worked on both fronts. I don't even really like chocolate, but among my tiny arsenal of recipes when we opened were a brown sugar–chocolate pot de crème, a crème-fraîche caramel, and a chocolate shortbread. So I tweaked the shortbread recipe to make it a compatible vehicle for the caramel and pot de crème, added a sprinkle of sea salt, and then finished it with a very Italian-style drizzle of olive oil.

ASSEMBLY

Brown Sugar–Chocolate Budino (recipe follows)

Chocolate Shortbread Crust (page 278)

Crème Fraîche Caramel (page 277)

Maldon or other flaky sea salt

8 teaspoons clean, light, floral olive oil

First make the **Brown Sugar–Chocolate Budino** and refrigerate for 8 hours. While the budino is refrigerated, make the **Chocolate Shortbread Crust** and set it aside to cool completely. Finally, make the **Crème Fraîche Caramel** and let cool to room temperature.

Gently smooth about 1½ teaspoons of the caramel evenly over the bottom of each tart shell. Fill each with about ⅓ cup of the budino. Crush a pinch Maldon salt over the top and drizzle with 1 teaspoon olive oil before serving.

BROWN SUGAR–CHOCOLATE BUDINO

2⅔ cups (635 grams) heavy cream

½ vanilla bean, seeds scraped, pod reserved

Pinch of kosher salt

9 ounces (255 grams) bittersweet chocolate (70 percent cacao)

2 ounces (57 grams) milk chocolate (36 percent cacao)

⅔ cup (151 grams) whole milk

½ cup plus 1 teaspoon (107 grams) packed light muscovado sugar or light brown sugar

8 large egg yolks

Preheat the oven to 350°F.

In a small saucepan over low heat, combine the heavy cream, vanilla seeds and pod, and salt and bring to a low simmer. Remove from the heat and let cool and infuse for 10 minutes. Set aside.

Prepare a double boiler or make one by filling a saucepan with 2 inches of water and bringing to a simmer over low heat. Nestle a heatproof bowl in the saucepan over the boiling water, making sure the bottom of the bowl isn't touching the water. Add the bittersweet and milk chocolates to the top pan of the double boiler or the bowl and let melt, stirring occasionally with a spatula, until completely smooth, about 10 minutes. Remove from the heat

continued

and set aside until cool enough to handle but still warm. Slowly begin pouring in small amounts of the warm vanilla-cream mixture, gently folding with a spatula, until all of the cream has been incorporated into the chocolate. Set aside.

In a small saucepan, heat the milk to a simmer. In a bowl, whisk together the brown sugar and the egg yolks. Slowly pour the warm milk into the egg mixture to temper the yolks, whisking until the sugar is mostly dissolved, then slowly pour it into the chocolate while gently stirring with a spatula until the mixture is smooth and all of the ingredients are evenly incorporated.

Using a chinois or extra-fine-mesh strainer, strain the budino into a standard 9-by-5-inch loaf pan and cover it with ovenproof plastic wrap twice. Create a bain marie by placing the loaf pan into a 9-by-13-inch baking pan, then pour warm water into the bottom pan until it reaches three-fourths of the way up the sides of the budino. Cover the whole bain marie with aluminum foil to create an airtight seal and bake for 20 to 25 minutes, until the budino is set around the edges but still jiggly in the center.

Using a whisk, stir the budino a few times, gently scraping down the sides of the pan, until the texture is smooth and even, then pour it into a bowl. Gently stir it once more with the whisk, then press a sheet of plastic wrap directly to the surface to prevent it from forming a skin. Refrigerate for at least 8 hours or up to overnight.

CRÈME FRAÎCHE CARAMEL

1 cup (200 grams) sugar

2 tablespoons (40 grams) light corn syrup

1 teaspoon plus heaping ⅛ teaspoon (10 grams) kosher salt

¼ cup (60 grams) heavy cream

4 tablespoons (55 grams) unsalted butter, cubed

3 tablespoons (40 grams) crème fraîche

In a saucepan over medium heat, combine the sugar, corn syrup, salt, and ¼ cup (55 grams) water and bring to a simmer. Using a pastry brush dipped in water, gently brush down the inner sides of the pan to make sure no sugar crystals form. Heat until the bubbles begin to slow and the mixture starts to caramelize. If needed, you can occasionally tilt the pan from side to side to make sure no one part browns quicker than any other. Cook until the mixture is fully caramelized and amber in color, 10 to 15 minutes.

Remove the pan from the heat and immediately drizzle in the cream. Whisk carefully away from your face (the steam will be hot) to combine. Add the cubed butter and whisk until the butter is completely melted, about 1 minute, then add the crème fraîche and whisk until the mixture is smooth and velvety. Allow the caramel to cool to room temperature, then cover and refrigerate until ready to use, up to 5 days.

continued

CHOCOLATE SHORTBREAD CRUST

½ cup (113 grams) unsalted butter, at room temperature

¼ cup plus 1 teaspoon (55 grams) sugar

¼ teaspoon kosher salt

½ teaspoon vanilla extract

⅓ cup (30 grams) cocoa powder

1¼ cups (150 grams) all-purpose flour

In the bowl of a stand mixer fitted with the paddle attachment, whip the butter on low speed until glossy, about 2 minutes. Add the sugar and whip until fluffy, about 5 minutes. Add the salt and vanilla and mix until combined. Turn off the mixer and add the cocoa powder, then mix on low speed until incorporated, scraping the bowl periodically with a rubber spatula to make sure all of the butter is incorporated.

Once evenly mixed, turn off the mixer and add the flour all at once. Mix on low speed until almost incorporated but bits of flour are still visible. Then, take the bowl off the mixer and finish mixing with a spatula or spoon by hand, scraping the sides and gently folding in the remaining flour.

Form the dough into a loose ball and wrap in plastic wrap. Press the dough into a disk and refrigerate for at least 2 hours or freeze for up to 1 week. Butter eight 4-inch removeable-bottom tart pans and put them in the freezer for 2 hours (see Note).

When ready to roll out, bring the dough to room temperature and, on a lightly floured surface, roll out 1⁄16 inch thick. Cut the dough into eight circles each 3½ or 4 inches in diameter and press into the chilled tart pans, trimming off any overhang. Use scraps of dough to fill cracks in the tart shells as needed. Prick the bottoms with a fork two or three times to help prevent bubbling. Cover with plastic wrap and freeze or refrigerate until cold, at least 30 minutes or up to 3 days.

When ready to bake, preheat the oven to 325°F. Bake until the crusts have lost their shine, about 20 minutes. Let cool completely, then remove from the pans and transfer to a parchment paper–lined baking sheet and recrisp at 325°F for about 10 minutes more. This should give the crusts a light, short texture and makes them a great counterpoint to the heavy filling.

NOTE

For this delicate, decadent dough, we heavily butter the tart pans and put them in the freezer on a baking sheet until we are ready to press in the dough rounds. It helps the dough remain firm and stay in place while pressing. (You can make the tarts smaller if you like, but don't make them larger than 4 inches; the filling will be too heavy.)

VARIATION

If you don't have individual tart pans handy, you can make the elements of this recipe into a delicious parfait: Roll out the chocolate shortbread dough into pieces about ⅛ inch thick and 4 inches square. Transfer to a baking sheet and bake according to the recipe instructions. Then simply break the crusts into bite-size pieces and arrange them in the bottom individual glass parfait cups followed by a layer of the caramel, then the chocolate budino, and finally a drizzle with olive oil. Top with a pinch of flaky sea salt. It's a rustic look, but the parfaits are still pretty, and will taste just as good.

MASCARPONE RICE PUDDING WITH PERSIMMON CARAMEL, HACHIYA PERSIMMONS, AND ORANGE BLOSSOM PISTACHIOS

SERVES 8

This is the dessert I'm the most proud of. It's a dessert that is unique and complex, yet manages to evoke familiarity, and the whole creation came from happenstance.

Somewhere along the way, I began layering beautiful peak-of-ripeness Hachiya persimmons over the pudding, followed by a caramel made from the persimmons too ripe to cut. The pistachios are a nod to the nuts you would find in a traditional rice pudding, but with the floral notes of orange blossom rather than cardamom or cinnamon.

The key to this rice pudding is to cook the rice enough to remove the chalkiness, but to leave just a touch of chewy texture. This allows the rice to keep its identity amidst all of that creaminess.

---

8 cups whole milk, plus more if needed

½ cup plus 2 tablespoons plus 1 teaspoon (130 grams) sugar

1 vanilla bean, seeds scraped, pod reserved

2 fresh bay leaves or 2 small dried

3 large strips orange zest

Pinch of saffron threads

½ teaspoon kosher salt

Slightly rounded 1 cup (200 grams) Carnaroli rice

1¼ cups (283 grams) mascarpone

½ cup plus 2 tablespoons (142 grams) crème fraîche

4 large, very ripe Hachiya persimmons, sliced

Persimmon Caramel for serving (recipe follows)

Orange Blossom Pistachios for serving (recipe follows)

In a large, heavy saucepan over high heat, combine the milk, sugar, vanilla seeds and pod, bay leaves, orange zest, saffron, and salt and bring to a boil, whisking occasionally. Once boiling, stir in the rice. Cook, uncovered, over high heat, stirring constantly with a wooden spoon or spatula, until the grains are fully cooked and the mixture is the consistency of a loose oatmeal, about 30 minutes. If the liquid gets too thick before the rice is finished, add more milk, a little at a time and up to ¼ cup, and continue to cook. You want to cook the rice just until it becomes completely tender and soft all the way through. It will harden up a bit and have a chew once it cools down.

Have ready a large bowl full of ice and water. Transfer the rice mixture to a large glass or metal baking dish and set it in the ice bath. Stir for about 2 minutes to release the steam and stop the cooking process. With tongs, pick out and discard the orange zest, bay leaf, and vanilla pod. When the rice is completely cool, cover with a sheet of plastic wrap pressed to the surface and refrigerate for at least 2 hours or until cold.

Once chilled, test the texture. It should be very thick, but you should be able to stir it easily. If it's too thick, slowly mix in a small drizzle of milk. The texture should be such that if you spooned the rice onto a plate it would hold in a soft pile, not spread.

continued

Meanwhile, in the bowl of a stand mixer fitted with the whisk attachment or in a bowl with a hand mixer, combine the mascarpone and crème fraîche on medium speed until light and fluffy, 5 to 7 minutes.

Using a rubber spatula, spread the mascarpone mixture over the cooled rice, then gently fold it into the rice until just incorporated. It's okay if a few streaks remain. Divide among serving bowls and top with caramel and pistachios before serving.

MAKES ABOUT 1 CUP

PERSIMMON CARAMEL

4 very ripe Hachiya persimmons, stems removed

½ cup sugar

¼ teaspoon vanilla extract

2 teaspoons kirsch

1 tablespoon freshly squeezed lemon juice

Place the persimmons in a food processor or a blender and purée until smooth. Then, using your hand or a scraper, push the mixture through a tamis or extra-fine-mesh strainer into a large bowl.

In a small saucepan, combine the sugar and just enough water to cover (about 2 tablespoons). Add the vanilla and place over medium-high heat. Using a pastry brush dipped in water, gently brush down the inner sides of the pan to make sure no sugar crystals form. Cook undisturbed about 10 minutes, gently tilting the pan from side to side if any hot spots emerge, until the mixture turns a deep golden amber color.

Remove from the heat and whisk in 1 cup of the persimmon purée. The caramel will naturally stiffen. Return the pan to very low heat and whisk continuously until all of the sugar is dissolved and the mixture is smooth. Remove from the heat and stir in the kirsch and lemon juice. Let cool to room temperature. Use immediately, or refrigerate in an airtight container for up to 2 weeks.

MAKES ENOUGH FOR 8 SERVINGS

ORANGE BLOSSOM PISTACHIOS

¼ cup raw pistachio oil

¼ teaspoon food-grade orange blossom oil (see Note)

¼ cup raw whole pistachios

In a bowl, whisk together the two oils, then stir in the pistachios. When ready to serve, use 8 or 9 pistachios and a few drops of oil per plate.

NOTE

Do not substitute orange blossom water for the orange blossom oil. The orange water will not emulsify with the pistachio oil and will make the nuts soggy.

CRÈME FRAîCHE PANNA COTTA WITH WILDFLOWER HONEY SYRUP

SERVES 8

My panna cotta has just enough gelatin to barely hold it together on the spoon, the goal being for it *not* to be recognizable as a gelatin dessert. I love how the crème fraîche adds a refreshing dairy tanginess, and I cut the cream with some whole milk, which makes it feel incredibly light on the palate. I never get tired of eating it.

⅓ cup plus 2 teaspoons (75 grams) sugar

2 cups (475 grams) heavy cream

1 cup (235 grams) whole milk

Generous pinch of kosher salt

⅛ teaspoon freshly grated lemon zest

½ vanilla bean, seeds scraped, pod reserved

1½ teaspoons powdered gelatin

1 cup (225 grams) crème fraîche

Fresh fruit such as blueberries, sliced strawberries, or sliced figs for serving

8 teaspoons Wildflower Honey Syrup (recipe follows)

In a saucepan, combine the sugar, cream, ¾ cup (175 grams) of the milk, the salt, lemon zest, and vanilla seeds and pod and stir to mix. Refrigerate the remaining ¼ cup (60 grams) milk to keep cold.

Place the saucepan over medium-low heat and cook, whisking occasionally, until just lightly simmering or an instant-read thermometer registers 170°F, about 8 minutes. Remove from the heat and let cool until it feels like a hot bath or an instant-read thermometer registers 120°F, about 10 minutes.

Meanwhile, in a small bowl, sprinkle the gelatin evenly over the reserved cold milk and let stand until softened, 5 to 10 minutes. Pour a little bit of the warm mixture into the bowl and stir until the gelatin is completely dissolved, then pour the gelatin mixture into the saucepan. Add the crème fraîche and whisk to remove any lumps. Strain the panna cotta mixture through a chinois or extra-fine-mesh strainer into a clean bowl with a pouring spout or a large glass measuring cup. Divide evenly among eight individual ramekins or jars. Cover and refrigerate until set, about 2 hours.

Serve the panna cotta in their ramekins. Top with fresh fruit and drizzle each with 1 teaspoon of the honey syrup.

WILDFLOWER HONEY SYRUP

MAKES ABOUT 1¼ CUPS

½ cup raw sugar

⅓ cup wildflower honey

⅔ cup water

Combine all of the ingredients in a small saucepan and bring to a boil over medium-high heat. Turn the heat to medium-low and simmer, stirring a few times, until all of the sugar is dissolved, about 2 minutes. Remove from the heat and let cool, then refrigerate until well chilled before using. Refrigerate in an airtight container for up to 2 months.

ZABAGLIONE AL MOSCATO WITH BLOOD ORANGE SORBET, PINE NUT MERINGUE, AND CANDIED ORANGE PEEL

SERVES 8

A meal at Bestia can be an intense experience—full of big flavors and heavier meats. Sometimes you want to end your meal in a light and refreshing way, but a plain sorbet feels too spartan. Out of all of our desserts, I think this is actually, truly my favorite. It has all of the satisfaction of our richer desserts, but at the same time it's incredibly light and palate cleansing.

Blood Orange Sorbet (see facing page)

Pine Nut Meringue (see facing page)

Candied Blood Orange Peel (page 29)

½ cup cold heavy cream

8 large egg yolks

⅔ cup moscato wine

⅓ cup sugar

Small pinch of kosher salt

Make the sorbet at least 2 days in advance, so it's frozen firm. Make the meringues at least 1 day in advance and, after completely cool, store in an airtight container in a cool place until ready to use. Make the candied orange peel at least a few hours in advance.

In a bowl, vigorously whisk the cream by hand—or with a stand mixer fitted with the whisk attachment—until it is fluffy and holds stiff peaks. Cover and refrigerate for up to 3 hours until ready to use.

Have ready a large bowl filled with water and ice.

Prepare a double boiler or make one by filling a saucepan with 2 inches of water and bringing to a simmer over low heat. Nestle a heatproof bowl in the saucepan over the boiling water, making sure the bottom of the bowl isn't touching the water. Add the egg yolks, moscato, sugar, and salt to the top pan of the double boiler or bowl and whisk to combine. Turn the heat to very low while making sure that your water remains simmering during the whole cooking process. Slowly rotating the bowl with your hand, whisk the yolk mixture until it is thickened and starts to pull away from the sides of the bowl, 8 to 10 minutes.

Remove from the heat and continue to whisk until the bowl is cool to the touch. Nest the zabaglione bowl in the ice bath and let cool completely, stirring often. Gently fold in the whipped cream with a rubber spatula. (Cover and refrigerate until ready to serve, or up to 4 hours.)

If you've refrigerated the zabaglione after whisking, give it a few folds with a rubber spatula to reincorporate everything. Spoon about ⅓ cup of the zabaglione into each serving bowl and top each with a meringue and two small scoops or quenelles of the sorbet. Sprinkle with the candied orange peel and serve immediately.

MAKES ABOUT 1 QUART

BLOOD ORANGE SORBET

4¼ cups freshly squeezed blood orange juice

1 cup sugar

Small pinch of kosher salt

1 tablespoon vodka

1 tablespoon freshly squeezed lemon juice

In a saucepan, combine 1 cup of the blood orange juice with the sugar and salt, place over low heat, and cook, stirring, just until all of the sugar has dissolved. Remove from the heat and transfer the mixture to a large bowl. Stir in the remaining 3¼ cups blood orange juice, the vodka, and the lemon juice. Cover and refrigerate until very cold, at least 6 hours or up to overnight. Once chilled, churn in an ice-cream maker according to the manufacturer's instructions. Transfer to an airtight container and freeze until firm, at least 2 days and up to 1 week.

MAKES 12 MERINGUES

PINE NUT MERINGUE

¼ cup egg whites (from about 2 large eggs)

¼ cup packed muscovado sugar or dark brown sugar

⅓ cup granulated sugar

⅛ teaspoon vanilla extract

⅛ teaspoon Grand Marnier

Small pinch of kosher salt

3 tablespoons pine nuts

Preheat the oven to 225°F. Line a baking sheet with parchment paper.

In the bowl of a stand mixer, combine the egg whites, both sugars, vanilla, Grand Marnier, and salt. Fill a large, heavy pot with 1 inch of very hot water. Nest the mixer bowl over the pot so the bottom is almost touching the water. Then, using your fingers, gently stir the mixture to help dissolve the sugars, crumbling any lumps and stirring gently until you can feel the mixture is no longer grainy, about 5 minutes.

Transfer the bowl to the mixer stand fitted with the whisk attachment and beat on medium speed until the egg whites are shiny and hold very stiff peaks. Remove the bowl from the mixer and stir in the pine nuts.

Transfer the meringue mixture to a piping bag fitted with a medium plain tip (alternatively, transfer it to a zippered plastic bag and snip off one corner) and, in a spiral motion, pipe the batter onto the prepared baking sheet into disks about 2½ inches in diameter and ¼ inch thick. Bake for 1¼ hours, until the meringues are dry to the touch. Turn off the oven, crack the oven door, and let cool completely in the oven. The meringues should be crisp. Store in an airtight container at room temperature for at least 1 day and up to 1 week.

ROASTED BANANA MALT AND MUSCOVADO PEANUT ICE CREAM BARS WITH DARK ROASTED PEANUT CREAM AND CARAMELIZED BANANAS

MAKES ABOUT 18 BARS

Ori originally felt this dessert wasn't Italian enough to put on the menu. That's totally true. It's as American as can be—basically a cross between a Snickers bar and bananas Foster. Banana malt milk-shaky ice cream with salted peanut crunchy layers, served with contrasting warm caramelized bananas. My whole pastry team loved it, so I put it on the menu. And now Ori eats it all the time.

The ice cream is a wonderful thing on its own. For a simple sundae, crumble the nougatine on top and serve with slices of caramelized banana, a dollop of whipped cream, and, of course, a cherry. Roast extra bananas for my favorite banana bread on page 310, if you like.

ASSEMBLY

Peanut Nougatine (page 288)
Peanut Crunch Crust (page 289)
Roasted Banana Ice Cream (page 290)
Peanut Cream (page 289)
Peanut Muscovado Caramel (page 291)
Banana Fosters Caramel (page 291)
6 bananas, peeled and sliced ¼ inch thick (54 slices total)

NOTE

There are a lot of components, and some yield more than you'll need for one batch of bars; but all are perfect for any number of delicious other uses, or future rounds of bars. See the details in the recipe for storage.

First make the **Peanut Nougatine** up to 2 weeks in advance and store in an airtight container at room temperature. (This will be used in the Peanut Crunch Crust batter, which forms the base of the ice cream bars.)

Next, make the **Peanut Crunch Crust.** Assemble the crust in the pan as directed, cover with plastic wrap, and freeze until solid, at least 1 hour or up to 3 days.

Make the **Roasted Banana Ice Cream.** Once it is churned, spread it in an even layer over the frozen Peanut Crunch Crust, cover with plastic wrap, and freeze for at least 1 hour.

Make the **Peanut Cream** and refrigerate in an airtight container until ready to use or up to 3 days.

Make the **Peanut Muscovado Caramel.** If using immediately, stir in the peanuts. If making ahead, you can refrigerate for up to 3 days, bring to room temperature, and then stir in the peanuts before use.

When ready to assemble, remove the ice cream–covered crust from the freezer and, using an offset spatula, spread all the Peanut Muscovado Caramel over the ice cream as quickly as possible. Return to the freezer for at least 1 hour or up to 2 days before serving.

continued

Make the **Banana Fosters Caramel**. Use immediately, or refrigerate in an airtight container for up to 3 days.

Carefully unmold the ice cream base—either by removing the pan extender or by lifting up on the overhanging parchment. (At the restaurant we use a small blowtorch to heat the sides for easy removal, but you can also dip the base in a warm water bath for a few seconds.) Cut into 1¼-by-4-inch bars. Return the bars to the freezer until the bananas and caramel are ready.

Place a small saucepan over medium heat and add about one-third of the Bananas Foster Caramel. When the caramel is bubbling, add 18 banana slices and allow them to caramelize and heat through, about 1 minute. Repeat in two more batches, using the remaining caramel and banana slices.

Spread a dollop of the Peanut Cream on each plate and place an ice cream bar next to it. Spoon a few slices of caramelized banana beside the bar and serve immediately.

PEANUT NOUGATINE

½ cup sugar
¼ cup water
¼ teaspoon vanilla extract
Pinch of kosher salt
1 teaspoon unsalted butter
1 cup salted roasted peanuts

SPECIAL EQUIPMENT
Candy thermometer

Line a baking sheet with a nonstick silicone mat. In a saucepan over medium-high heat, combine the sugar, water, vanilla, and salt. Using a pastry brush dipped in water, gently brush down the inner sides the pan to make sure no sugar crystals form. Cook undisturbed for about 7 to 10 minutes, gently tilting the pan from side to side if any hot spots emerge, until all of the sugar has dissolved and the mixture is golden and registers 300°F on a candy thermometer.

Remove the pan from the heat. Add the butter and gently stir with a heatproof spatula, then fold in the nuts until just coated. Turn the mixture out onto the prepared baking sheet and spread in a ¼-inch-thick layer with a spatula. Let cool at room temperature until hard, then finely chop the nougatine.

Store the nougatine in an airtight container at room temperature for up to 2 weeks.

PEANUT CRUNCH CRUST

⅓ cup packed muscovado sugar

¾ cup roasted, salted peanut butter, at room temperature

¾ cup Peanut Nougatine (facing page)

1¼ cups feuilletine flakes (see Note)

1 tablespoon plus 1 teaspoon coconut oil

Rounded ¼ teaspoon kosher salt

SPECIAL EQUIPMENT

One 9-by-13-inch pan with 2-inch sides or 9-by-13-inch pan with a pan extender

Pass the sugar through a tamis or extra-fine-mesh strainer to remove any lumps. In a bowl, combine the sugar and peanut butter and stir with a rubber spatula until smooth and there are no longer any sugar lumps. Fold in the nougatine followed by the feuilletine flakes, then drizzle in the coconut oil, sprinkle the salt evenly over the mixture, and stir.

Line a 9-by-13-inch pan with 2-inch sides—or a 9-by-13-inch pan with a pan extender—with a double layer of parchment paper, allowing a few inches of overhang to drape over the sides of the pan. Dump the mixture into the pan and, using an offset spatula, press into all the corners, being sure to break up any large chunks of peanut nougatine. Cover with plastic wrap and freeze until solid, at least 1 hour or up to 3 days.

NOTE

Feuilletine flakes are crisp, thin, brittle, tiny caramelized wheat flakes available in specialty stores or online.

PEANUT CREAM

1 cup raw peanuts

2 cups heavy cream

⅓ cup packed muscovado sugar or light brown sugar (the flavor will be slightly different and not as rich with light brown sugar)

⅛ teaspoon kosher salt

Preheat the oven to 350°F. Spread the peanuts evenly over a baking sheet and bake for 15 to 20 minutes, until toasted to a deep golden brown. Let cool on the sheet on a wire rack. Finely chop the peanuts by hand or lightly pulse in a food processor. In a bowl, stir together the cream and chopped nuts, then cover and refrigerate for at least 8 hours or up to overnight.

Transfer the chilled peanut-cream mixture to a saucepan and bring to a low simmer over very low heat. Add the sugar and salt and whisk just until the sugar is completely dissolved. Immediately remove from the heat and strain the mixture through a chionois or extra-fine-mesh strainer into a bowl, pressing down on the solids with a spoon to extract as much cream as possible. Place a sheet of plastic wrap directly on the surface of the cream to prevent a skin from forming and refrigerate for 2 hours, until ice-cold. If you need it sooner, place the bowl in an ice bath to speed up the chilling process.

Fill a very large bowl with ice. Nest the cold peanut cream bowl in the ice bowl and whisk by hand until the cream forms loose peaks. Do not overmix or it will separate and become grainy. Refrigerate in an airtight container until ready to use or up to 3 days.

continued

ROASTED BANANA ICE CREAM

5 large or 6 medium very ripe bananas, unpeeled

⅓ cup plus 2 tablespoons malted milk powder

8 tablespoons granulated sugar

1¾ cups heavy cream

¾ cup whole milk

½ vanilla bean, seeds scraped, pod reserved

Pinch of kosher salt

6 large egg yolks

1½ teaspoons freshly squeezed lemon juice

Preheat the oven to 350°F. Lay the whole, unpeeled bananas on a rimmed baking sheet and bake until black and blistered with juices running out, about 25 minutes. Let them cool completely before peeling, picking out any spots with visible bruises. (You will be able to see the bruises because they are gray and hard.) Put the fruit and any accumulated juices from the baking sheet into a blender or food processor and purée. Transfer the purée to a zippered plastic bag and refrigerate until very cold. You can do this up to 24 hours in advance of using them in the ice cream.

In a small bowl, whisk together the malted milk powder and 6 tablespoons of the sugar. (This is important, as it prevents the malted milk from clumping.) Combine the cream, ¼ cup of the milk, the vanilla seeds and pod, salt, and sugar-malt mixture in a saucepan and cook over medium heat, stirring occasionally with a whisk, until the mixture comes to a simmer. Remove from the heat.

In a large bowl, whisk together the remaining 2 tablespoons sugar and the egg yolks. Slowly drizzle in the warm cream mixture while whisking until thoroughly incorporated. Return the whole mixture to the saucepan and cook over low heat while stirring continuously with a heatproof spatula, scraping the bottom and sides of the pan to make sure the eggs don't start to scramble. Cook until the mixture thickens enough to coat the back of a spoon, about 15 minutes.

Pour the mixture through a chinois or extra-fine-mesh strainer into a large bowl to get out any bits of cooked egg, then stir in the remaining ½ cup milk to stop the cooking process. Press a sheet of plastic wrap on the surface of the liquid to prevent a skin from forming and refrigerate for at least 8 hours or up to 2 days.

Once the base is chilled, stir in the chilled roasted banana purée and lemon juice. Before transferring to your ice-cream maker and churning, have the frozen Peanut Crunch Crust ready. Churn the banana mixture in an ice-cream maker according to the manufacturer's instructions. (Makes about 1 quart. Transfer any extra to an airtight container and freeze.)

PEANUT MUSCOVADO CARAMEL

¾ cup (150 grams) very tightly packed muscovado sugar or light brown sugar (the taste will be less rich if you use the light brown sugar)

¾ cup (180 grams) heavy cream

1 tablespoon plus 1 teaspoon (25 grams) glucose, or 1 tablespoon plus 1½ teaspoons (30 grams) light corn syrup

1 teaspoon vanilla extract

½ teaspoon kosher salt

1½ cups (200 grams) salted roasted peanuts

SPECIAL EQUIPMENT

Candy thermometer

In a small saucepan, whisk together the sugar, ½ cup (120 grams) of the cream, the glucose, vanilla, and salt, breaking up any large sugar lumps. Cook over medium-high heat, whisking frequently at first, then slowly and continuously as it begins to thicken, until a candy thermometer registers 250°F, 5 to 7 minutes.

Remove the pan from the heat and slowly whisk in the remaining ¼ cup (60 grams) cream to stop the cooking process. Let the caramel cool completely to room temperature. If using immediately, stir in the peanuts. If making ahead, you can refrigerate for up to 3 days, bring to room temperature, then stir in the peanuts before use.

BANANA FOSTERS CARAMEL

¾ cup plus 3 tablespoons (170 grams) packed muscovado sugar or light brown sugar (the taste will be less rich with light brown sugar)

½ teaspoon kosher salt

⅛ teaspoon ground cinnamon

½ cup (113 grams) unsalted butter

½ cup (120 grams) heavy cream

⅓ cup plus 1 tablespoon dark rum

6 fresh ripe bananas

In a saucepan, combine the sugar, salt, cinnamon, and butter and cook over medium-high heat while whisking continuously until the butter is melted and the mixture is smooth, about 2 minutes. When it starts to bubble, add the cream and whisk until combined.

Remove the pan from the heat and add the rum, then return the pan to the heat and flambé. To do this, carefully tilt the pan so the caramel reaches the very rim, then dip the pan down to allow the burner flame to hit the surface of the caramel. Once it ignites, flambé until the fire goes out, then remove from the heat. You should have about 1¾ cups. Use immediately, or refrigerate in an airtight container for up to 3 days.

NOTE

The flambé process for the Banana Fosters Caramel isn't just for show. Cooking off the rum quickly lets you keep a thin caramel while getting rid of the burn of the alcohol. If the tilting method seems too tricky, you can also use a match. But a disclaimer: the match is more dangerous than the tilting.

FROZEN STRAWBERRY TORTE

MAKES ONE 9-INCH TORTE

Strawberries are delicious, but more often than not you're eating them on their own or as a sort of garnish on top of waffles. If you think about it, there aren't many composed desserts that really showcase strawberries in a strong and flavorful way. So that's what makes this torte really unique: it's all about the strawberry. There's the intensified strawberry buttermilk ice cream. A layer of strawberry sorbet that tastes of strawberry amplified in its purest, most potent form. Followed by a layer of dulce de leche that counterbalances that potency with just a little bit of creaminess. At the bottom, the whole dessert is anchored by a buttery, satisfyingly dense pound cake–style butter cake. As a final note, we top the torte with a sprinkle of something that we call Jesus Dust, so that the first thing that hits your mouth is a shock of vibrant berry acidity. Only make this recipe when strawberries are in season.

ASSEMBLY

Butter Cake (page 294)

Strawberry Buttermilk Ice Cream (page 295)

Strawberry Sorbet (page 296)

Dulce Whip (page 296)

Dehydrated Coconut (page 297)

Jesus Dust (page 297)

First, make the **Butter Cake**. Let the cake cool completely in the pan, then cover the pan with plastic wrap and freeze for at least 1 hour or up to 3 days before assembly.

Make the **Strawberry Buttermilk Ice Cream**. Once the ice cream has churned and is still soft and pliable, using an offset spatula, spread 3 cups of the ice cream in an even layer on top of the cake, then return the pan to the freezer until the ice cream is very firm, about 1 hour.

Make the **Strawberry Sorbet**. Once the sorbet has churned and is still soft and pliable, remove the pan from the freezer again and, using an offset spatula, spread 3 cups of the sorbet in an even layer on top of the ice cream. Cover with plastic wrap and return to the freezer until firm, 1 hour.

Make the **Dulce Whip**. Remove the cake from the freezer and spread the whip to cover the top. Wrap in plastic, and return to the freezer for at least 2 hours or up to 3 days before serving.

Make the **Dehydrated Coconut** and **Jesus Dust**.

Remove the pan sides, slice the cake into 12 equal slices, and arrange on dessert plates. Top with the Dehydrated Coconut bits and then give the cake a heavy dusting of Jesus Dust. Serve immediately.

continued

BUTTER CAKE

- ¼ cup (58 grams) crème fraîche
- 1 tablespoon plus 1 teaspoon (18 grams) whole milk
- ¾ cup plus 1 tablespoon (95 grams) all-purpose flour
- ¼ teaspoon baking powder
- ¼ teaspoon kosher salt
- 4 tablespoons (55 grams) unsalted butter, at room temperature
- 2 tablespoons plus 1 teaspoon (25 grams) vegetable shortening
- ¾ cup (150 grams) sugar
- 1½ teaspoons freshly grated lemon zest
- ¼ teaspoon freshly squeezed lemon juice
- ¼ teaspoon vanilla extract
- ¼ teaspoon almond extract
- 1 extra-large egg

Butter a 9-inch springform pan. Cut out a 9-inch-diameter circle of parchment, press it on the bottom of the pan, and then brush the parchment with butter.

Combine the crème fraîche and milk in a small bowl and stir to combine. Set aside.

In another small bowl, whisk together the flour, baking powder, and salt and whisk well. Set aside.

In the bowl of a stand mixer fitted with the paddle attachment, combine the butter and vegetable shortening and beat on medium speed until smooth and creamy. Scrape down the bowl with a rubber spatula, then add the sugar and beat on medium speed until light and fluffy, about 5 minutes. Add the lemon zest, lemon juice, vanilla, and almond extract and continue to mix for another 30 seconds. Scrape down the sides of the bowl with a spatula as needed, then add the egg and beat until incorporated.

Add half of the flour mixture to the bowl and mix on low speed for a few seconds to combine, scraping down the sides of the bowl with the spatula to make sure the batter is mixing evenly. Add the milk mixture and gently mix on low speed until just incorporated. Finish with the remaining flour, being careful not to overmix. Scrape down the sides and bottom of the bowl to make sure everything is combined evenly.

Transfer the batter to the prepared pan and spread into an even layer. Bake until a toothpick inserted in the center comes out with moist crumbs, 25 to 30 minutes. Let the cake cool completely in the pan, on a wire rack, then cover the pan with plastic wrap and freeze for at least 1 hour or up to 3 days before final assembly.

NOTE

The cake is formatted to be a base for this frozen dessert, so I don't recommend making it if you're just looking for a pound cake recipe. Feel free to use it as the base for any ice-cream cake you want. Bake it, cool it, freeze it, fill the rest of the pan with any ice cream of your choice. Unmold, top with whipped cream, and freeze again.

STRAWBERRY BUTTERMILK ICE CREAM

STRAWBERRY PURÉE

1 pound strawberries, hulled and halved

⅓ cup plus 1½ teaspoons sugar

½ teaspoon freshly squeezed lemon juice

1½ teaspoons fraise des bois liqueur

BUTTERMILK BASE

1⅔ cups heavy cream

8 tablespoons sugar, plus more as needed

½ vanilla bean, seeds scraped, pod reserved

⅛ teaspoon kosher salt

6 large egg yolks

1 cup plus 2 tablespoons buttermilk

NOTE

We have been known to serve this ice cream on its own and so could you.

To make the strawberry purée, in a large bowl, combine the strawberries, sugar, and lemon juice and toss well. Cover with plastic wrap and let sit at room temperature for 1 hour to macerate, then strain through a fine-mesh strainer into a bowl, pressing down on the berries to extract all of the juices; set the berries aside. Combine the strawberry juice and fraise des bois liqueur in a small saucepan and cook over medium-high heat, stirring occasionally, until the mixture begins to thicken and the bubbles slow, about 5 minutes.

Turn the heat to low and continue cooking until the liquid is dark and thick, about 10 minutes. Transfer the mixture to a bowl and refrigerate for 30 minutes, until cold. Meanwhile, place the berries in the bowl of a food processor and pulse until you have a chunky purée, then transfer to a bowl and refrigerate until cold. Stir together the chilled reduced juice and berry purée. Use immediately, or store in an airtight container in the refrigerator until ready to churn or up to 2 weeks.

To make the buttermilk base, in a saucepan over medium heat, combine the cream, 6 tablespoons of the sugar, the vanilla seeds and pod, and salt and heat to a simmer.

Meanwhile, in a large bowl, whisk together the egg yolks and the remaining 2 tablespoons sugar. Slowly pour the warm cream mixture into the yolks while whisking constantly until fully incorporated. Return the whole mixture to the saucepan and cook over very low heat while stirring continuously with a heatproof spatula until thick enough to coat the back of a spoon, about 10 minutes.

When thickened, remove the mixture from the heat, pour through a chinois or extra-fine-mesh strainer into a large bowl, and stir in the buttermilk. Cover and refrigerate until very cold, 8 hours or up to overnight.

Fold the strawberry purée into the base, then taste and add sugar, if needed, but no more than 2 tablespoons. Pour the mixture into your ice-cream maker and churn according to the manufacturer's instructions. Use immediately and freeze any leftover in an airtight container for up to 2 weeks.

continued

STRAWBERRY SORBET

- 5½ cups small, peak-season strawberries, hulled
- ½ lemon, sliced, seeds removed
- ⅔ cup sugar
- Pinch of kosher salt
- 1 tablespoon plus 1½ teaspoons vodka
- 1 teaspoon fraise des bois liqueur

In a food processor, combine the strawberries, lemon, sugar, and salt and process to a smooth purée. (Process in two batches if necessary.) Transfer the purée to a large bowl and stir in the vodka and fraise des bois liqueur. Add the mixture to your ice-cream maker and churn according to the manufacturers instructions. Use immediately and freeze any leftover in an airtight container for up to 2 weeks.

NOTE

The sorbet is delicious on its own, particularly in summer. Using the whole lemon slices here, provides a little bitterness and complexity to a normally basic dessert.

DULCE WHIP

- 1 (14-ounce) can sweetened condensed milk
- ¾ cup heavy cream
- ⅛ teaspoon vanilla extract
- Small pinch of kosher salt

NOTE

Dulce de leche gives whipped cream a beautiful rich caramel flavor without the graininess of a brown sugar. Top your coffee or cakes with the leftovers.

Partially open the can of sweetened condensed milk, leaving the lid ajar. Place the open can in the center of a saucepan and fill the pan with water to reach about three-fourths of the way up the sides of the can. Bring to a boil over medium-high heat and continue boiling for about 2½ hours, until the condensed milk is golden brown. Check the pan periodically to make sure there's enough water and add more as needed to maintain the original level. Remove from the heat and let sit until cool enough to handle.

In the bowl of a stand mixer fitted with the whisk attachment, combine the cream, vanilla, salt, and 2 tablespoons of the dulce de leche. (Use the leftover dulce de leche in almost anything, even your morning coffee.) Beat on medium speed until the cream begins to form loose peaks, about 5 minutes. Use immediately, or refrigerate in an airtight container until ready to use or up to 24 hours. Lightly rewhip before using if it's been longer than 1 hour.

DEHYDRATED COCONUT

2 cups sweetened shredded dried coconut

Preheat the oven to 200°F. Spread the coconut evenly on a baking sheet and bake for 2 hours. Remove from the oven and let cool. Transfer to a food processor and pulse a few times until reduced to small bits for easy sprinkling. Set aside in a small bowl until ready to serve.

JESUS DUST

1 (1.2-ounce) bag freeze-dried strawberries

¼ teaspoon citric acid

In a very dry, cool food processor, grind the freeze-dried strawberries into a fine powder. Pass the powder through a fine-mesh sieve into a small bowl. Whisk in the citric acid until combined. Store in an airtight container at room temperature for up to 2 days (see Note).

NOTE

Keep the little packet that comes in the bag of freeze-dried strawberries and add it to the storage container to help keep the dust from forming clumps.

RAINBOW SHERBET

MAKES ABOUT 3 QUARTS

One day during morning prep, the kitchen conversation turned to our favorite Thrifty ice cream flavors. Rainbow sherbet came up several times, and so I asked everyone, "What if we made a rainbow sherbet out of real fruit instead of just food dye?" Everyone agreed that would be awesome, so we decided to go ahead and do it. We ended up putting it on the menu as mini scoops served in mini cones that every day we had to hand-roll while scalding hot, leaving all of our fingertips a permanent burnt bright red.

It didn't occur to me to put this in the cookbook, but Daniela insisted upon it. When I told her we would need to test the recipe, she responded, "Don't threaten me with a good time." She loves making it that much.

There are four different fruit-flavored sherbets here, but we only mix three together at a time at the restaurant for our Rainbow Sherbet, so just pick your three favorites. All of these flavors are also delicious on their own, so I encourage you to make solo batches. But when they're mixed together they become something magical.

ASSEMBLY

Blackberry-Buttermilk Sherbet (page 300)

Raspberry Sherbet (Page 300)

Lime Sherbet (Page 301)

Orange Sherbet (page 301)

Choose just three sherbet flavors from the four flavors listed here and freeze them as directed. When it is time to assemble the rainbow, transfer them to the refrigerator until they are soft enough to scoop but still frozen, about 30 minutes. Then, in a large, freezer-safe container, add scoops of the three flavors in alternating layers until you've reached the desired amount of rainbow sherbet. Smooth the surface into an even layer, then cover and freeze until ready to serve.

continued

MAKES ABOUT 1 QUART

BLACKBERRY-BUTTERMILK SHERBET

1 cup plus 2 tablespoons sugar
Pinch of kosher salt
¼ cup whole milk
¼ cup heavy cream
1¾ cups buttermilk
3 cups fresh blackberries
1½ teaspoons raspberry liqueur
1½ teaspoons freshly squeezed lemon juice

In a small saucepan over medium heat, combine the sugar, salt, milk, and cream and bring to a simmer. Continue to cook until the sugar is almost completely dissolved. (Because of the small amount of liquid, it may not be possible to dissolve it completely. That's OK.) Remove from the heat and transfer the liquid to a large bowl to let cool for about 10 minutes. Stir in the buttermilk, cover with plastic wrap, and refrigerate for at least 2 hours or up to 2 days.

In a blender or food processor, process the blackberries until smooth, then strain the purée through a chinois or extra-fine-mesh strainer to remove the seeds. Refrigerate for 1 hour, then stir the purée, raspberry liqueur, and lemon juice into the cold buttermilk base.

Transfer to your ice-cream maker and churn according to the manufacturer's instructions. Transfer to an airtight container and freeze until ready to use or store for up to 1 week.

MAKES ABOUT 1 QUART

RASPBERRY SHERBET

1 cup plus 2 tablespoons sugar
Pinch of kosher salt
2 cups whole milk
¼ cup heavy cream
3 cups fresh raspberries
1½ teaspoons raspberry liqueur
1½ teaspoons freshly squeezed lemon juice

In a small saucepan over medium heat, combine the sugar, salt, milk, and cream and bring to a simmer. Continue to cook until the sugar is almost completely dissolved. (Because of the small amount of liquid, it may not be possible to dissolve it completely. That's OK.) Remove from the heat and transfer the liquid to a large bowl to let cool for about 10 minutes. Cover with plastic wrap and refrigerate for at least 2 hours or up to 2 days.

In a blender or food processor, process the raspberries until smooth, then strain the purée through a chinois or extra-fine-mesh strainer to remove the seeds. Refrigerate for 1 hour, then stir the purée, raspberry liqueur, and lemon juice into the cold milk base.

Transfer to your ice-cream maker and churn according to the manufacturer's instructions. Transfer to an airtight container and freeze until ready to use or store for up to 1 week.

MAKES ABOUT 1 QUART

LIME SHERBET

¾ cup plus 3 tablespoons sugar
Pinch of kosher salt
2 cups whole milk
1 cup heavy cream
1 tablespoon falernum
¾ cup freshly squeezed lime juice

In a small saucepan over medium heat, combine the sugar, salt, milk, and cream and bring to a simmer. Continue to cook until the sugar is almost completely dissolved. (Because of the small amount of liquid, it may not be possible to dissolve it completely. That's OK.) Remove from the heat and transfer the liquid to a large bowl to let cool for about 10 minutes. Cover with plastic wrap and refrigerate for at least 6 hours or up to overnight.

Stir in the falernum and lime juice, then transfer to your ice-cream maker and churn according to the manufacturer's instructions. Transfer to an airtight container and freeze until ready to use or store for up to 1 week.

MAKES ABOUT 1 QUART

ORANGE SHERBET

1 cup sugar
Pinch of kosher salt
1 cup whole milk
⅔ cup heavy cream
2¼ cups freshly squeezed orange juice or tangerine juice, strained of pulp and chilled
1 tablespoon Combier or other orange liqueur
Big pinch of citric acid
2 teaspoons freshly squeezed lemon juice

In a small saucepan over medium heat, combine the sugar, salt, milk, and cream and bring to a simmer. Continue to cook until the sugar is almost completely dissolved. (Because of the small amount of liquid, it may not be possible to dissolve it completely. That's OK.) Remove from the heat and transfer the liquid to a large bowl to let cool for about 10 minutes. Cover with plastic wrap and refrigerate for at least 6 hours or overnight.

Stir in the orange juice, Combier, citric acid, and lemon juice, then transfer to your ice-cream maker and churn according to the manufacturer's instructions. Transfer to an airtight container and freeze until ready to use or store for up to 1 week.

LEMON VERBENA SHERBET

MAKES ABOUT 1 QUART

One of our most beloved regulars is a woman named June, who happens to have an amazing fruit and vegetable garden. She is always bringing stuff that she grows to the restaurant to see if we can use it. One day she brought in a giant bunch of beautiful lemon verbena branches and asked if I could do anything with them. I decided I would try to make a sorbet and made a bright-green lemon verbena syrup from the leaves. It tasted insane on its own, but when I made it into a sorbet, it was too perfumy. I figured out that you need to balance that verbena flavor with something, or else it's a bit like eating a bar of soap. I made it again, this time into a sherbet, adding some fresh lemon juice, lemon liqueur, and some dairy to soften it. Suddenly it had all the wonderful perfumy qualities of the lemon verbena without any of the soapiness. It's super-tart and refreshing, and it goes well with any of your favorite subtly flavored cakes or pound cakes.

---

1 cup sugar

2 cups loosely packed fresh lemon verbena leaves (from the farmers' market or borrowed from your neighbor . . . in the middle of the night)

2 cups whole milk

1 cup heavy cream

Pinch of kosher salt

¾ cup freshly squeezed lemon juice, chilled

1 tablespoon Acqua di Cedro liqueur or limoncello

In a food processor, combine the sugar and lemon verbena leaves and blend until thoroughly incorporated and small bits of leaf are no longer visible in the sugar.

In a saucepan over medium heat, combine the milk, cream, salt, and lemon verbena–sugar mixture and bring to a simmer. Remove from the heat and strain through a chinois or extra-fine-mesh strainer into an airtight container. Refrigerate until completely cold, about 6 hours or up to overnight.

Stir the lemon juice and Acqua di Cedro into the cold base. Pour the mixture into your ice-cream maker and churn according to the manufacturer's instructions. Transfer to an airtight container and freeze for 2 hours before serving or up to 1 week.

BLUEBERRY MASCARPONE ICE CREAM

MAKES ABOUT 1 QUART

The only description I can come up with for this ice cream is that it is a little like a sophisticated blueberry cheesecake. The mascarpone gives it that slightly cheesy flavor while also making it extra creamy. (Pictured on page 250.)

1¼ cups whole milk

⅛ teaspoon kosher salt

8 tablespoons sugar

6 large egg yolks

1½ cups mascarpone, at room temperature

1¾ cups Blueberry Jam Purée (recipe follows)

In a saucepan over medium heat, combine the milk, salt, and 6 tablespoons of the sugar and cook, stirring occasionally, until the mixture comes to a simmer. Remove from the heat.

Meanwhile, in a bowl, whisk together the egg yolks and the remaining 2 tablespoons sugar. Slowly pour the warm cream mixture into the yolks while whisking constantly until fully incorporated. Return the whole mixture to the saucepan and cook over low heat while stirring continuously with a heatproof spatula until thick enough to coat the back of a spoon, about 10 minutes.

Place the mascarpone in a large bowl. Strain the yolk mixture through a chinois or extra-fine-mesh strainer into the mascarpone and whisk until smooth. Press a sheet of plastic wrap on the surface of the liquid to keep it from forming a skin and refrigerate for at least 8 hours or up to overnight.

Stir the jam purée into the cold base. Pour the mixture into your ice-cream maker and churn according to the manufacturer's instructions. Transfer to an airtight container and freeze for 2 hours before serving or up to 1 week.

BLUEBERRY JAM PURÉE

MAKES 1¾ CUPS

4 cups (about 1¼ pounds) fresh blueberries

½ cup sugar

1 tablespoon plus 1 teaspoon crème de cassis

2 tablespoons freshly squeezed lemon juice

In a saucepan over medium-high heat, combine all of the ingredients and bring to a boil, stirring occasionally with a wooden spoon. Once boiling, stir the mixture continually until the volume has reduced by one-third, 8 to 10 minutes. Remove from the heat and let cool to room temperature.

Transfer the mixture to a blender and blend until smooth, then push it through a tamis or extra-fine-mesh strainer to remove any fibers. Cover and refrigerate for up to 7 days or freeze for up to 1 month.

COFFEE ICE CREAM

MAKES ABOUT 1 QUART

Use whatever coffee you like to drink to make this caffeinated ice cream. Personally, I like a dark chocolatey roast, which is enhanced by caramel notes from the addition of brown sugar, but go with whatever style of coffee is your favorite.

---

2 cups whole coffee beans

2 cups whole milk

2 cups heavy cream

¾ cup plus 2 teaspoons granulated sugar

¼ cup packed moscovado or light brown sugar

¼ vanilla bean, seeds scraped, pod reserved

⅛ teaspoon kosher salt

8 large egg yolks

⅔ cup boiling water

SPECIAL EQUIPMENT

Paper coffee filter

In a saucepan over low heat, combine 1½ cups of the coffee beans, 1 cup of the milk, the cream, ½ cup plus 2 teaspoons of the granulated sugar, the brown sugar, vanilla seeds and pod, and salt and slowly bring to a simmer, whisking occasionally. Just before it comes to a boil, remove from the heat, cover, and let steep for 2 hours at room temperature.

Return the saucepan to low heat and bring to a very low boil, whisking occasionally. Remove from the heat and strain the infused cream mixture through a colander or other strainer into a large heatproof bowl. Discard the coffee beans and vanilla bean pod.

In a large bowl, whisk together the egg yolks and the remaining ¼ cup granulated sugar. Slowly pour the warm coffee-cream mixture into the yolks while whisking constantly until fully incorporated. Return the whole mixture to the saucepan and cook over very low heat, stirring continuously with a heatproof spatula, until thick enough to coat the back of the spatula, about 10 minutes.

Remove the mixture from the heat and pour through a chinois or extra-fine-mesh strainer into a large heatproof bowl. Place the strainer over the bowl and pour the remaining 1 cup milk through the strainer into the bowl, helping to push all the thickened bits off the strainer and into the bowl. Cover with plastic wrap, pressing it directly on the surface to prevent a skin from forming. Refrigerate for at least 8 hours or up to overnight.

Just before churning, grind the remaining ½ cup coffee beans to an extra-fine espresso grind and transfer to a small heatproof bowl. Pour the boiling water over the ground coffee and let sit for 5 minutes. Strain the coffee through a paper coffee filter into a small bowl, gently squeezing the filter to make sure you have a full ¼ cup of coffee concentrate. Fill a larger bowl with ice and nest the bowl with the coffee concentrate in the ice until cold.

Stir the chilled concentrate into the cold base. Pour the mixture into your ice-cream maker and churn according to the manufacturer's instructions. Transfer to an airtight container and freeze for 2 hours before serving or up to 1 week.

SOUR CREAM ICE CREAM WITH HUCKLEBERRY JAM

MAKES ABOUT 1 QUART

Sour cream makes everything better, and ice cream is no exception. If you're a purist, you could even make this without the swirl of jam, but I think the fruit bolsters it with a decadent, woodsy berry note.

---

1 cup whole milk

1 cup heavy cream

⅛ teaspoon kosher salt

1 cup sugar

6 large egg yolks

2 cups sour cream

¼ teaspoon vanilla extract

½ to ¾ cup huckleberry jam, homemade (recipe follows), or store-bought huckleberry or blackberry jam

In a saucepan, combine the milk, cream, salt, and ¾ cup of the sugar and cook over medium heat, stirring occasionally, until the mixture just begins to bubble. Remove from the heat.

In a large bowl, whisk together the egg yolks and the remaining ¼ cup sugar. Slowly pour the warm cream mixture into the yolks while whisking constantly until fully incorporated. Return the whole mixture to the saucepan and cook over very low heat while stirring continuously until thick enough to coat the back of a spoon, about 10 minutes. Pour through a chinois or extra-fine-mesh strainer into a large bowl. Stir in the sour cream and vanilla, then cover with plastic wrap, pressing it directly on the surface to prevent a skin from forming. Refrigerate for at least 8 hours or up to overnight.

Pour the mixture into your ice-cream maker and churn according to the manufacturer's instructions. Drop spoonfuls of the jam on the ice cream and swirl them in. Transfer to an airtight container and freeze for 2 hours before serving or up to 1 week.

HUCKLEBERRY JAM

MAKES ABOUT 1¼ CUPS

1½ cups fresh huckleberries

¾ cup sugar

¾ teaspoon crème de cassis

In a saucepan over medium-high heat, combine the berries, sugar, and crème de cassis and bring to a boil, stirring occasionally with a wooden spoon. Boil, stirring continuously, until the consistency of a heavy syrup, 10 to 15 minutes.

Remove from the heat and let cool to room temperature. It should have the consistency of a loose jam, easily spread but not drippy. If too thick, return to the heat for 1 minute and add water, 1 teaspoon at a time, to thin. If too thin, return to a boil and allow to reduce for a few minutes, then let cool again.

Refrigerate for at 2 hours before adding to the ice cream base. Refrigerate the leftover for up to 1 month or freeze for up to 2 months.

MEXICAN WEDDING COOKIES

MAKES ABOUT 40 COOKIES

These cookies have been a family holiday staple for as long as I can remember. My mom and sister used to use a recipe from some generic Christmas cookie book, but my version of Mexican wedding cookies are nicely salted, extra buttery, and have a good amount of nuts. I whip the butter first, which makes a delicate, melt-in-your-mouth cookie, but Ori prefers his denser and meatier. If you do too, you can skip whipping the butter in the first step and the cookies will still be great, just sturdier. Whichever way I make these, Saffron will put an entire cookie in her mouth and chew it really slowly in her adorable little chipmunk cheeks until it melts.

---

1 cup (227 grams) unsalted butter, at room temperature

½ cup (65 grams) powdered sugar, plus more for dusting

2 teaspoons vanilla extract

1¾ cups (170 grams) pecan halves, very finely chopped

1¾ cups (210 grams) all-purpose flour

1 teaspoon kosher salt

In the bowl of a stand mixer fitted with the paddle attachment, beat the butter on medium speed until pale and glossy, about 5 minutes. Stop the mixer and scrape down the sides of the bowl with a rubber spatula, then add the powdered sugar and beat on low speed until incorporated. Raise the speed to high and beat until very light and fluffy, about 5 minutes, scraping down the sides of the bowl again about halfway through.

Add the vanilla and beat for 1 minute, then add the nuts and beat briefly on low speed just until incorporated.

In a small bowl, whisk together the flour and salt, then add it to the batter and mix on very low speed until just incorporated and the mixture forms a loose, shaggy dough. Wrap in plastic wrap and refrigerate for 2 hours.

Preheat the oven to 325°F. Line a baking sheet with parchment paper.

Once chilled, shape the dough into smallish Ping-Pong-size balls and place them about 2 inches apart on the prepared baking sheet. Transfer the whole sheet to the refrigerator for 5 minutes to rechill briefly, then bake until just barely golden on top, 20 to 25 minutes.

Transfer to a wire rack and let cool on the sheet briefly, then use a spatula to transfer the cookies to the rack and let cool completely. Dust with powdered sugar before serving. Store in an airtight container at room temperature for up to 1 week.

BUTTER-TOPPED BANANA BREAD

MAKES 2 LOAVES

My mother's idea of cookies were always some sort of bready, most-often-banana-based drop cookies. They weren't what I wanted as a kid, but as I got older, I began to appreciate those cookies and how comforting they can be.

In college, I started making banana bread, but I wanted to make it more banana-y and buttery. I decided to roast the bananas to amplify their flavor, added in enough walnuts to bring it to the brink of collapse, and brushed the top of each loaf with melted butter after baking.

This banana bread isn't on the menu at Bestia, but still, I love baking up a few loaves for the staff and doling out the slices in a one-for-you, two-for-me manner.

---

4 cups (480 grams) all-purpose flour

2 teaspoons baking powder

1 teaspoon baking soda

1½ teaspoons kosher salt

2 cups (510 grams) mashed roasted banana (see Roasted Banana Ice Cream, page 290)

3 tablespoons buttermilk

1 tablespoon vanilla extract

1 tablespoon freshly squeezed lemon juice

1½ cups (340 grams) unsalted butter, at room temperature

2 cups (400 grams) sugar

2 large eggs, at room temperature

2½ cups (280 grams) walnut halves and pieces

Preheat the oven to 325°F. Liberally butter two 9-by-5-inch loaf pans, then line each pan along the bottom and up the two short sides with a strip of parchment, leaving plenty of overhang. Tape down the overhang with ovenproof tape (masking or other), then butter the parchment. This will help you to lift the banana bread out of the pan with ease when cooled.

In a large bowl, combine the flour, baking powder, baking soda, and salt and whisk thoroughly. Set aside. In a second large bowl, whisk together the roasted banana, buttermilk, vanilla, and lemon juice and set aside.

In the bowl of a stand mixer fitted with the paddle attachment, beat 1 cup (227 grams) of the butter on high speed until light and glossy, about 3 minutes. Add the sugar and continue beating on high speed until very light and fluffy, 5 to 7 minutes longer. Turn the speed to medium-low and add the eggs one at a time, beating after each addition until fully incorporated, then stop the mixer and scrape down the sides of the bowl with a spatula. Add the wet ingredients and mix on very low speed until just combined, then add the flour mixture all at once and mix on low speed just until you no longer see any flour.

Remove the bowl from the mixer stand and, with the spatula, fold in the walnuts, then scrape the bottom of the bowl to ensure all of the ingredients are thoroughly incorporated.

continued

Divide the batter evenly between the prepared loaf pans. Bake for 1 to 1¼ hours, until a toothpick inserted in the center comes out with moist crumbs.

When the loaves are almost done, melt the remaining ½ cup (113 grams) butter in a small saucepan over low heat. When the loaves are finished baking and still very hot, use a pastry brush and liberally brush the top of each with the melted butter until all of the butter is absorbed.

Let the loaves cool completely in the pans on wire racks. When cool, lift up on the overhanging edges of the parchment paper to remove the loaves from the pans. The bread can be wrapped in aluminum foil and stored in a cool, dark spot for up to 3 days.

OPTIONAL

To create a sugar-butter crust, sprinkle the top liberally with granulated sugar right after brushing on the butter.

NOTE

Do not open your oven to check until it's been at least 55 minutes; the loaves will deflate and become dense and gummy.

THE TEAM

MELISSA LOPEZ

People like Melissa make me better at what I do. Everyone will tell you that she has an aura about her—no matter how crazy it gets in the kitchen, she exudes a calmness that's contagious. And she's a great leader. Whenever she guides The Huddle (see page 57), she almost starts crying. And that's not because she's sensitive—though she can be—it's that she's so intensely invested in the restaurant and the people in it. She cares so much about being successful that whenever she speaks to the staff, it's directly from her heart, never from her head.

Of course, none of that compares to how good a cook she is. She's consistent, and I trust her inherently. Melissa came to me from Barbuto in New York and is the only person I've ever hired directly as a sous chef. She didn't need a month or two of training; she just had it. And everybody knows it. It's unfortunate to admit, but normally women have a hard time getting total support and respect from a group of alpha-male line cooks. But not Melissa. She owns it—that's not something you see often.

—ORI

MIKEY PRIORE

Mikey is like my annoying little brother who I love, but he drives me insane. I first met him back at Angelini almost a decade ago. I had just gotten back from a two-week vacation, and when I walked through the kitchen door, there was this kid, fresh out of culinary school, just standing there. Gino had been desperate for help and hired him without even caring that he had no résumé, so I was already skeptical. I said hello and asked, "Where are you from?" He says, "From Italy." "Really?" I said. "You don't sound Italian." "No, no," he insisted, "I'm from Italy." So I ask him to say a word in Italian. He couldn't. "Oh, so you're not Italian?" I asked. "My grandmother's Italian." "Oh, so you're American?" "Yes, I'm American," he said. "OK," I said. "I'm happy we got that clear." (Our relationship has been a little like this ever since.)

In the beginning, Mikey proved to be exactly like I thought he would be. He was young and a troublemaker, and after one particularly bad service, I told him not to come back to Angelini unless he started taking his job seriously. He walked in the next morning like a different person. Overnight, he began to approach cooking with a whole other level of skill and dedication. Years later, when I left to open Bestia, Mikey called me and asked if I needed anyone. He had grown considerably as a chef, but at twenty-three wasn't quite ready for the sous chef position.

I hired him as a line cook and he thrived. He started as the pizza guy, then moved on to quickly master every station. At three months, I made him the sous chef.

Being a great sous chef is not just about cooking and having a great palate—which Mikey has—it's also about leadership, and that's where he shines the most. He's like a coach, motivating you: "We're going to be serving five hundred people! It's going to be aggressive! I need everyone to be loud! I need good energy! I need everyone to take double shots of espresso!" He has a way of firing everyone up, including me. When it comes down to it, my faith in Mikey is one of the only reasons I ever allow myself a day off. He's there when you need him, and my wife and I trust him like family. Because he is.

—ORI

YUVAL BAR-ZEMER

Yuval is the patriarch of the modern L.A. Arts District. He and his partner were the first people to see the incredible potential amid the abandoned lofts and disheveled warehouses just east of downtown. The first and most beautifully rehabbed properties here are all theirs. But to us, Yuval is the reason for Bestia's location. Long before Bestia opened, we were scouting locations with our original business partner. We looked at more than a dozen places with him all over Los Angeles, mostly on the West Side. But then we fell in love with a beautiful space in the Arts District. Our partner couldn't get on board with our vision and immediately pulled out.

We were devastated. We figured that was the end of the road, and that we would have to start looking for jobs. When we told Yuval that we wouldn't be signing the lease after all, he told us he didn't care that we didn't have a partner anymore. He'd hold the space until we found new investors and a new partner. We were shocked. He hadn't even tasted Ori's food and he'd only just met us. When we asked him why, he said he had a feeling in his gut that he'd never had before. He saw a fire and a drive in Ori and knew that he was capable of great things. "I only want you for this space," he said. "Do what you need to do on your end. When you do, I will do everything I can from my end to make this happen."

Yuval and Ori actually have a lot in common. Both are Israeli, and both have these incredibly soft centers, but on the surface they are two of the toughest, most stubborn people to deal with. If you ever want some high-quality entertainment, watch Ori and Yuval debate something. You'll just have to learn Hebrew.

—**GENEVIEVE**

DIEGO VINICIO ARGOTI

Diego had worked on the line only a few short months when he made a big mistake. I was debating on whether or not to keep him when he confessed, "Chef, I'm not ready to work here." But I liked him—and he liked working for us—so I kept him on as our farmers' market forager while he went on to work in other kitchens across L.A., learning and growing as a chef. Three years later, he came back to Bestia, and he was definitely ready. Now he works with confidence. That small amount of fear that caused him to make mistakes early on is now the thing that drives him to be the best at what he does.

Today, Diego is still responsible for buying all of our farmers' market produce, and he's great at it. He doesn't just shop for flavor, but also for texture, color, and ripeness. Then, after waking up at 5 a.m. three days a week to get to the early-morning markets, he also helps make all of the bread, pizza dough, and pasta for the restaurant. It's a lot of work, but he's like me: he's obsessed, and he never stops. On his days off, he reads everything he can get his hands on about food, and he's a maniac about baking bread at home. Every once in a while he even hosts his own pop-up dinners, with these crazy-out-there menus. A guy like that, with that kind of drive, you don't ever have to be his mentor. He's his own mentor and will no doubt be running his own restaurant someday soon. I can't wait.

—ORI

JOSE GARCIA

Jose has been the man in charge of everything dough-related since two months after Bestia opened. He's the caretaker of our precious sourdough starter—the guy who takes it home over the holidays and feeds it like a pet. He knows how it works, why it behaves certain ways in cold temperatures or hot, why it becomes sour or stays sweet. He understands it scientifically—he's really smart—but he also knows it by feel. He can touch a dough and know exactly what's going on with it. Sometimes I'll test a new pasta recipe and he will touch it and say, "Chef, it needs more flour." You don't get that way by reading books. You get that way through constant repetition and touching. That talent is all in his hands. You know how old Italian women who make pasta have these amazing hands? Jose's hands are like that—they're magic. Just look at his perfect tortellini (see page 191) and you'll know what I mean.

—ORI

RYAN IBSEN

People don't understand Ryan. They confuse his passion for anger. Much like me, he can sometimes snap and unintentionally offend people, but it all comes from him wanting to be as great as he can be for the restaurant, for the staff, and for himself. He's a perfectionist—that's just how he is—and it makes him wonderful at his job. The love of his life, whom he met at the restaurant and now has a beautiful daughter with, agrees. Every bottle he brings to the table he chooses with confidence, and that's an achievement considering how challenging Bestia's menu can be for a sommelier. Many of our dishes are uniquely potent and flavorful, but Ryan manages to find equally unique wines to round them out and complement them. I give him 100 percent creative control of the program, and our highly regarded wine list is a reflection of that.

—ORI

LAURA D'LAVARA

It would be very hard for me to walk into work in the morning and not see Laura's sweet face. I give her a hug as soon as I arrive—it's part of my routine, and I'm pretty sure it's part of everyone's routine. She's that kind of lady. But mostly it'd be difficult to work a day without her because, in effect, the entire restaurant hinges on her pulling off the nearly impossible: she's responsible for completing a daily prep list that will efficiently feed five hundred people every night.

Six or so months after Bestia opened, an employee told me about a burrito he'd gotten the night before from a taco spot, and how the woman who made it was looking for a job. I met with Laura the next day, and I'm not sure what I saw in her, but I knew she was something special. Just a great human being with genuine care in her voice. Five years later that has translated into one of the most important employees at the restaurant.

I'm emphasizing her warmth, but Laura is also incredibly tough. She comes to work every day and busts her ass, and trust me when I say that you don't want to disappoint her. Because if the prep list doesn't get done, the entire restaurant breaks down and she knows it. She's also one hell of a cook—her family meals could almost be on the menu.

—ORI

ABOUT GENEVIEVE GERGIS, BY ORI MENASHE

The first time I saw Genevieve was her first day as a hostess at La Terza. I was working as a cook and I thought she was beautiful and she had an energy about her that intrigued me. The next day, while everyone was on break, I shouted, "Are you Jewish?" She responded, "Why?" "Because you look like one of the beautiful women from my country," I answered. It was the dumbest thing I could have said, but I'd choked. "No," she answered and walked away. Everyone laughed, so I bet them all a case of beer that we would start dating by the end of one month. A month passed and she wouldn't even speak to me. And I continued to lose that bet for another six months. Eventually she began to warm up to me. I asked her to coffee, then a date, and we've been together ever since.

Until Bestia, Genevieve cooked only at home for fun. She grew up in Thousand Oaks, California, and spent her twenties traveling the world playing the French horn professionally and working in design. As we began putting together our dream of Bestia, we planned for Genevieve to manage the front-of-house operations. But then, as the restaurant was being built, friend and fellow chef Amy Pressman passed away. We were heartbroken and subsequently offered to make some food and desserts for the funeral.

After the service, chef Nancy Silverton took a nibble of one of Genevieve's shortbreads. She immediately asked who had made them. When Genevieve raised her hand, Nancy asked her what she was planning on doing at Bestia, and Genevieve responded "front of house." "No you're not," Nancy declared. "You're going to be the pastry chef. Who are you going to hire that makes pastries better than you? No one." That's the moment we decided Genevieve would be the pastry chef at Bestia.

Nancy was right—Genevieve is a natural. In all my years, I've never seen such dedication. Genevieve has fairly severe attention deficit disorder, but in the kitchen, she's extremely focused. She doesn't use cookbooks, either. Her dad was a scientist, and she shares his scientific approach to cooking, understanding the chemical reactions needed to achieve exactly the flavor and texture she wants.

The desserts were wonderful from Day One, and within a few weeks of opening, I went from not being sure if she should be a part of the restaurant to not knowing how it could exist without her. Both of us were so stressed out that first year that at least once a day we would meet up on one of the couches in the dining room and lay on each other. It was the two of us against the world, and it was beautiful.

Genevieve's desserts have become an essential part of the Bestia experience, and her warm, welcoming personality softens everything she touches. In 2014, we had our daughter, Saffron, and I discovered one other thing that Genevieve was born to do: be a mother. She gives every ounce of herself to raising our child but somehow still finds a piece of her heart to pour into her professional work. I don't know what I'd do—or what this restaurant would be—without her.

ABOUT ORI MENASHE, BY GENEVIEVE GERGIS

I first met Ori at La Terza. Rough and lax, with a cigarette dangling out of his mouth and a crazy Mohawk, he looked like the kind of guy who didn't care about anything. But even then, when passing through the kitchen and seeing him work, you could tell by his movements and his speed that he was leagues better than everyone else. I once asked him how he mastered everything so quickly, and he said, "I come in before my shift, and I stay after my shift." I remember thinking, "This so does not go with the persona you're giving off."

Ori was born in L.A., but, when he was ten, his father moved the family to Israel where Ori continued to live until after he finished his military service at twenty. He spent the next six months traveling the world snowboarding, partying, and cooking for his friends, a latent talent he discovered he enjoyed. He enrolled in culinary school in L.A. but dropped out after one month, deciding instead to learn on the job. He worked with Gino Angelini at La Terza and later moved on to the kitchens of such legendary L.A. chefs as Nancy Silverton and Mirko Paderno. Eventually he teamed up again with Gino at Angelini Osteria, where he became the executive chef, a life-changing position he almost didn't take.

"It's going to be hell," he said. "That is the hardest kitchen in all of Los Angeles." But his biggest worry was that I'd break up with him because I'd never see him anymore. I said, "Who cares about me? Will you get anything out of it?" He said, "Yeah, it's the hardest kitchen ever. If I do that, I can do anything." I could suddenly see the wheels turning in his head. "If I do it, I'll have mastered something big," he said. "Should I do it?"

He did. And Ori was right, I never saw him. But during that time he also grew immensely as a chef and a leader. He successfully ran the Angelini kitchen for three years before the grind got to him and he started to burn out. He even considered quitting cooking altogether. Then one day he said, "The only way I can continue is if it's my own place. I can't kill myself every day unless it's entirely my vision—unless I'm putting 100 percent of my soul into the cooking." And that was the start of Bestia. It came from one of the most dedicated people I've ever met giving everything to a job, and then knowing he had to push himself even further.

If you talk to Ori, he will tell you this restaurant is a fifty-fifty effort. But in reality, it's much more Ori than myself. He can coax out the best in people in ways that I didn't even think was possible. Watching his drive to be a better chef, a better dad, and a better mentor motivates me to want more for myself and the people around me. And that is the true reason Bestia is successful. It's not just about the food or drinks or being in a cool spot. It's Ori's essence, vibrating through the whole restaurant, that makes it what it is.

ACKNOWLEDGMENTS

We would like to thank our families and friends, Lola, and our daughter, Saffron, for putting up with our horrendous schedules and perpetual exhaustion. All of the people who invested and helped build Bestia, who believed in us when all indications pointed otherwise. The amazingly talented people who were involved in the creation and completion of this book. Additionally, we'd like to thank the people behind the scenes at Bestia, both in the kitchen and out, because without their unparalleled dedication and attention to detail, this book would not be what it is. Lastly, to all of our amazing guests who have come back so many times that they have now become part of our family.

INDEX

Published in the United States by Ten Speed Press,
an imprint of the Crown Publishing Group, a division
of Penguin Random House LLC, New York.
www.crownpublishing.com
www.tenspeed.com

Ten Speed Press and the Ten Speed Press colophon are
registered trademarks of Penguin Random House LLC.

Library of Congress Cataloging-in-Publication Data
Names: Menashe, Ori, author. | Gergis, Genevieve, author. |
Franzen, Nicole, photographer.
Title: Bestia : italian recipes created in the Heart of L.A. / by Ori
Menashe and Genevieve Gergis, with Lesley Suter ; photographs
by Nicole Franzen.
Description: California, New York : Ten Speed Press, [2018] |
Includes bibliographical references and index.
Identifiers: LCCN 2018014042
Subjects: LCSH: Cooking, Italian. | Bestia (Restaurant) |
LCGFT: Cookbooks.
Classification: LCC TX723 .M4585 2018 | DDC 641.5945—dc23
LC record available at https://lccn.loc.gov/2018014042

Hardcover ISBN: 978-0-399-58090-1
eBook ISBN: 978-0-399-58091-8

Printed in China

Design by Emma Campion
Prop styling by Joni Noe

10 9 8 7 6 5 4 3 2 1

First Edition